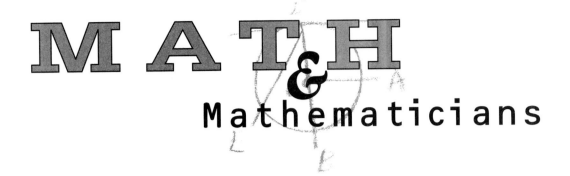

MATH

&

Mathematicians

MATH & Mathematicians:

The History of Math Discoveries Around the World

Volume  2 I-Z

Leonard C. Bruno

Lawrence W. Baker, Editor

UXL®

AN IMPRINT OF THE GALE GROUP

DETROIT · SAN FRANCISCO · LONDON
BOSTON · WOODBRIDGE, CT

Math and Mathematicians: The History of Math Discoveries Around the World
Leonard C. Bruno

Staff

Lawrence W. Baker, *U•X•L Senior Editor*
Carol DeKane Nagel, *U•X•L Managing Editor*
Thomas L. Romig, *U•X•L Publisher*

Meggin Condino, *Senior Analyst, New Product Development*

Margaret Chamberlain, *Permissions Specialist (Pictures)*

Rita Wimberley, *Senior Buyer*
Evi Seoud, *Assistant Production Manager*
Dorothy Maki, *Manufacturing Manager*

Eric Johnson, *Page Designer*
Tracey Rowens, *Page Designer*
Martha Schiebold, *Cover Designer*
Cynthia Baldwin, *Product Design Manager*

Pamela Reed, *Imaging Coordinator*
Robert Duncan, *Senior Imaging Specialist*
Randy A. Bassett, *Image Database Supervisor*
Barbara J. Yarrow, *Graphic Services Manager*

Marco Di Vita, Graphix Group, *Typesetting*

Copyright © 1999
U•X•L, an imprint of The Gale Group
27500 Drake Rd.
Farmington Hills, MI 48331-3535

Library of Congress Catalog-in-Publication Data

Bruno, Leonard C.
　　Math and mathematicians : the history of math discoveries around the world / Leonard C. Bruno ; Lawrence W. Baker, editor.
　　　　p.　　cm.
　　Includes index.
　　Contents: v. 1. A-H – v. 2. I-Z.
　　Summary: Compilation of fifty biographies of mathematicians from throughout history and approximately thirty-five articles describing math concepts and principles.
　　　　ISBN 0-7876-3812-9 (set). – ISBN 0-7876-3813-7 (vol. 1). – ISBN 0-7876-3814-5 (vol. 2).
　　　　1. Mathematicians—Biography, Juvenile literature.　2. Mathematics–History Encyclopedias, Juvenile.　[1. Mathematicians Encyclopedias.　2. Mathematics Encyclopedias.]　I. Baker, Lawrence W.　II. Title.
　　QA28.B78　1999
　　510'.92'2–dc21
　　[B]

99-32424
CIP

Printed in the United States of America

10 9 8 7 6 5 4 3 2

Contents

Contents

Contents

Contents

Entries by Mathematical Field

Algebra

Analysis

Applied mathematics

Boldface type indicates volume number; regular type indicates page numbers.

Game theory

Geometry

Group theory

Logic

Number theory

Probability and ratio

Set theory

Statistics

Time

Entries by
Mathematical Field

Biographical Entries by Ethnicity

Boldface type indicates volume number; regular type indicates page numbers.

Biographical
Entries by
Ethnicity

Reader's Guide

Unlike many other fields of science, mathematics has only a few really well-known individuals whose names most people easily recognize. Although by high school we all know something of the contributions of Euclid, Pythagoras, and Isaac Newton, the history of mathematics contains a far greater number of individuals whose accomplishments were nearly as important and whose lives may have been even more interesting, but about whom most of us know very little. *Math and Mathematicians: The History of Math Discoveries Around the World* is intended therefore not only to summarize and describe the lives of those better-known achievers, but to tell the stories of those other greats and near-greats whose contributions have not become an integral part of our popular mathematical knowledge. This two-volume set covers the early life, influences, and career of each individual.

Altogether, fifty such individuals have been selected on the basis not only of their mathematical contributions, but also with the intent of offering young readers a sampling of just how rich the history of mathematics is and how diverse are its contributors. The biographies in *Math and Mathematicians* include representatives from every major part of the world—ancient and modern—as well as

mathematicians who were and are young and old, male and female. If there is one common thread that links all these biographies, it is that genius, hard work, determination, inspiration, and courage are multicultural, multiracial, and totally ignorant of gender.

Surveyed as a group, the fifty biographies in *Math and Mathematicians* include fourteen people who either were born or did their major work in the twentieth century—six of whom are still living. This should suggest that not all the great mathematicians are musty names found in old history books. The oldest historical figure included here, Thales of Miletus, harks back to seventh century B.C., while the youngest living mathematician in this book, Andrew Wiles, was born in 1953. Ranging over the entire history of mathematics and selecting only fifty individuals obviously suggests that many more mathematicians were excluded than included, and it should not be surprising that some truly deserving individuals were left out. But with the help of an advisory board, we selected a solid core of mathematicians that spans the centuries: seven were born before the sixteenth century, six in the sixteenth century, five in the seventeenth century, ten in the eighteenth century, eleven in the nineteenth century, and eleven in the twentieth century.

Besides the mathematical accomplishments that earned these individuals a high place in the history of mathematics, there are many fascinating personal stories that make them extremely interesting from a human perspective. While the number of child prodigies like Carl Friedrich Gauss, William Rowan Hamilton, John von Neumann, Norbert Wiener, and others may not be surprising, the number of what might be called martyrs to mathematics certainly is. Archimedes and Hypatia were in fact killed because of their work, and the number of shortened and wrecked lives (Niels Abel, René Descartes, Évariste Galois, Sofya Kovalevskaya, and Alan Turing, among others) is truly shocking. The eccentric or "nutty" professors are also represented here, with the likes of Charles Babbage, Girolamo Cardano, Paul Erdös, Joseph Fourier, Kurt Gödel, John Napier, and Srinivasa A. Ramanujan doing their best to uphold the stereotype of the misfit or oddball scientist.

In addition to the fifty biographical essays, *Math and Mathematicians* also contains thirty-four essays describing math concepts and principles important to the middle school curriculum. These concepts, again chosen with the assistance of our advisory board, are arranged and interfiled alphabetically with the biographies to form one encyclopedic set. Each essay describes, when relevant, the time period, culture, and circumstances in which the concept or theory evolved or was discovered. Each entry also explains the concept in nontechnical language and offers examples.

All entries are easy to read and written in a straightforward style. Difficult words are defined within the text. Each of the thirty-four concept entries also includes a "Words to Know" sidebar that defines technical words and scientific terms. This enables students to learn vocabulary appropriate to mathematics without having to consult other sources for definitions.

Added features

Math and Mathematicians: The History of Math Discoveries Around the World includes a number of additional features that help make the connection between math concepts and theories, the people who discovered and worked with them, and common uses of mathematics.

- Three tables of contents—alphabetically by mathematician or concept, by mathematical field, and by mathematician's ethnicity—provide varied access to the entries.

- A timeline at the beginning of each volume provides a chronology of highlights in the history of mathematics.

- A cumulative "Words to Know" section gives definitions of key mathematical terms.

- More than one hundred photographs and illustrations bring to life the mathematicians, concepts, and ways in which mathematics is commonly used.

- Sidebars provide fascinating supplemental information about important terms, mathematicians, and theories.

- Extensive cross references make it easy to refer to other mathematicians and concepts covered in both volumes; cross references to other entries are boldfaced upon the first mention in an entry.

- Sources for more information are found at the end of each entry so students know where to delve even deeper.

• A comprehensive index quickly points readers to the mathematicians, concepts, theories, and organizations mentioned in *Math and Mathematicians*.

Special thanks

The author wishes to thank his wife, Jane, and children Nat, Ben, and Nina, for their patience, understanding, and actual help when I often needed something explained in a simple, direct manner. The excellent index was prepared by Michelle B. Cadoree, whose knowledge, ability, and professionalism made that part of the book a worry-free experience for the author. Thanks also to copyeditor Theresa Murray and proofreader Mya Nelson for their adept work.

Additional appreciation goes to the folks at U•X•L. Thanks to senior market analyst Meggin Condino for selecting the author and for her work early on, and to publisher Tom Romig for being so pleasant a negotiator. Finally, all praise should go to senior editor Larry Baker, who not only worked long and hard on every aspect of this book, but who actually made the author look forward to each and every contact with him, whether by phone or by email. His wit, "simpatico" for writers, high standards, and simple pride in hard work (not to mention encyclopedic baseball knowledge) made him the perfect editor for me.

Comments and suggestions

We welcome your comments on *Math and Mathematicians* as well as your suggestions for biographies and concepts to be featured in future volumes. Please write: Editors, *Math and Mathematicians*, U•X•L, 27500 Drake Rd., Farmington Hills, Michigan, 48331-3535; call toll-free: 1-800-877-4253; fax to 248-699-8097; or send e-mail via www.gale.com.

Advisory Board

Elaine Ezell
Library Media Specialist
Bowling Green Junior High School
Bowling Green, Ohio

Marie-Claire Kelin
Library Media Teacher
Lincoln Middle School
Santa Monica, California

Eric Stromberg
Mathematics Teacher
Riley Middle School
Livonia, Michigan

Words to Know

A

Abacus a manual computing device consisting of a frame holding parallel rods or wires strung with movable, bead-like counters

Abstract something thought of or stated without reference to anything specific; theoretical rather than practical

Abstraction something that is general and not particular; an idea or concept that is theoretical rather than practical

Acute triangle a triangle in which the measure of every angle is less than 90 degrees

Addend one of a set of numbers to be added; in 4 + 1 = 5, 4 and 1 are the addends

Adjoining touching or having a common point

Algorithm any systematic method of doing mathematics that involves a step-by-step procedure

Analog clock an instrument that indicates the time of day by its moving hands on a numbered dial

Analog computer an early type of computer that converts numbers or quantities into another model or form, such as the column of mercury in a thermometer

Analogy a form of reasoning that assumes if two things are alike in some ways, then they are probably alike in other ways as well

Angle what is formed inside a triangle by two sides meeting at the vertex

Arbitrary something not determined by a reason or necessity but by individual preference

Area the amount of space a flat geometrical shape occupies; the region inside a given boundary

Arithmetic operations the four fundamental actions or processes—addition, subtraction, multiplication, and division—that are performed in a specified sequence and in accordance with specific rules

Associative a property that applies to addition and multiplication (but not subtraction or division) in which addends or factors can be grouped in any order without changing the sum or product

Avoirdupois weight a system of weights and measures based on a pound containing 16 ounces

Axes the intersecting lines of a coordinate system; made up of the horizontal axis (x-axis) and the vertical axis (y-axis)

Axiom a statement that is accepted without proof; something self-evident

B

Bank note a note or piece of paper issued by a bank that represents its promise to pay a certain amount upon demand to the holder of the note; acceptable as money

Barter to trade goods or services instead of using money

Base the number being raised to a certain power or being repeatedly multiplied by itself

Binary a numeral system used by modern computers that contains only two digits, 0 and 1; any number is represented by some sequence of the two

Binary operation an operation that is performed on exactly two numbers at a time

Boundary a line that separates a figure into its interior and its exterior

C

Capacity the ability to receive, hold, or contain; a measure on content

Certified the confirmation that something is genuine; a guarantee that something is worth what it says it is

Chord a line segment that joins any two points on a circle and does not go through its center

Circadian rhythm the daily rhythm or cycle of activity that many organisms exhibit during a single 24-hour period

Circumference the distance completely around the outside of a circle; its perimeter

Clepsydra an ancient timekeeping device that marked the passage of time by the regulated flow of water through a small opening; a water clock

Commutative a property that applies to addition and multiplication (but not subtraction or division) in which the order in which the numbers are added or multiplied does not change the sum; for example, $1 \times 2 = 2 \times 1$

Component an element or part that makes up some sort of system

Composite number a whole number that is not a prime number; any number that can be obtained by multiplying two whole numbers other than itself and 1; the first ten composites are 4, 6, 8, 9, 10, 12, 14, 15, 16, 18

Computation the act or method of carrying out a mathematical process

Compute to carry out a mathematical process; to calculate

Concave polygon a polygon with at least one interior angle that measures more than 180 degrees; at least one straight line can intersect more than two sides

Convex polygon a polygon whose every interior angle measures less than 180 degrees; any straight line intersects no more than two sides

Concentric two or more circles of different size that have the same point as their center; circles that are inside one another

Conversion the exchange of one type of money for another

Cross-multiplication rule the product of the means equals the product of the extremes; for example, in the proportion 1:3 = 2:6, the means (3 and 2) can be multiplied and will equal the product of the extremes (1 and 6)

D

Decimal fraction a fractional number expressed in decimal form; one in which the denominator is some power of ten; for example, .3 is the decimal version of $\frac{3}{10}$

Decimal system a number written using the base of 10

Deductive reasoning or **deduction** a type of reasoning in which a conclusion follows necessarily from a set of axioms or givens; it proceeds logically from the general to the specific

Denomination a particular value, size, or kind of money

Denominator in a fraction, the numeral written below the bar or line; it tells how many parts the whole has

Descriptive statistics the science of collecting, organizing, and summarizing data that characterize a particular group

Diameter a line segment that joins two points on a circle and passes through its center; the longest chord possible in a circle

Difference the result of subtraction

Digital clock an instrument that indicates the time of day by giving its reading in actual digits or numbers

Digital computer a modern type of computer that processes information in the form of numbers or digits

Distributive in multiplying one number times a sum of two other numbers, the sum may be taken first and then the multiplication performed, or each of the numbers to be summed can first be multiplied by the common factor and the results added together; for example, with $3 \times (3 + 4)$, 3 and 4 are added and their sum (7) multiplied by 3 equals 21; or 3 and 4 can each be multiplied by 3 and their products (9 and 12) can then be added to get 21

Dividend the number that is to be divided by another number

Divisor the number by which the dividend is to be divided

E

Electromechanical a mechanical device or system that is controlled by electricity

Equation a mathematical sentence with an equal sign (=) between two expressions; a statement of equality; for example, $3 + x = 10$ and $a + b = b + a$ are both equations

Equator the imaginary circle drawn around the center of the Earth's surface; a line equidistant from the North and South poles

Equiangular polygon a polygon in which every interior angle measures the same number of degrees

Equilateral polygon a polygon in which every side measures the same length

Equilateral triangle a triangle in which all three sides are of equal length

Equivalent something that is essentially equal to something else

Equivalent fraction fractions that are of equal value; for example $\frac{5}{10}$ is the same as $\frac{1}{2}$

Evolution the theory that groups of organisms change with the passage of time as a result of natural selection

Exchange rate the cost of changing one country's currency into that of another; costs or rates fluctuate daily

Exponential increase and decrease when something grows or declines at a particular rate or designated power; often at a massive or dramatic rate

Extract to determine or calculate the root of a number

Extremes the first and fourth terms in a proportion; for example, in the proportion 1:3 = 2:6, 1 and 6 are the extremes

F

Factor in a given number, that which divides that number evenly; for example, the factors of the number 12 are 1, 2, 3, 4, 6, and 12

Factors the numbers multiplied to form a product; both the multiplier and the multiplicand

Force strength, energy, or power that causes motion or change

Formula a general answer, rule, or principle stated in a mathematical way (with an equal sign between two expressions)

Fractional divided into smaller parts or pieces of a whole

G

Genetics the branch of biology that deals with heredity, especially the transmission of characteristics

Gravitation the natural phenomenon of attraction between massive celestial bodies

Grid a pattern of regularly spaced horizontal and vertical lines forming squares, as on a map or chart

H

Hardware the physical equipment or machinery of a computer; its processor, monitor, and other devices

Heretical characterized by a radical departure from traditional standards

Hierarchy a series in which each element is graded or ranked

Hypotenuse the longest side in a right triangle

I

Improper fraction a fraction in which the numerator is equal to or greater than the denominator; the value of the fraction is always equal to or larger than 1; for example, ⅝ is an improper fraction

Incertitude uncertainty or doubt about something

Index the number in the upper left-hand corner of the radical sign that tells which root is to be extracted

Indigenous people who are original to a certain area or environment; native

Inductive reasoning or **induction** a type of reasoning conducted first by observing patterns of something and then by predicting answers for similar future cases; it proceeds logically from the specific to the general

Inertia the tendency of a body to resist being moved and to remain at rest

Inference the act of reasoning or making a logical conclusion based on evidence or something known to be true

Inferential statistics the science of making inferences or predictions about a group based on characteristics of a sample of that group

Infinite set a set whose elements cannot be counted because they are unlimited

Integers a set of numbers that includes the positive numbers, negative numbers, and zero

Integrated circuit a tiny piece of material on which is imprinted a complex series of electronic components and their interconnections; a computer chip

Interaction the state or process of two things acting upon each other; mutual influence

Intersect to cut across or through; to cross or overlap

Intersection two lines that have a common point and necessarily cross each other

Intuition the act or faculty of knowing or sensing something without having any rational thought or doing any reasoning

Irrational number a number that is expressed as a nonrepeating decimal fraction and which, when carried out, simply goes on forever; contrasted to a rational number, which has either a terminating decimal (it comes out even with no remainder) or a repeating decimal (as .33333333...)

Isosceles triangle a triangle with at least two sides of equal length

L

Latitude the angular distance north or south of the Earth's equator; indicated by horizontal lines on a map

Least common denominator in the case of two fractions, it is the smallest multiple common to both denominators; for example, with the fractions ⅚, ¼, and ½, the least common denominator is 12 (the lowest number into which 6, 4, and 2 can be divided)

Legs the sides of a right triangle perpendicular to each other; they have a common point of intersection and are adjacent to the right angle

Length the measure of a line segment or an object from end to end

Like fractions fractions with the same denominator; for example, 2/7 and 4/7 are like fractions

Line a set of points joined together and extending in both directions; it has no thickness and is one-dimensional

Longitude the angular distance east or west from the prime meridian at Greenwich, England; indicated by vertical lines on a map

Linear equation also called a first-degree equation since none of its terms is raised to a power of 2 or higher, it is graphed as a straight line; $y = x + 1$ is a linear equation

Logic the study of the principles of proper or correct reasoning

M

Mass the measure of the quantity of matter that a body contains

Means the second and third terms in a proportion; for example, in the proportion 1:3 = 2:6, 2 and 3 are the means

Memory the part of a computer that stores and preserves information and programs for retrieval

Mercantile of or relating to merchants or trade

Minuend in subtraction, the larger number from which a smaller number is taken away; in 10 − 5, 10 is the minuend

Minute a measure of time equal to $\frac{1}{60}$th of an hour

Mixed number a number consisting of an integer and a proper fraction; for example, $1\frac{3}{4}$ is a mixed number

Mortality tables statistical tables based on death data compiled over a number of years

Multiplicand the number that is being multiplied by another number; for example, in 3 × 4 = 12, 3 is the multiplicand

Multiplier the number that does the multiplying; for example, in 3 × 4 = 12, 4 is the multiplier

N

Natural numbers all the cardinal numbers or counting numbers (1, 2, 3, . . .) except 0

Natural selection the process in nature by which only those organisms best suited to their environment survive and transmit their genetic characteristics to succeeding generations

Negative number a number less than 0; a minus (−) sign is always written before the numeral to indicate it is to the left of 0 on a number line

Number theory a branch of mathematics concerned generally with the properties and relationships of integers

Numeral a symbol or name that stands for a number

Numerator in a fraction, the numeral written above the bar or line; it tells how many parts are being considered

O

Obtuse triangle a triangle with one angle that measures greater than 90 degrees

P

Papyrus an early form of writing paper made by the Egyptians from the stems of the papyrus plant

Parallelogram a quadrilateral in which both pairs of opposite sides are parallel

Parchment the treated skin of a goat or sheep that in ancient times was treated so that it could be written on

Pentagon a polygon with five sides

Perimeter the distance around a polygon, obtained by adding the lengths of its sides; the perimeter or distance completely around a circle is called its circumference

Perpendicular when lines intersect and form a right angle

Perspective the technique of representing three-dimensional objects and depth relationships on a two-dimensional surface

Pi (π) a number defined as the ratio of the circumference to the diameter of a circle; it cannot be represented exactly as a decimal, but it is between 3.1415 and 3.1416

Place value (positional notation) the system in which the position or place of a symbol or digit in a numeral determines its value; for example, in the numeral 1,234, the 1 occupies the 1000 place, the 2 is in the 100 place, the 3 is in the 10 place, and the 4 is in the unit (1) place

Polygon a geometric figure composed of three or more line segments (straight sides) that never cross each other

Population all of the individuals, events, or objects that make up a group

Positive number a number greater than 0 (and to the right of 0 on a number line)

Prime factorization the process of finding all the prime factors of a given number

Prime meridian the zero meridian (0 degrees) used as a reference or baseline from which longitude east or west is measured; by international agreement, it passes through Greenwich, England

Probability likely to happen or to be true; likelihood

Probability theory the branch of mathematics that studies the likelihood of random events occurring in order to predict the behavior of defined systems

Product the result in a multiplication problem

Projection the image of a figure reproduced atop a grid of intersecting lines

Proper fraction a fraction in which the numerator is less than the denominator; for example, ⅔ is a proper fraction

Property a characteristic of something that is assumed

Proposition a statement that makes an assertion; something that is stated as either true or false

Q

Qualifier a word or phrase that limits or modifies the meaning of another word

Quotient the result when one number is divided by another; for example, 2 is the quotient when 10 is divided by 5

R

Radicand the number under a radical sign

Radioactive decay the natural disintegration or breakdown of a radioactive substance that allows it to be dated

Radius a line drawn from the center of a circle to some point on the circle's boundary or edge; it is half the length of the diameter

Random something done unsystematically, without purpose, pattern, or method

Ratio the relationship between two quantities, which is obtained by dividing two things; for instance, the ratio of 3 to 2 is written 3:2 or $\frac{3}{2}$

Rational consistent with or based on reason; logical; reasonable

Rectangle a parallelogram whose angles are all right angles

Regular polygon a polygon in which all sides have equal length and all interior angles have equal measure; a polygon that is both equilateral and equiangular

Remainder the number left over when division does not come out evenly; for example, 2 is the remainder when 17 is divided by 5

Renaissance the period between the fourteenth and sixteenth century in Europe characterized by the revival of classical art, architecture, and literature

Rhombus a parallelogram whose four sides are of equal length

Right angle an angle of 90 degrees

Right triangle a triangle in which one of its angles measures 90 degrees (a right angle)

Rigor strict precision or exactness

S

Sample a number of individuals, events, or objects chosen from a given population that are representative of the entire group

Scalene triangle a triangle in which each side is of a different length

Scientific notation writing a number as the product of a number between 1 and 10 and a power of 10; used to represent very large or very small numbers

Secant any straight line that intersects a circle at two points or cuts through its outer edges

Second a measure of time equal to $\frac{1}{60}$th of a minute

Set a collection or group of particular things

Sexagesimal a numeration system using 60 as a base; used by the Babylonians

Side one of the line segments of a polygon; also called "legs" for a triangle

Sieve a device with holes or mesh that allows liquid or only particles of a very small size to pass through but which captures larger particles

Simulation representation or imitation of an event, process, or system

Slide rule a device operated by hand that uses sliding logarithmic scales to reduce complex computations to addition and subtraction; replaced by the hand-held calculator

Software all of the programs, routines, and instructions that control a computer's hardware and direct its operation

Spherical having the shape of a sphere; round; globular

Square a rectangle whose four sides are the same length

Square of a number a number raised to the second power or multiplied by itself

Statistics the branch of mathematics consisting of methods for collecting, organizing, and summarizing data in order to make predictions based on these data

Storage the memory system of a computer that keeps information for later retrieval

Subtrahend in subtraction, the smaller number being taken away from a larger number; in $10 - 5$, 5 is the subtrahend

Sum in addition, the result of adding two or more numbers or addends; for example, in $4 + 1 = 5$, 5 is the sum

Subset a set contained within a set

Sundial an instrument that indicates solar time by the shadow cast by its central pointer onto a numbered dial

Surface in terms of area, the region that is inside a given boundary

Syllogism a logical argument that involves three propositions, usually two premises and a conclusion, whose conclusion necessarily is true if the premises are true

Symbolic logic a system of mathematical logic that uses symbols instead of words to solve problems, and whose symbols can be manipulated much like an equation

Symbolic notation a mathematical shorthand in which a sign is used to represent an operation, element, quantity, or relationship

Symmetry the exact correspondence of a form or shape on opposite sides of a center dividing line

T

Tangent a straight line that intersects a circle at only one point or touches its outer edge at only one point

Terms the numerator and denominator of a fraction

Theorem a statement or generalization that can be demonstrated to be true

Transistor a small electronic device containing a semiconductor that acts as an amplifier, detector, or switch; it replaced old, glass vacuum tubes and was itself replaced by silicon chips

Trapezium a quadrilateral with no pairs of opposite sides parallel

Trapezoid a quadrilateral with only two sides parallel

Triangulation the location of an unknown point by forming a triangle whose two points are known

Troy weight a system of weight in which a pound contains 12 ounces

V

Vertex the point at which any two sides of a polygon meet or intersect; plural is "vertices"

Volume a number describing the three-dimensional amount of a space; a measure of the capacity or how much something will hold; the number of cubic units in a solid figure

W

Whole numbers the set of natural or counting numbers (1, 2, 3, . . .) plus 0

Z

Zero a real number that separates positive and negative numbers on a number line; it also functions as an empty set and as a place holder

Milestones in the History of Mathematics

50,000 B.C.   Primitive humans leave behind evidence of their ability to count. Paleolithic people in central Europe make notches on animal bones to tally.

c. 15,000 B.C.   Cave dwellers in the Middle East make notches on bones to keep count and possibly to track the lunar cycle.

c. 8000 B.C.   Clay tokens are used in Mesopotamia to record numbers of animals. This eventually develops into the first system of numeration.

75,000 B.C.
Neanderthal man
can communicate
by speech.

38,000 B.C.
Homo sapiens
species evolves from
Neanderthal man.

12,000 B.C.
The dog is
domesticated from
the Asian wolf.

8000 B.C.
Earth's human
population soars to
5.3 million.

50,000 B.C.   40,000 B.C.   30,000 B.C.   20,000 B.C.   8000 B.C.

Milestones in the History of Mathematics

3500 B.C. The Egyptian number system reaches the point where they now can record numbers as large as necessary by introducing new symbols.

c. 2400 B.C. Mathematical tablets dated to this period are found at Ur, a city of ancient Sumer (present-day Iraq).

c. 2000 B.C. Babylonians and Egyptians use **fractions** as a way to help them tell **time** and measure angles.

c. 1800 B.C. The Babylonians know and use what is later called the **Pythagorean theorem**, but they do not yet have a proof for it.

c. 1650 B.C. The Rhind papyrus (also known as the Ahmes papyrus) is prepared by Egyptian scribe Ahmes, which contains solutions to simple equations. It becomes a primary source of knowledge about early Egyptian mathematics, describing their methods of **multiplication, division,** and **algebra.**

876 B.C. The first known reference to the usage of the symbol for zero is made in India.

c. 585 B.C. Greek geometer and philosopher **Thales of Miletus** converts Egyptian **geometry** into an abstract study. He removes mathematics from a sole consideration of practical problems and proves mathematical statements by a series of logical arguments. Doing this, Thales invents deductive mathematics.

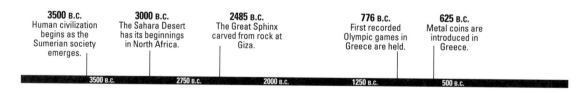

3500 B.C.
Human civilization begins as the Sumerian society emerges.

3000 B.C.
The Sahara Desert has its beginnings in North Africa.

2485 B.C.
The Great Sphinx carved from rock at Giza.

776 B.C.
First recorded Olympic games in Greece are held.

625 B.C.
Metal coins are introduced in Greece.

3500 B.C. 2750 B.C. 2000 B.C. 1250 B.C. 500 B.C.

c. 500 B.C.   Greek geometer and philosopher **Pythagoras of Samos** formulates the idea that the entire universe rests on numbers and their relationships. He deduces that the square of the length of the hypotenuse of a right **triangle** is equal to the sum of the squares of the lengths of its sides. It becomes known as the **Pythagorean theorem.**

c. 300 B.C.   Greek geometer **Euclid of Alexandria** writes a textbook on **geometry** called the *Elements*. It becomes the standard work on its subject for over 2,000 years.

c. 240 B.C.   Greek geometer **Archimedes of Syracuse** calculates the most accurate arithmetical value for **pi (π)** to date. He also uses a system for expressing large numbers that uses an exponential-like method. Archimedes also finds **areas** and **volumes** of special curved surfaces and solids.

c. 230 B.C.   Greek astronomer Eratosthenes develops a system for determining **prime numbers** that becomes known as the "sieve of Eratosthenes."

c. 100 B.C.   Negative numbers are used in China.

A.D. c. 250   Greek algebraist Diophantus of Alexandria is the first Greek to write a significant work on **algebra.**

c. 320   Greek geometer Pappus of Alexandria summarizes in a book all acquired knowledge of

429 B.C.
The plague kills at least one-third of the population of Athens, Greece.

214 B.C.
Construction begins on the Great Wall of China.

153 B.C.
January 1 becomes the first day of the civil year in Rome.

c. 6 B.C.
Jesus Christ is born.

A.D. 222
Chinese alchemists invent gunpowder.

500 B.C.   300 B.C.   100 B.C.   A.D. 100   350

Greek mathematics, making it the best source for Greek mathematics. French number theorist **Pierre de Fermat** later restores and studies Pappus's work.

c. 400 Greek geometer, astronomer, and philosopher **Hypatia of Alexandria** writes commentaries on Greek mathematicians Apollonius of Perga and Diophantus of Alexandria. She is the only woman scholar of ancient times and the first woman mentioned in the history of mathematics.

499 Hindu mathematician and astronomer Aryabhata the Elder describes the Indian numerical system. He also uses **division** to popularize a method for finding the greatest common divisor of two numbers.

700 Negative numbers are introduced by the Hindus to represent a negative balance.

820 Arab algebraist and astronomer **al-Khwārizmī** writes a mathematics book that introduces the Arabic word *al-jabr,* which becomes transliterated as **algebra.** His own name is distorted by translation into "algorism," which comes to mean the art of calculating or arithmetic. Al-Khwārizmī also uses Hindu numerals, including zero, and when his work is translated into Latin and published in the West, those numerals are called "Arabic numerals."

422
The walls of Rome's
Colosseum crack
during an
earthquake.

629
The Koran is
established as the
holy book of Islam.

752
Japan's 55-foot
Buddha statue is
completed.

400   500   600   700   825

c. 825	Arab algebraist and astronomer **al-Khwārizmī** recommends the use of a **decimal** system.
1202	Italian number theorist **Leonardo Pisano Fibonacci** writes about the abacus, the use of zero and Arabic (Hindu) numerals, the importance of positional notations, and the merits of the **decimal** system.
1225	Italian number theorist **Leonardo Pisano Fibonacci** writes *Liber Quadratorum* in which he uses **algebra** based on the Arabic system.
1299	A law is passed in Florence, Italy, forbidding the use of Hindu-Arabic numbers by bankers. Authorities believe such numbers are more easily forged than Roman numerals.
1482	The first printed edition of Greek geometer **Euclid of Alexandria**'s **geometry** book, *Elements,* is published in Venice, Italy.
1489	The plus (+) and minus (−) symbols are first used in a book by German mathematician Johannes Widmann. They are not used as symbols of operation but merely to indicate excess and deficiency.
1535	Italian mathematician Niccolò Tartaglia demonstrates in a public forum his correct solution to the cubic equation. He later discloses in confidence his secret methods to another Italian mathematician, **Girolamo Car-**

850
Coffee is discovered in East Africa.

1139
Civil war breaks out in England.

1254
Explorer Marco Polo is born.

1492
Christopher Columbus discovers America.

825   1000   1200   1400   1550

dano, who later publishes the solution after learning that another Italian mathematician, Scipione dal Ferro, had discovered the solution as early as 1515. Cardano's paper correctly gives credit to both Tartaglia and dal Ferro.

1557 English mathematician Robert Recorde is the first to use the modern symbol for equality (=) in a book.

1570 The first complete English translation of *Elements,* by Greek geometer **Euclid of Alexandria,** appears.

1581 Italian mathematician **Galileo** discovers that the amount of **time** for a pendulum to swing back and forth is the same, regardless of the size of the arc. Dutch astronomer and mathematical physicist **Christiaan Huygens** would later use this principle to build the first pendulum clock.

1585 Dutch mathematician **Simon Stevin** writes about the first comprehensive system of **decimal fractions** and their practical applications.

1594 Scottish mathematician **John Napier** first conceives of the notion of obtaining exponential expressions for various numbers, and begins work on the complicated formulas for what he eventually calls **logarithms.**

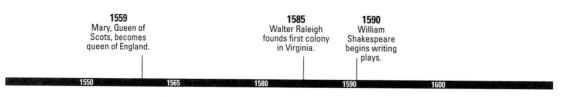

1559
Mary, Queen of Scots, becomes queen of England.

1585
Walter Raleigh founds first colony in Virginia.

1590
William Shakespeare begins writing plays.

1550   1565   1580   1590   1600

| 1609 | German astronomer and mathematician **Johannes Kepler** advances the development of the **geometry** of the ellipse as he attempts to prove that planets move in elliptical orbits. |

| 1609 | Italian mathematician **Galileo** improves upon the invention of the telescope by building a version with a magnification of about thirty times. |

| 1614 | Scottish mathematician **John Napier** invents "Napier's bones." This calculating machine consists of sticks with a **multiplication** table on the face of each stick. Calculations can be done by turning the rods by hand. He also publishes a book on **logarithms.** |

| 1619 | German astronomer and mathematician **Johannes Kepler** shows that a planet's revolution is proportional to the cube of its average distance from the Sun. |

| 1622 | English mathemetician William Oughtred invents the straight logarithmic slide rule. |

| 1629 | French number theorist **Pierre de Fermat** pioneers the application of **algebra** to **geometry.** Although French algebraist and philosopher **René Descartes** is credited with the invention and full development of analytic geometry, Fermat develops it earlier but does not publish his findings. |

1603
Russian famine kills
tens of thousands.

1620
Pilgrims land in
Plymouth Colony.

1628
Salem,
Massachusetts, is
founded.

1600   1610   1620   1625   1630

1631   English mathematician William Oughtred includes a large amount of mathematical symbolism in a book he publishes, including the notation "×" for multiplication and "::" for proportion.

1632   Italian mathematician **Galileo** discounts the theory of an Earth-centered universe. As a result, the Roman Inquisition sentences him to life imprisonment.

1636   French number theorist **Pierre de Fermat** introduces the modern theory of numbers. His work includes theories on **prime numbers.**

1637   French algebraist and philosopher **René Descartes** introduces analytic **geometry** by demonstrating how geometric forms may be systematically studied by analytic or algebraical means. He is the first person to use the letters near the beginning of the alphabet for constants and those near the end for variables. He also includes a notation system for expressing **exponents.**

c. 1637   French number theorist **Pierre de Fermat** writes in the margin of a book a reference to what comes to be known as "Fermat's last theorem." This theorem remains the most famous unsolved problem in mathematics until it is solved in 1993 by **Andrew J. Wiles.** Fermat says he has a proof for the particular problem

---

1630
Lemonade is invented in Paris, France.

1632
Galileo says that the Earth is not the center of the universe.

1636
Harvard College in Massachusetts opens.

1640
The first English stagecoach lines begin.

| 1630 | 1632 | 1635 | 1638 | 1640 |

posed, but that the margin is too small to include it there.

1642   French mathematician Blaise Pascal invents the first automatic calculator. It performs **addition** and **subtraction** by means of a set of wheels linked together by gears.

1644   French number theorist Marin Mersenne suggests a formula that will yield **prime numbers.** These "Mersenne numbers" are not always correct, but they stimulate research into the theory of numbers.

1654   French number theorist **Pierre de Fermat** exchanges letters with French mathematician Blaise Pascal in which they discuss the basic laws of **probability** and essentially found the theory of probability.

1657   Dutch astronomer and mathematical physicist **Christiaan Huygens** writes about **probability.**

1659   Swiss mathematician Johann Heinrich Rahn is the first to use today's division sign ($\div$) in a book. Later, English mathematician John Wallis adopts it and popularizes it through his works.

1662   English statistician John Graunt is the first to apply mathematics to the integration of vital **statistics.** As the first to establish life expectancy and to publish a table of demographic data,

Milestones in the History of Mathematics

1641
The first sugar factory in the English new world is built.

1652
Capetown, South Africa, is founded.

1659
Typhoid fever is described for the first time.

1640   1645   1650   1660   1665

Graunt is considered the founder of vital statistics.

1666   German logician **Gottfried Leibniz** begins the study of symbolic **logic** by calling for a "calculus of reasoning" in mathematics.

1668   German mathematician and astronomer Nicolaus Mercator is the first to calculate the **area** under a curve using the newly developed analytical **geometry.**

1673   German logician **Gottfried Leibniz** begins his development of differential and integral calculus independently of English physicist **Isaac Newton.**

1674   Japanese mathematician **Seki Kōwa** publishes his only book, in which he solves 15 supposedly "unsolvable" problems.

1684   German logician **Gottfried Leibniz** publishes an account of his discovery of calculus. He discovers it independently of English physicist **Isaac Newton,** although later than him. Newton, however, publishes his discovery after Leibniz in 1687. The timing of the discovery produces a feud between the two men.

1687   English physicist **Isaac Newton** introduces the laws of motion and universal gravitation and his invention of calculus.

1667
The first
recorded blood
transfusion is
performed.

1670
Minute hands
appear on watches
for the first time.

1682
Philadelphia,
Pennsylvania, is
founded.

| 1665 | 1670 | 1675 | 1680 | 1690 |

1690	Massachusetts is the first colony to produce paper **currency.**

1693	English astronomer Edmund Halley compiles the first set of detailed mortality tables, making use of **statistics** in the study of life and death.

1706	English geometer William Jones is the first to use the sixteenth letter of the Greek alphabet, **pi** (π), as the symbol for the **ratio** of the circumference to the diameter of a **circle.**

1713	The first full-length treatment of the theory of **probability** appears in a work by Swiss mathematician Jakob Bernoulli.

1737	Swiss geometer and number theorist **Leonhard Euler** formally adopts the sixteenth letter of the Greek alphabet (π) as the symbol for the **ratio** of the circumference to the diameter of a **circle.** The ratio itself becomes known as **pi.** Following his adoption and use, it is generally accepted.

1748	Italian mathematician **Maria Agnesi** publishes *Analytical Institutions,* a large, two-volume work that surveys elementary and advanced mathematics. Agnesi is best known for her consideration of the cubic curve or what comes to be translated as the "witch of Agnesi."

1704
America's first regular newspaper begins publication.

1705
Thomas Newcomen invents the steam engine.

1714
Daniel Fahrenheit builds a mercury thermometer.

1725
Antonio Vivaldi composes *The Four Seasons.*

1732
Benjamin Franklin revolutionizes the colonial postal service.

| 1690 | 1705 | 1720 | 1735 | 1750 |

1755	Nineteen-year-old French algebraist **Joseph-Louis Lagrange** sends a paper to Swiss geometer and number theorist **Leonhard Euler** concerning Lagrange's "calculus of variations." Euler is so impressed with the young man's work that he holds back his own writings on the subject, thus allowing Lagrange priority of publication.
1767	German geometer Johann Heinrich Lambert proves that the number for **pi** (π) is irrational.
1791	African American mathematician **Benjamin Banneker** assists in the surveying process of the new city of Washington, D.C.
1792	African American mathematician **Benjamin Banneker** publishes his first *Almanac*.
1792	The United States establishes its first monetary system, making the dollar its basic unit of **currency.**
1795	France adopts the metric system.
1797	German mathematician **Carl Friedrich Gauss** gives the first wholly satisfactory proof of the fundamental theorem of **algebra.**
1813	English mathematician **Charles Babbage** cofounds The Analytical Society, whose general purpose is to revive mathematical analysis in England.

1754
Seven Years' War
between the French
and Indians begins.

1776
Declaration of
Independence is
written.

1789
French
Revolution
begins.

1794
Eli Whitney
invents the
cotton gin.

1803
The United States
nearly doubles,
following the
Louisiana Purchase.

1755   1770   1785   1800   1815

| 1816 | French mathematician **Sophie Germain** receives an award for her paper on the mathematical theory of elasticity. |

| 1820 | English mathematician **Charles Babbage** conceives of the idea of calculation "by machinery." Over the next fifty years, he works on developing the "difference engine," but never succeeds. The technical requirements for such a machine turn out to be beyond the engineering ability of his time. |

| 1821 | French mathematician **Augustin-Louis Cauchy** publishes the first of three books on calculus. |

| 1825 | Norwegian mathematician **Niels Abel** first proves the impossibility of solving the general quintic equation by means of radicals. This problem had puzzled mathematicians for two and a half centuries. |

| 1829 | Russian geometer **Nicolay Lobachevsky** describes his discovery of non-Euclidean **geometry**. This system includes the concept that an indefinite number of lines can be drawn in a plane parallel to a given line through a given point. |

| 1830 | French algebraist and group theorist **Évariste Galois** is the first to use the word "group" in the technical sense and to apply groups of sub- |

1818
Russian socialist leader Karl Marx is born.

1827
Contact lenses are invented.

1829
George Stephenson develops the railroad.

1815   1818   1821   1825   1830

stitutions to the question of reducibility of algebraic equations.

1832 Hungarian geometer János Bolyai announces his discovery of non-Euclidean **geometry**, which he makes at about the same time as Russian geometer **Nikolay Lobachevsky**. His discovery is totally independent of Lobachevsky's, and when Bolyai finally sees Lobachevsky's work, he thinks it has been plagarized from his own.

1833 Irish algebraist **William Rowan Hamilton** makes one of the first attempts at analyzing the basis of irrational numbers. His theory views both **rational and irrational numbers** as based on algebraic number couples.

1847 English logician **George Boole** maintains that the essential character of mathematics lies in its form rather than in its content. His work focuses on mathematics as symbolic rather than only "the science of measurement and number."

1854 English logician **George Boole** establishes both formal **logic** and Boolean **algebra**.

1854 German geometer **Bernhard Riemann** offers a global view of **geometry**. He develops further the ideas of Russian geometer **Nikolay Lobachevsky** and Hungarian geometer János Bolyai and introduces a new, non-Euclidean system of geometry.

1834
The Braille system for the blind is invented.

1836
Siege of the Alamo takes place in Texas.

1844
Gottlob Keller invents the wood pulp paper process.

1846
Mexican War begins.

1856
Neanderthal man fossils are found.

| 1830 | 1835 | 1840 | 1850 | 1855 |

| 1860 | German geometer **Bernhard Riemann** uses the complex number theory to form the basis for most of the research in **prime numbers** for the next century. |

| 1874 | German mathematician **Georg Cantor** begins his revolutionary work on set theory and the theory of the infinite and creates a whole new field of mathematical research. |

| 1874 | Russian mathematician **Sofya Kovalevskaya** writes two papers on differential equations. |

| 1884 | Greenwich, England, is chosen as the site where the world's 24 **time** zones begin. |

| 1888 | Russian mathematician **Sofya Kovalevskaya** receives an award for her paper on the problem of how Saturn's rings rotate the planet. |

| 1905 | German American physicist and mathematician **Albert Einstein** writes five landmark papers that cover Brownian motion, the photoelectric effect, and his theory of relativity. It was with relativity that he devised his famous formula, $E = mc^2$. |

| 1913 | Indian number theorist **Srinivasa A. Ramanujan** begins a five-year collaboration with English mathematician Godfrey Harold Hardy during which Ramanujan works on and solves many mathematical problems. |

1859
Charles Darwin publishes his theory of evolution.

1865
U.S. president Abraham Lincoln is assassinated.

1876
Alexander Graham Bell invents the telephone.

1903
Wright Brothers take first airplane flight.

1908
Henry Ford introduces the Model T.

1860   1875   1890   1905   1920

Milestones in the History of Mathematics

1921 — German algebraist **Emmy Noether** publishes her studies on abstract rings and ideal theory which become important in the development of modern **algebra.**

1931 — Austrian American mathematician **Kurt Gödel** publishes a paper whose incompleteness theorem startles the mathematical community. It states that within any rigidly logical mathematical system there are propositions that cannot be proved or disproved on the basis of the axioms within that system.

1933 — Hungarian number theorist **Paul Erdös** discovers a proof for Chebyshev's theorem, which says that for each **integer** greater than one, there is always at least one **prime number** between it and its double.

1936 — Chinese American geometrist **Shiing-Shen Chern** begins working with French number theorist Elie-Joseph Cartan on differential **geometry.**

1937 — American mathematician **Claude E. Shannon** arrives at a connection between a **computer's** relay circuit and Boolean **algebra.**

1937 — English algebraist and logician **Alan Turing** envisions an imaginary machine that would solve all computable problems and help prove the existence of undecidable mathematical statements.

1914 World War I begins.

1917 V. I. Lenin leads communist takeover of Russia.

1923 Edwin Hubble identifies galaxies beyond the Milky Way.

1928 Alexander Fleming discovers penicillin.

1933 Nazis take control of Germany.

1939 The Baseball Hall of Fame is established.

1920   1925   1930   1935   1940

| 1943 | American computer scientist **Grace Hopper** joins the U.S. Navy, with whom she serves for 43 years. |

| 1943 | English algebraist and logician **Alan Turing** helps the World War II allies crack German codes. |

| 1944 | Harvard scientists, including American computer scientist **Grace Hopper,** build the Mark I, the world's first digital **computer.** |

| 1944 | Hungarian American number theorist **John von Neumann** and Austrian American economist Oskar Morgenstren develop a mathematical theory of games that comes to be known as game theory. |

| 1945 | Hungarian American number theorist **John von Neumann** presents the first description of the concept of a stored **computer** program. |

| 1947 | African American statistician **David Blackwell** describes "sufficiency," the process of simplifying a statistical problem by summarizing data. |

| 1946 | The Electronic Numerical Integrator and Computer (ENIAC), the first fully electronic **computer,** is invented. |

| 1948 | American logician **Norbert Wiener** produces a landmark paper that marks the beginning of cybernetics. |

1939
World War II begins.

1941
Japanese attack U.S. naval base Pearl Harbor in Hawaii.

1945
U.S. president Franklin Roosevelt dies during his fourth term.

1948
Jews in Palestine form the State of Israel.

1949
Mao Zedong becomes first leader of People's Republic of China.

1940   1942   1944   1946   1948

1949 University of Michigan students **Evelyn Boyd Granville** and Marjorie Lee Browne become the first African American women to receive Ph.D.'s in mathematics.

1949 American mathematician **Claude E. Shannon** formulates basic information theory, upon which much of today's **computer** and communications technology is based.

1951 Fifteen nations found the International Mathematical Union to promote cooperation among the world's mathematicians and to more widely disseminate the results of mathematical research.

1953 American mathematician **Claude E. Shannon** publishes his pioneering work on artificial intelligence.

1956 African American mathematician **Evelyn Boyd Granville** begins working at IBM as a **computer** programmer.

1960 The metric system is adopted by nearly every country in the world.

1982 Polish-born Lithuanian mathematician **Benoit B. Mandelbrot** founds fractal **geometry,** a new branch of mathematics based on the study of the irregularities in nature.

1993 English-born mathematician **Andrew J. Wiles** announces his proof of "Fermat's last theo-

1963
U.S. president John
F. Kennedy is
assassinated.

1978
John Paul II
becomes pope.

1985
Microsoft releases
Windows.

1954
Elvis Presley makes
his first commercial
recording.

1989
Berlin Wall is
torn down.

1948   1958   1970   1980   1993

rem." His 200-page paper is the result of a seven-year study on a problem left unsolved by French number theorist **Pierre de Fermat** 325 years earlier. Over the years, many mathematicians had declared it unsolvable.

1994   English-born mathematician **Andrew J. Wiles** publishes a corrected, improved version of his proof of "Fermat's last theorem."

1999   The euro becomes legal tender throughout Europe, beginning a three-year transition to January 1, 2002, when the euro becomes common **currency** throughout most of Europe.

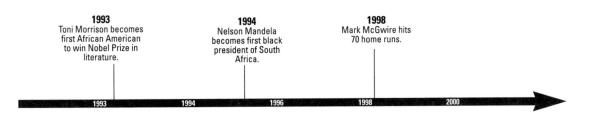

1993
Toni Morrison becomes first African American to win Nobel Prize in literature.

1994
Nelson Mandela becomes first black president of South Africa.

1998
Mark McGwire hits 70 home runs.

1993   1994   1996   1998   2000

Integers

Integers are a set of numbers that include the positive numbers, negative numbers, and zero. They are therefore a broader category than that of **whole numbers** since they also include negative numbers.

Description and use

It is often said that the idea of integers is a man-made concept that came about in order to create a number system in which **subtraction** would always be possible. In arithmetic, **addition** can always be performed using regular counting numbers (1, 2, 3. . .), but subtraction cannot, since how can a larger quantity be taken away from a smaller (2 – 3)? While at first glance such an operation might seem illogical, there is an obvious and real need for what are called negative numbers. Common examples are everywhere. Writing a check for more money than is present in a bank account will result in a negative bank balance (say, -$50.00). When the temperature drops below zero, it is recorded as, for instance, -5 degrees Fahrenheit. When the price of a stock drops, it is shown as, for example, -$2.00 or -3 **percent** (see also **Ratio, proportion, and percent**). And when divers swim below the surface of the ocean, they descend to a certain number of feet below sea level (say, -50 feet).

When integers are shown on a number line, the idea of negative numbers becomes more concrete and more understandable. With zero at the center of the line and therefore acting as the starting point, or point of origin, integers to the right of zero indicate positive integers and integers to the left of zero indicated negative integers.

Integers

$$-6 \ -5 \ -4 \ -3 \ -2 \ -1 \ 0 \ +1 \ +2 \ +3 \ +4 \ +5 \ +6$$

Numbers that are written using positive signs (+1) and negative signs (-1) are called signed numbers. The key for signed numbers is their relation to zero, since every negative number (-1) has its opposite (+1). In a mathematical sense, -1 is something that when added to +1 gives 0. Therefore, the notion of zero as a number and not just as nothing had to be understood before negative numbers could be invented.

Negative numbers were introduced sometime around A.D 700. by the Hindus to represent a minus balance. Some say that the idea of negative numbers came about in connection with a banking system in India in which people were constantly in debt. Negative numbers were then adopted by the Arabs who later transmitted them to the West where it took a long time for them to be understood and actually used. During the fifteenth century, German business arithmetic books used the + sign to indicate a surplus (more) and the − sign to show a deficiency (less). Although negative numbers also were used in Europe in the sixteenth century to do some **algebra,** Europeans never seemed comfortable with the idea of a number that was smaller than zero.

Today, negative numbers are recognized as highly practical. But their use requires an understanding of several special rules. Although one can add, subtract, multiply, and divide positive and negative numbers, the rules of their operations are quite different from those of ordinary arithmetic and sometimes seem illogical. One example is that the subtraction of integers is actually done by addition, with the rule stating, "To subtract, add the opposite of the numbers to be subtracted." This becomes understandable if the problem is done on the number line while remembering what "to the right" and "to the left" of zero really mean. Thus, while add

Negative number a number less than 0; a minus (–) sign is always written before the numeral to indicate it is to the left of 0 on a number line

Positive number a number greater than 0 (and to the right of 0 on a number line)

Whole numbers the set of natural or counting numbers (1, 2, 3, . . .) plus 0

Zero a real number that separates positive and negative numbers on a number line; it also functions as an empty set and as a place holder

means "move to the right" of the zero and subtract means "move to the left," a negative sign on the number reverses this direction. This also means that unlike ordinary arithmetic in which numbers indicate only size or quantity (telling how much or how many), integers also indicate *direction* in relation to something (such as zero).

Integers and their negative numbers should be recognized as friendly and very useful. Descriptive phrases like "in the hole" to describe a financial situation or B.C.E. ("before the common era") for a date in history are examples of negative numbers without the minus signs.

For More Information

Adler, Irving. *Integers: Positive and Negative.* New York: John Day, 1972.

Asimov, Isaac. *Realm of Numbers.* Boston: Houghton Mifflin, 1959.

Flegg, Graham. *Numbers: Their History and Meaning.* New York: Schocken Books, 1983.

Humez, Alexander, et al. *Zero to Lazy Eight: The Romance of Numbers.* New York: Simon & Schuster, 1993.

Lappan, Glenda, et al. *Accenturate the Negative: Integers.* White Plains, NY: Dale Seymour Publications, 1997.

**Born December 27, 1571
Weil der Stadt, Holy Roman Empire (present-day Germany)**

**Died November 15, 1630
Regensburg, Germany**

German astronomer and mathematician

Johannes Kepler

Best remembered for his discovery of the three laws of planetary motion, Johannes Kepler was a student of the works of the great Polish astronomer Nicolas Copernicus (1473–1543). Kepler shared Copernicus's view that the solar system was centered around the Sun, not the Earth. He further believed that God had created a universe that was mathematical. As a mathematician, he therefore dedicated himself to finding the mathematical relations and laws on which the universe is based.

Early life and education

Born in Weil der Stadt, now part of Württemberg in southern Germany, Kepler was the oldest son of Heinrich Kepler and Katharina Guldenmann. His grandfather, Sebald Kepler, had once been mayor of Weil der Stadt. Although the family was of the Lutheran faith, when Kepler was only three years old, his father joined a group of hired soldiers to fight for a Catholic army and thus disgraced the family. By the time Kepler was 17, his father had abandoned the family altogether. Kepler later described his father as "criminally inclined, quarrel-

> *"I used to measure the heavens, now I shall measure the shadows of the earth."*

some," and said his mother "could not overcome the inhumanity of her husband."

Kepler first attended a church school in Leonberg, where his family had moved in 1576. When he was 13, he entered the Adelberg monastery school to prepare for a religious career. Two years later, he attended a college preparatory school. In October 1587, he formally entered the University of Tübingen on a scholarship.

Although still intent on a religious career, Kepler studied science and mathematics. As a straight-A student, he was described by one teacher as having "such a superior and magnificent mind that something special may be expected of him." At Tübingen, Kepler was strongly influenced by his astronomy professor, Michael Maestlin (1550–1631), who also believed in the Sun-centered theory of Copernicus. Kepler began to study Copernicus's theory and started to consider astronomy more seriously.

Switches from religion to mathematics

After receiving his degree in 1591, Kepler was still planning to have a religious career. His life changed, however, when a mathematics teacher at a Lutheran school in the city of Graz, Austria, suddenly died and the University of Tübingen was asked to nominate a replacement. The university selected Kepler because of his demonstrated brilliance in mathematics. Although he protested at first, he eventually accepted.

In April 1594, the 22-year-old Kepler arrived in southern Austria to teach mathematics and mathematical astronomy. At that time, astronomy professors were also expected to cast horoscopes and make predictions. Kepler did so but always tried to do it in a scientific way. Although he described astrology as the "foolish little daughter" of respectable astronomy, he issued many calendars that contained all sorts of predictions.

Mathematical astronomy

Teaching in Graz and casting horoscopes left Kepler unsatisfied. He began to wonder about some of the basic questions of astronomy. Why are there only six planets? How can their distance from the Sun be determined? Why do planets farthest from the Sun move the slowest? In seeking the answers to such difficult questions, Kepler used mathematics and the new Copernican theory of a Sun-centered universe. The mathematics he used was the **geometry** of **Euclid of Alexandria** (c. 325–c. 270 B.C.).

In 1596, Kepler published a book called *Mysterium cosmographicum.* Although the ideas he proposed in the book were incorrect, it contained the seeds of his future mathematical explanations of the universe. Kepler's small book made its way to other European scientists, one of whom, Danish astronomer Tycho Brahe (1546–1601), invited Kepler to come to Prague and work with him.

In 1597, Kepler married Barbara Müller, the oldest daughter of a wealthy mill owner. The couple would have five children (two of whom would die young). When 1598 brought religious conflict between Protestants and Catholics, conditions for the Protestants in the largely Catholic city of Graz became increasingly tense. Most of the Protestants were asked to leave. Kepler gladly accepted Brahe's invitation to move to Prague. His wife's fortune, however, was tied to her properties in Graz, so when the Keplers left that city, they left their financial assets behind.

Kepler joined Brahe at the Benatky Castle observatory outside Prague in February 1600. Brahe had left Germany and become part of the court of Emperor Rudolf II (1552–1612) at Prague only a few years before. Despite some difficulties working with the feisty and secretive Brahe, Kepler remained with him. Kepler worked on determining the orbit of Mars until Brahe died suddenly in October 1601. Kepler then inherited Brahe's valuable data collected over the years on the stars and planets and also received the position of imperial mathematician, in which he cast the horoscope of Emperor Rudolf. Kepler then set out to fit all of Brahe's data into a model or theory of the universe.

Kepler's three laws

Kepler found that no matter how hard he tried, he could not get Brahe's data to fit into the traditional model in which the planets moved in perfect **circles.** This led him to start searching for some noncircular curve that would work, and his mathematics showed him the way. He was familiar with the ellipse—a shape resembling a flattened circle that was first studied by third-century B.C. Greek mathematician Apollonius of Perga (c. 262–c. 190 B.C.). Kepler applied the ellipse to

TABVLA III. ORBIVM PLANETARVM DIMENSIONES, ET DISTANTIAS PER QVINQVE
REGVLARIA CORPORA GEOMETRICA EXHIBENS.
ILLVSTRISS: PRINCIPI, AC DÑO, DÑO, FRIDERICO, DVCI WIR-
TENBERGICO, ET TECCIO, COMITI MONTIS BELGARVM, ETC. CONSECRATA.

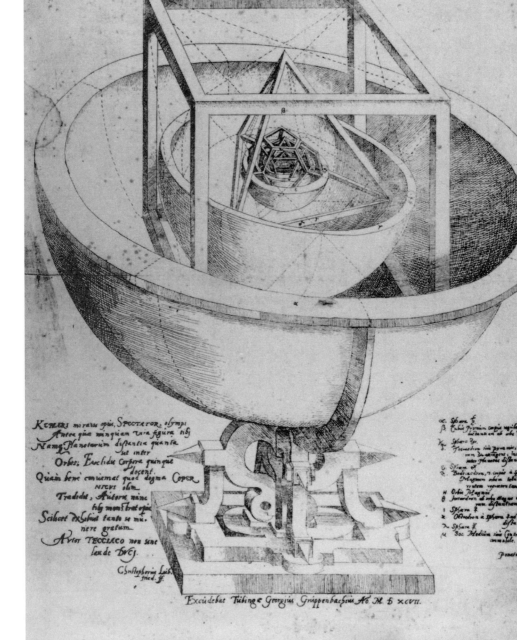

Excudebat Tübingæ Georgius Gruppenbachius Aᵒ M. D. XCVII.

the data he had gathered on the orbit of Mars. To his delight, Kepler found that the positions of Mars fit into an elliptical orbit around the Sun with a high degree of accuracy. With further study, Kepler was able to put forth his first two laws of planetary motion.

Kepler's first law showed that every planet's orbit is an ellipse with the sun at one focus. His second law concerned the speed of the planets and showed that the closer a planet was to the Sun the faster it would move. These two laws were eventually published in 1609 in his aptly titled *Astronomia nova (New Astronomy).*

In 1619, Kepler published another book, *Harmonice mundi (Harmony of the World)*, which also contained his third law. Stated mathematically, the law said that a planet's revolution (the time it takes to make one complete circle) is proportional to the cube of its average distance from the Sun. Kepler's laws would eventually put an end to the incorrect astronomy of the Greeks, especially the astronomy of Ptolemy, the second-century astronomer who believed that all astronomical bodies revolved around the Earth. Kepler's laws featured mathematical laws and concepts as the foundation of this new astronomy.

Moves to Linz and remarries

In 1611, Protestant and Catholic conflict finally resulted in bloodshed in Prague, and Rudolph II was forced to abdicate (leave his throne). Kepler had already been invited by the city of Linz, Austria, to fill the position of provincial mathematician, a job created just for him. He agreed to accept since his wife liked Linz. Before they could leave however, she caught a disease called typhus, which the soldiers had brought to Prague, and she died. Kepler eventually was allowed to leave Prague and would remain in Linz for 14 years.

In Linz, the 42-year-old Kepler met and married 24-year-old Susanna Reuttinger, with whom he had seven children, only two of whom survived childhood. Apparently Kepler applied mathematics to everything, even to the selection of a wife. When he decided to remarry, he compiled a list of 11 eligible women and rated each according to a series of desirable qualities. He then averaged the grades and made a selection. When the highest-ranking prospect refused his request, he recalculated and married Reuttinger, the previously fifth-rated woman on the list.

Johannes Kepler

Opposite page:
Johannes Kepler's model of the orbits of the planets.

Johannes Kepler

Kepler went on to publish several more important works. During his career, he did enough research on the nature of light to found the modern study of geometrical optics. This area of science involves the use of the laws of geometry to trace a light ray through a system of lenses. Religious war seemed to follow Kepler wherever he lived. He eventually sought a place where Protestants were at least tolerated. After living in Regensburg, Germany, for a time, he moved to the duchy (a territory ruled by a duke or duchess) of Sagan, where Ferdinand III (1608–57), king of Bohemia, had promised to give him a position. Unhappy in this strange city and with never being paid, Kepler eventually decided to return to Linz, but died in Regensburg on November 15, 1630, of a fever.

For a man who believed that the universe was governed by discoverable mathematical laws, the first line of Kepler's epitaph (inscription on a tomb)—written by Kepler himself—is appropriate. It reads, "I used to measure the heavens, now I shall measure the shadows of the earth."

For More Information

Asimov, Isaac. *Asimov's Biographical Encyclopedia of Science and Technology.* Garden City, NY: Doubleday & Co., 1982.

Caspar, Max. *Kepler.* Edited and translated by C. Doris Hellman. Also translated by Owen Gingerich. Reprint, Mineola, NY: Dover Publications, 1993.

Gillispie, Charles C. *Dictionary of Scientific Biography.* New York: Charles Scribner's Sons, 1972.

Kline, Morris. *Mathematics in Western Culture.* New York: Oxford University Press, 1953.

MacTutor History of Mathematics Archive. "Johannes Kepler." http://www-groups.dcs.st-and.ac.uk/~history/Mathematicians/Kepler.html (accessed on April 23, 1999).

Tiner, John Hudson. *Johannes Kepler: Giant of Faith and Science.* Milford, MI: Mott Media, 1977.

Young, Robyn V., ed. *Notable Mathematicians: From Ancient Times to the Present.* Detroit: Gale Research, 1998.

Born c. 780
Baghdad (in present-day Iraq)

Died c. 850
Location unknown

Arab algebraist and astronomer

al-Khwārizmī

Often called the "father of algebra," al-Khwārizmī composed the first **algebra** text to be written in Arabic. This Arab scholar is also responsible for the Arab adoption of Hindu numerals. He is an essential link in their eventual acceptance by the West. Because of both his writings and his own name, two words—"algebra" and "algorithm"—were introduced into the language of mathematics.

Origins

Few details of the early life and education of al-Khwārizmī (pronounced al-KWAR-iz-mee) are known. Historians usually focus on any meanings contained in his full name, which is Abu Ja'Far Muhammad Ibn Mūsā al-Khwārizmī, as well as examining other names he was called. "Al-Khwārizmī" means that he came "from Khwārizm," which is now the city of Khiva (pronounced KEE-va) in the central Asian country of Uzbekistan (pronounced uhz-BEK-i-stan). However, because al-Khwārizmī was also called *Qutrubbulli,* he may have been from the region between the Tigris and the Euphrates rivers, which corresponds to present-day Baghdad in Iraq. (Perhaps only his ancestors came from Khwārizm.) A further claim that he was of Persian ancestry because he was sometimes called *al-*

Muslim "House of Wisdom"

Around the year A.D. 800, during what is known in Europe as the Middle Ages, when learning and progress were almost at a standstill, the Arab city of Baghdad was becoming an international center of learning. From 813 to 833, during the reign of the Caliph al-Ma'mūn (786–833), a school was officially established in Baghdad (now in Iraq) that resembled the ancient "Museum" founded in Alexandria, Egypt, in Euclid's time. The Caliph was a great patron of learning and science. As Arab knowledge was just then becoming enriched by its translations of many ancient Greek works, the Caliph sponsored and set up what became known as the "Dar al-Hikma," or the "House of Wisdom."

As a kind of academy established to promote science, the House of Wisdom attracted the best Arab scholars of the day. It was there that many important Greek manuscripts in science were translated and made available to other Arab scholars. One of the more famous members of the House of Wisdom was al-Khwārizmī. It was because of the Arab respect, understanding, and actual care for Greek knowledge (including mathematics) that the House of Wisdom was eventually preserved, improved upon, and finally passed on to the West.

Majusi may mean only that he or his forebears were members of an old Persian religion. However, regardless of which region he is from, al-Khwārizmī was always an orthodox Muslim, so most scholars consider him to be an Arab.

Scholarly career

As an adult, al-Khwārizmī was a scholar in astronomy and mathematics at Dar al-Hikma, or the "House of Wisdom." This was an Arab institution similar to the ancient Museum at Alexandria (set up in that city by Ptolemy after the death of Alexander the Great). Created in Baghdad by the caliph (spiritual leader), al-Ma'mūn (786–833), who was its patron, Dar al-Hikma drew scholars from all parts of the Arab world. The city of Baghdad became for a time the new Alexandria. (See accompanying sidebar for more information on the House of Wisdom.)

Al-Khwārizmī was one of the first to join Dar al-Hikma, which was dedicated to the promotion of science. He became a faculty member, specializing in both mathematics and astronomy. As an astronomer, he was often required to work with astrology as well. In the year 847, when al-Khwārizmī was called upon to cast the horoscope (to tell the future using a person's birth date and the positions of the stars and planets) of a dying caliph, he predicted that the caliph would live another 50 years. Although the caliph died ten days later, al-Khwārizmī was able to survive his mistake.

Mathematical contributions: algebra

Although he wrote many books in different fields (such as geography), two books were to play an especially important role in the history of mathematics. The first of these was his work on algebra. In this first book, part of whose title contained the Arab words *al-jabr,* he dealt with the development of solutions to mathematical problems in which there was an unknown quantity. His purpose in writing such a book was for it to have a real, practical usefulness, "such as men constantly require . . . in all their dealings with one another, or where the measuring of lands, the digging of canals, geometrical computations . . . are concerned," he wrote.

Ancient algebra was very different from today's algebra. It used no symbols at all but instead used actual words for functions and even for numbers (which were also written out). Although his work is the first Arab book on algebra, al-Khwārizmī should not be considered the "inventor" of algebra but rather one who best represented and summarized the teachings of his time.

There is no doubt, however, that algebra got its European name through the title of al-Khwārizmī's book. His long title contained the Arabic word *al-jabr,* meaning "transposing," "restoring," or "completion." The Western monks who were translating his book into Latin often would simply shorten the long Arabic title to the words *al-jabir.* Because mathematicians in the West first learned about the new techniques of algebra through his book, it is not surprising that they came to describe any aspect of the mathematics of solving for unknown quantities—or even any other Arabic book on the same subject—after the well-known shortened version of his Arabic title. Thus, when *al-jabir* was transliterated (spelled using the characters of the Latin alphabet), it became "algebra."

Mathematical contributions: Hindu numbering system

Al-Khwārizmī's second book on mathematics contained an equally significant if not greater contribution—the description and explanation of the Hindu system of number symbols. Number symbols that are similar to those used today were a very ancient accomplishment in India. The related ideas of positional value and the use of zero were introduced into India not too long before al-Khwārizmī lived. In fact, al-Khwārizmī wrote what is considered the earliest text that deals with the new Hindu symbols for numbers; he is therefore responsible for their eventual adoption by Arab mathematicians.

al-Khwārizmī

"Arabic" numerals of the West

The symbols used today in the West for the numbers zero through nine are called "Arabic numerals." But, in fact, they really came from India. Properly called the Hindu-Arabic numeral system, the symbols 0, 1, 2, 3, 4, 5, 6, 7, 8, and 9 were invented by the Hindus of northern India. It was the Arabs who, after adopting them, eventually transmitted them to western Europe. After crossing into Spain and Sicily early in the seventh century, the Arabs introduced the Greek learning that they had been using (and improving) for centuries, as well as much knowledge from the East that they also had adopted. Thus, the knowledge of the East made its way to the West via the Arabs.

Once Western scholars understood the superiority of this "new arithmetic" over both the abacus and the traditional system of Roman numerals, they began calling the numerals "Arabic" after the people from whom they learned it.

Because Europeans learned them from the Arabs about 400 years later, they came to be called Arabic numerals instead of Hindu numerals. Today they are correctly described as Hindu-Arabic numerals. (See accompanying sidebar for more information.)

Al-Khwārizmī's book introduced the nine characters (the number symbols for 1 through 9) as well as the use of a **circle** for zero. The use of a zero was most important, since it functioned mainly as a place-holder. The number 307, therefore, means that there are 3 hundreds, 0 tens, and 7 ones.

Although the value would be written as three hundred seven, the number could not be written in symbols without a zero. A key part of this example is also the concept called "positional notation," or place value. In the previous example, the 3 in 307 is in the third place from the right, meaning it signifies groups, or units, of a hundred. The second place is for groups of ten, and the first is for groups of ones. The Hindu system was based on the value ten, and each change (to the left) in the position of a number meant an increase by ten. Thus, the fourth position was for thousands, the fifth for ten thousands, and so on.

With the support of this system by al-Khwārizmī and its eventual acceptance in the Arab world, the benefits of this system, especially to the world of business and commerce, inevitably became obvious to those in the West. Nonetheless, this took a very long time to be introduced into Europe and then to be really accepted.

As the Western word "algebra" was derived from al-Khwārizmī's work, so too was the word "algorithm." Once Europe fully understood the Hindu-Arabic system and began to use it regularly, Europeans also attributed the algorithm completely to al-Khwārizmī. Soon, today's "algorithm" was called *al-khwārizmī,* or more carelessly, *algorismi*. Eventually, "algorithm" began to be used to name any step-by-step procedure for solving a mathematical problem.

Al-Khwārizmī's algebra and his introduction of the Hindu numeral system to the Arab world make him a highly significant link between time and cultures. Because of his study and writings, the West was eventually able to benefit, via the Arabs, from the mathematical learning and experience of the East.

For More Information

Biographical Dictionary of Mathematicians. New York: Charles Scribner's Sons, 1991.

Boyer, Carl B., and Uta C. Merzbach. *A History of Mathematics.* New York: John Wiley & Sons, 1989.

Katz, Victor J. *A History of Mathematics: An Introduction.* New York: HarperCollins College Publishers, 1993.

MacTutor History of Mathematics Archive. "Abu Abd-Allah ibn Musa al-Khwārizmī." http://www-groups.dcs.st-and.ac.uk/~history/Mathematicians/Al'Khwārizmī.html (accessed on April 23, 1999).

Young, Robyn V., ed. *Notable Mathematicians: From Ancient Times to the Present.* Detroit: Gale Research, 1998.

**Born January 15, 1850
Moscow, Russia**

**Died February 10, 1891
Stockholm, Sweden**

Russian mathematician

Sofya Kovalevskaya

The first woman to hold a full university professorship in modern Europe, Sofya Kovalevskaya has been described as a dazzling mathematical genius. Her life was spent battling and overcoming the many barriers nineteenth-century women faced in the sciences. Although she died at age 41 and published only ten papers, her mathematical achievements and contributions are considerable. Her name lives on through a theorem named after her.

> *"Mathematics [is] an exalted and mysterious science which opens up to its initiates a new world of wonders, inaccessible to ordinary mortals."*

Early life and education

The second of three children born into a family of wealthy aristocrats (government by privileged individuals), Sofya Vasilyevna Kovalevskaya (pronounced kuh-vul-YAFE-skuh-yuh) was born in Moscow, Russia, on January 15, 1850. (There are various transliterations of both her first and last name.) Her father, Vasily Korvin-Krukovsky, was a well-educated man who rose to the rank of artillery general in the czar's (Russian ruler) army. Her mother, Elizaveta Schubert, was also well-educated and a member of the Russian nobility. Her father's family was probably Ukrainian; her mother's people were German. Kovalevskaya's maternal

Sofya Kovalevskaya

grandfather, Fyodor Fyodorovich Schubert, and great-grandfather, Fyodor Ivanovich Schubert, were noted mathematicians.

Kovalevskaya was the middle child, and always felt that her parents loved her brother and sister more than they did her. As with most noble families in Russia, the children had nannies and governesses (women who take care of children in a household) as tutors. They did not see much of their parents while they were very young. When her father retired, the family moved to their country estate in a remote part of Russia near the Lithuanian border.

In the isolated countryside in which the Kovalevskaya family lived, young Sofya had her first encounter with mathematics in a most unusual manner. As the large country house was being redecorated with fancy imported wallpaper, the workers ran out of paper. They resorted to using anything they could find as a temporary wall covering. Kovalevskaya came upon a room whose walls had been covered with separate sheets consisting of a lecture on calculus that had been left over from her father's college days. She later wrote how she sat before the mysterious wall for hours, trying to make some sense of a phrase or a formula.

After her governess left when Kovalevskaya was 12, the young girl decided to continue her studies on her own and borrowed a physics book from a neighbor. When she was unable to understand the formulas in the book (since they related to trigonometry), she actually worked them out on her own from scratch.

Kovalevskaya's physicist neighbor was so impressed by her work that eventually he was able to persuade her father to let her study with a tutor in the Russian city of St. Petersburg. This was a significant achievement, because her father was initially alarmed by his daughter's talents. He believed that it was not a woman's role to be educated. However, by the time his daughter was 18, she had decided on making mathematics her career. This decision created a serious dilemma for her: no Russian university would admit a woman as a student. Her only other option was to go to school in another country, yet Russian women could not travel on their own. A single woman was listed on her father's passport until she was married, and then she became her husband's responsibility.

Marriage of convenience

Although Russia was an extremely conservative society—it had only recently abolished its system of near-slavery called serfdom—many new ideas and movements based on greater freedom were beginning to sweep the country. In some ways, Russian society was like the United States in the 1960s when anti-establishment movements like hippies were becoming popular with young people. The hippies of 1860 Russia, called "nihilists," questioned any and all authority.

One popular way of rebelling against parents who would not allow their daughters any freedom was for the girl to marry "on paper" a male friend who would be willing to let her travel on her own. In this way, Kovalevskaya chose to break free from her parents. In 1868, she met Vladimir Kovalensky, a geology student, and married him in September. Together with Kovalevskaya's older sister, Anyuta, they left for Germany in early 1869. The three of them then split up: Kovalensky went to Vienna, Austria; Anyuta went to Paris, France; and Sofya remained in Heidelberg to study.

Studies with Weierstrass

Kovalevskaya soon found that Germany was little better than Russia concerning women and education. After receiving permission to attend lectures unofficially, she remained in Heidelberg for two years, after which she moved to Berlin. The university there also gave her problems. She eventually was able to persuade Karl T. Weierstrass (1815–97), a well-known German mathematician, to give her private lessons. Weierstrass agreed at first, possibly to get rid of her. When she quickly solved some of the most advanced problems he had given her (probably to discourage her and make her go away), however, he realized that she was potentially an original and imaginative mathematician.

Despite his prestige and authority, Weierstrass was unable to get Kovalevskaya admitted to the University of Berlin. So he simply allowed her to study with him for the next four years. By 1874, Kovalevskaya had written three original works, two on mathematics and one on astronomy. On the strength of the first of these papers, written on differential equations, she qualified for and received her doctorate degree *in absentia* from Göttingen University in Germany. (Her dissertation was so highly thought of that the

Sofya Kovalevskaya

university gave her the degree despite the fact that she was "absent," or never attended a class there.) The university also gave her the highest ranking, "summa cum laude," and did not even require her to take an examination.

Temporarily returns to Russia

Despite the continued help and support of Weierstrass, Kovalevskaya was unable to get a job teaching anywhere in Europe. So, after her long, hard years of study, she returned to Moscow with her husband, who expected to become a professor of paleontology (the science of fossils) there. In October 1878, the couple had a daughter, Sofya, whom they affectionately called Foufie. When Kovalensky's teaching job did not come through, however, he became involved in a bad business situation that eventually led to his disgrace and suicide. When this happened in 1883, his wife and daughter were already out of the country. Kovalevskaya had decided that, no matter what, she would attempt to become a true mathematician.

Recognition at last

Kovalevskaya returned to Berlin in order to follow her belief that she was born to be a mathematician. With the help of Weierstrass and some friends, she finally took a position in Sweden at Stockholm University as a *Privatdozent,* or unpaid lecturer. She was, however, able to receive payments directly from students.

In 1888, the real quality of her work became known when she submitted a mathematical paper for the Bordin Prize, one of the highest awards given in her field. Run by the French Academy, the contest for the Bordin Prize required that all papers be submitted anonymously so that the judges would not be influenced by the author's identity. Her paper—dealing with the problem of how Saturn's rings might rotate that planet—was chosen as the winner. The judges were so taken with its excellence that they raised the cash award from 3,000 francs to 5,000 francs. Little did they know that they had chosen the work of a woman.

The following year, Kovalevskaya was finally given the attention her work deserved: Stockholm University rewarded her with her first professorship position. This appointment made her the first woman mathematician to hold a chair at a European university. That same year, she won another prize from the Swedish Academy of Sciences and also was elected to membership in the Russian Academy of Sciences.

Less than two years later, at the height of her career, Kovalevskaya died suddenly at the age of 41 of influenza complicated by pneumonia. Two years before, she had met and fallen in love with Maxim Kovalensky, a distant relation of her dead husband. Although they at times had a stormy relationship, she had been vacationing with him in Paris after which she fell ill from the exhausting return trip to Sweden. She had not planned her trip well. More than once she found herself struggling all alone with her luggage, only to spend the night in a cold, empty train station. She died a few days after finally reaching Stockholm.

Often described as a mathematician with the soul of a poet, Kovalevskaya did indeed write plays, novels, and poetry in her short life. The shy yet strong-willed woman seemed to live her life according to the motto she used for her prize-winning paper: "Say what you know; do what you must, come what may."

For More Information

Biographical Dictionary of Mathematicians. New York: Charles Scribner's Sons, 1991.

Henderson, Harry. *Modern Mathematicians.* New York: Facts on File, 1996.

MacTutor History of Mathematics Archive. "Sofia Vasilyevna Kovalevskaya." http://www-groups.dcs.st-and.ac.uk/~history/Mathematicians/Kovalevskaya.html (accessed on April 23, 1999).

Morrow, Charlene, and Teri Perl, eds. *Notable Women in Mathematics: A Biographical Dictionary.* Westport, CT: Greenwood Press, 1998.

Osen, Lynn M. *Women in Mathematics.* Cambridge, MA: The MIT Press, 1974.

Sofya Kovalevskaya

Born January 25, 1736
Turin, Italy

Died April 10, 1813
Paris, France

French algebraist and number theorist

Joseph-Louis Lagrange

Considered the last great mathematician of the eighteenth century, Joseph-Louis Lagrange invented the calculus of variations, laid the foundations of modern mechanics, and helped establish the metric system. His many contributions to mathematics were always characterized by originality.

> "In [Joseph-Louis Lagrange, the city of] Turin possesses a treasure whose worth it perhaps does not know."
>
> —French mathematician
> Jean le Rond d'Alembert

Early life and education

Joseph-Louis Lagrange (pronounced lah-GRAHNZH) was born in Turin, Italy, of a French father and an Italian mother. Lagrange's great-grandfather was a French cavalry captain who went to northern Italy to serve the duke and remained there. Although French in descent, Lagrange's father's name appeared on the baptismal certificate as Giuseppe Francesco Lodovico Lagrangia. His mother, Teresa Grosso, was the daughter of a wealthy Italian physician. Lagrange was the youngest of eleven children. None but he lived long enough to reach adulthood.

Because Lagrange's family intended him to enter the legal profession, his early schooling focused on the classics. He showed little enthusiasm for mathematics during these years, although he did study the works of **Archimedes of Syracuse** (287–212 B.C.) and **Euclid of Alexandria** (c. 325–c. 270 B.C.). Lagrange himself later recalled that an article by English astronomer and mathematician Edmond Halley (1656–1742) convinced him that mathematics would be his field of work. After being inspired by Halley's article about calculus and how it was superior to ancient Greek **geometry,** Lagrange began teaching himself mathematics. (See sidebar on Edmond Halley in the **Statistics** entry.) By the time he was 19, Lagrange had become such a master in his new field that he was appointed professor of mathematics at the Royal Artillery School in Turin, Italy.

Early discoveries

Before he began teaching in Turin in 1755, Lagrange had already begun some of his best and most original work. In 1754, he produced an essay in which he had basically thought out the beginning principles of his first important discovery, the calculus of variations. Eventually, Lagrange would perfect this new calculus to the point where he worked out equations that were general enough to solve any problem in mechanics. Thus, instead of taking a geometrical approach to mechanical problems, he combined algebra and calculus and created an entirely new branch of mathematics—the calculus of variations.

Also in 1754, Lagrange began corresponding with Swiss mathematician **Leonhard Euler** (1707–83), who praised and encouraged the young man. Through Euler's influence, Lagrange was elected to the Berlin Academy at the age of 23. Lagrange continued teaching in Turin until he was 30. In 1759, he helped organize a research society called the Turin Academy of Sciences. In the publications of this new academy, Lagrange would publish a great deal of his early and very important material.

Also during his early years in Turin, Lagrange figured out how to deal with the motions of solar systems that contained more than two celestial bodies (such as our own universe with its many planets, Sun, and Moon). Newton's law of universal gravitation worked well when there were only two bodies in a system, but the real solar system had many bodies of all different sizes that influenced each other in different ways. Eventually, Lagrange would

Jean le Rond d'Alembert

French mathematician and physicist Jean le Rond d'Alembert (1717–83) began his life as an abandoned baby. On a cold and blustery night, a local policeman making his rounds found the infant on the steps of the little Church of Saint Jean-le-Rond. The newborn was baptized, given the name of the church, and sent to live with a nearby family.

The baby, who would grow to become a pioneer in the development of the calculus and would serve as science editor for the great French encyclopedia called *Encyclopedie,* was really the son of two of France's most powerful and connected people. His mother, the Marquise de Tencin (1685–1749), was the sister of a cardinal and a former nun who became mistress to many rich and powerful men. D'Alembert's father, Chevalier Louis-Camus Destouches, was a general in the French army. Abandoned and never recognized by his mother, d'Alembert was loved by his father who sent money to his foster parents and provided for his education.

It is not known why the child named after a saint later decided to take the name d'Alembert.

address what came to be called the three-body problem. This problem involves the complicated situation of trying to predict the motions of three different objects, each of which attracts and, therefore, influences the other. Lagrange would win a Grand Prize from the French Academy in 1766 for his solution. Two years earlier, Lagrange had won the same Grand Prize for determining the gravitational forces that caused the moon to always have its same side face the earth.

Accepts position in Berlin

With the intervention of his friend, French mathematician Jean le Rond d'Alembert (1717–83), Lagrange was offered the position of director of mathematics at the Berlin Academy (formerly held by Euler). (See accompanying sidebar for more information on Alembert.) The invitation came directly from Frederick II (1712–86), king of Prussia, who stated that as the "greatest king in Europe," he ought to have the "greatest mathematician in Europe" in his court. Since the Royal Artillery School did not even attempt to make him a better offer, Lagrange accepted the king's offer. After moving to Berlin, Lagrange began his new job as director in November 1766. The position paid him very well and did not require that he teach. Lagrange would keep it for 20 years.

Less than one year after he arrived in Berlin, Lagrange married his cousin, Vittoria Conti. Within a few years, however, she became ill and, after some years in decline, died in 1783. The couple had no children. Lagrange remained alone until 1792 when he married Renée-Françoise-Adélaide Lemonnier, the daughter of famous French astronomer Pierre-Charles Lemonnier. Although Lagrange was 56 and his new wife only a teenager, Lemonnier was devoted to him. She helped him regain his interest in mathematics following one of his more severe bouts of depression.

Returns to Paris

Lagrange suffered from depression from about 1780 to his death. When his first wife died in 1783 and King Frederick died in 1786, Lagrange's growing indifference to his work was not helped by an increasing resentment against foreigners that he was beginning to experience in Berlin. When a position with the French Academy opened up, he therefore sought it out, was selected, and returned to France in 1787. Although warmly welcomed, his depression worsened and he was not shaken from it until after the French Revolution began.

Despite the excesses of the Revolution and the political changes that occurred as a result of it, Lagrange's life was never in jeopardy. For his close friendship with French royalty, he should have been considered an enemy by the revolutionaries, but he was not treated so. In addition, in spite of his good treatment by the revolutionaries, French emperor Napoléon Bonaparte (1769–1821) gave Lagrange honors when he assumed power. Lagrange was never passionately involved in French politics and followed a single rule of conduct: "I believe that, in general, one of the first principles of every wise man is to conform strictly to the laws of the country in which he is living, even when they are unreasonable."

In 1790, Lagrange was appointed by the Revolution to head a commission to create a new system of weights and measures. Some of the best scientists in France were among its members. In 1795, the commission supported adoption of the metric system, founded on the base unit of ten. Eventually, the entire scientific community adopted the metric system as the universal language of science.

Although Lagrange never suffered at the hands of the Revolution's extremists, whose excesses were named The Terror, others did. When the Revolution guillotined French chemist Antoine Lavoisier (1743–94), the sad words of Lagrange survived him: "It took only a moment to strike off his head, and probably a hundred years will not be sufficient to produce another like it."

During the Revolution, Lagrange was made professor of mathematics at the newly formed L'École Normale. The school's goal was to train teachers and to standardize education. After the Revolution, Lagrange was appointed professor of mathematics at L'École Polytechnique, which exists today. In 1808 he was made a count of the Empire by Napoléon, and in 1811 was named *grand croix* by Napoléon. This award, meaning "grand cross," was created by Napoléon in 1811 to honor French individuals of high achievement. One of France's highest honors, it is still awarded today.

Lagrange died on April 10, 1813, and was buried with many other greats of France at the Pantheon. Of his many published works, his *Mécanique Analytique,* printed in 1788, is considered the most important. Based on his original work done more than 30 years before, this masterpiece systematized mechanics. It also transformed the study of the effects of forces on objects into a branch of mathematical analysis. By bringing his mathematics to the study of the solar system, Lagrange made the movements of celestial bodies in the solar system more understandable.

For More Information

Abbott, David, ed. *The Biographical Dictionary of Scientists: Mathematicians.* New York: Peter Bedrick Books, 1986.

Asimov, Isaac. *Asimov's Biographical Encyclopedia of Science and Technology.* Garden City, NY: Doubleday & Company, 1982.

Joseph-Louis Lagrange

Joseph-Louis Lagrange

Biographical Dictionary of Mathematicians. New York: Charles Scribner's Sons, 1991.

MacTutor History of Mathematics Archive. "Jean Le Rond d'Alembert." http://www-groups.dcs.st-and.ac.uk/~history/Mathematicians/D'Alembert.html (accessed on May 4, 1999).

MacTutor History of Mathematics Archive. "Joseph-Louis Lagrange." http://www-groups.dcs.st-and.ac.uk/~history/Mathematicians/Lagrange.html (accessed on April 23, 1999).

Young, Robyn V., ed. *Notable Mathematicians: From Ancient Times to the Present.* Detroit: Gale Research, 1998.

Born July 1, 1646
Leipzig, Saxony (present-day Germany)

Died November 14, 1716
Hannover, Hannover (present-day Germany)

German philosopher and logician

Gottfried Leibniz

Gottfried Leibniz was a multi-talented individual who is rightly considered one of the founders of calculus and symbolic **logic.** His invention of calculus was independent of that of English mathematician and physicist **Isaac Newton** (1642–1727) Leibniz not only expressed fundamental notions of calculus in the best way but named it as well. The last 15 years of his life were embittered by an international dispute with Newton over who first invented calculus.

> *"Nothing is more important than to see the sources of invention which are, in my opinion, more interesting than the inventions themselves."*

Early life and education

Gottfried Wilhelm von Leibniz (pronounced LIPE-nits) was born in Leipzig, Germany, into an educated family. His father, Friedrich, was a lawyer and a professor of moral philosophy at the University of Leipzig. His mother, Katherina Schmuck, was his father's third wife, and came from an academic family of good standing. Leibniz had one sister as well as a half-brother and a half-sister.

As a very young child, Leibniz was recognized by all as a prodigy (a child with a high degree of intelligence). At school, his teachers

Gottfried Leibniz

tried to get him to read books suitable to his age. Leibniz, however, wanted to read what was on the shelves of his father's library. Upon his father's death, when young Gottfried was six years old, a relative persuaded the school that the boy be given access to his father's books. It was then that his real education began, and the boy taught himself Latin by the time he was eight. Since he read nearly everything he could get his hands on regardless of subject matter, he also learned Greek at age 14 and had acquainted himself with most of the non-scientific classics.

In 1661, at the age of 15, Leibniz entered the University of Leipzig and received his formal training in the law. While there, he also began reading the important scientific works of others, like English philosopher Francis Bacon (1561–1626), French algebraist and philosopher **René Descartes** (1596–1650), Italian mathematician **Galileo** (1564–1642), and German astronomer and mathematician **Johannes Kepler** (1571–1630). Two years later, Leibniz received his bachelor's degree, and a master's degree in law followed the next year. However, when he completed his dissertation and applied for the doctor of law degree from Leipzig in 1666, he was turned down on the grounds that he was too young. So Leibniz simply presented his work to the University of Altdorf in Nuremburg, Germany. This school both gave him the degree and offered him a position. That same year, Leibniz wrote his first mathematical paper.

Foreign affairs career

Leibniz declined an academic career and took a government position involved with legal reform. In this capacity, he began corresponding with a large number of people about a wide range of topics. He would keep up his letter-writing all his life, and today more than 15,000 of his letters survive. This job also allowed him to travel a great deal, and he took advantage of his trips by meeting the leading scientists and mathematicians in each city.

During this time, Leibniz formed a lifelong friendship with Dutch physicist and astronomer **Christiaan Huygens** (1629–95), who lived in Paris. He also went to London and met English scientists Robert Boyle (1627–91) and Robert Hooke (1635–1702), among others. Later, Leibniz was elected a member of the Royal Society. During one diplomatic mission in France, he was able to live in

Gottfried Leibniz

English physicist Isaac Newton (left) and Gottfried Leibniz feuded over who first invented calculus.

Paris for three years and study unpublished manuscripts of the work of French mathematicians like Descartes and Blaise Pascal (1623–62). (See sidebar on Pascal in the **Probability** entry.)

Binary notation and calculating machine

As early as 1666, Leibniz had attempted to work out some type of symbolism for logic. This brilliant idea of reducing logical thought into some form of a mathematical calculation or equation led him to

Gottfried Leibniz

explore the possibilities of what came to be known as the "binary system." According to Leibniz, a binary system needed only two symbols: 0 and 1. The system, therefore, had the advantage of being extremely simple. Although Leibniz never developed his ideas entirely, they were taken up in the nineteenth century by English mathematician **George Boole** (1815–64). He developed Leibniz's ideas into his Boolean **algebra,** or symbolic logic. Symbolic logic, in turn, would lead to binary mathematics becoming the basis of twentieth-century modern **computer** systems. In today's computer technology, binary mathematics make it possible to represent systems that have a two-state nature—such as "on-off," "open-closed," or "go–no go."

Although Leibniz did not develop his binary ideas very far, he turned his thoughts about calculating machines into a workable reality. In 1671, while he was in Paris, he first began to work on what was the forerunner of the modern calculator. After two years of effort, he produced a calculating machine that was more advanced than any of its time. It could perform all four fundamental operations of arithmetic: **addition, subtraction, multiplication,** and **division.** Basically, the machine would multiply and divide by the mechanical repetition of adding and subtracting.

Leibniz's major technical innovation with the calculating machine was the stepped drum, which was a gear made of pins of different lengths. This gear was not improved upon until 1875. Although Leibniz presented his invention to the Royal Society in 1663, he did not write about it until 1685. The paper remained in a library for over 200 years until it was published in 1897.

Introduces calculus

A turning point in the mathematical life of Leibniz was his 1673 visit to London, where he became acquainted with the work of Isaac Newton and Newton's teacher, Isaac Barrow (1630–77). (See sidebar on Isaac Barrow in the **Isaac Newton** entry.) This intellectual stimulation, combined with Leibniz's friendship with Huygens and his familiarity with Pascal's work, led him to work long and hard on what he came to call "the calculus." In 1684, he submitted what would be the first published account of his calculus.

The invention of calculus marked the beginning of higher mathematics. Calculus would soon offer science a powerful new tool to

Gabrielle-Émilie Le Tonnelier de Breteuil

An aristocrat with the lengthy name of Gabrielle-Émilie Le Tonnelier de Breteuil (pronounced tun-lee-AY deu bruh-TOY), marquise du Châtelet (1706-49), was one of mathematics' more fascinating individuals. After receiving an exceptional education, Breteuil was told at the age of 19 that a marriage to the marquis du Châtelet, count of Lomont, had been arranged by her parents. She had little choice but to agree, and by the time she was 24, she had three children and a husband whose military and political career kept him away from Paris for extended periods of time.

After spending some years with her husband, Breteuil returned to Paris without him, where she began to live her own life. There, she met and fell in love with one of the great intellectual leaders of France, philosopher François-Marie Arouet de Voltaire. He encouraged her to cultivate her mind and to pursue her natural mathematical talents.

Breteuil proceeded to publish a mathematical work on Isaac Newton's physics and mechanics. She also became acquainted with the work of Gottfried Leibniz and did some writing on his ideas. As a member of Europe's intellectual elite, she managed an active social life while undertaking the huge task of translating Newton's *Principia Mathematica* into French. She completed this monument to French scholarship just before she died of an infection after giving birth to her fourth child at the age of 42.

solve problems that were previously far too complicated to even attempt. With it, scientists could work on a dynamic or rapidly changing problem that was influenced by several different factors (like velocity, **time,** distance, and force) at the same time.

Leibniz's calculus paper soon created a private disagreement between he and Newton. Newton all but accused Leibniz of stealing his ideas. The fact that the symbolism, or notation style, used by Leibniz would prove to be far more convenient and useful than Newton's did not help matters. Finally, Newton's friends and supporters joined in and argued that Leibniz must have taken Newton's ideas during Leibniz's visit to London in 1673. The disagreement then turned into a full-blown controversy that pitted England against Germany.

Gottfried Leibniz

The dispute between Leibniz and Newton was never resolved in their lifetimes. Only with the passage of centuries have passions cooled. Most historians now agree that each independently invented his own version of calculus, with Newton doing it first by eight to ten years. Leibniz published his first accounts, however, in 1684. The dispute proved harmful to British mathematics, since several generations of British mathematicians continued to be loyal to Newton's claim and deliberately shut themselves off from other important non-British advances in mathematics.

Founds Berlin Academy and labors for princes

Leibniz began his career working for royalty and state leaders, and in 1676 he accepted a position as librarian to the House of Brunswick. As with his earlier government job, this post enabled him to travel and meet with scientists in other countries. But this job also required him to research the genealogy, or family history, of the Brunswick family. Unfortunately, Leibniz worked as long and as hard doing genealogical research as he did on science and philosophy. He would remain in service to them for most of the rest of his life.

During the years Leibniz was the librarian, he *was* able to make some accomplishments in science and mathematics. In 1700, he persuaded King Frederick I of Prussia (1657–1713) to create the German equivalent of the Royal Society of London for the Improvement of Natural Knowledge (in England) or L'Académie de Sciences (in France). Named the Akademie der Wissenschaften (Academy of Sciences), the German science society was founded in Berlin that year with Leibniz serving as its first president.

Leibniz's inspiration for founding the Academy of Sciences in Germany came from his idea to create an international community of scholars who were linked by their national academies. He sought to have the scientists exchange ideas and share both their knowledge and their discoveries freely. Perhaps his dream for the Academy resulted from his long and bitter scientific controversy with Newton.

Leibniz, who never married or had children, had a sad end. His last years were spent suffering from gout and feeling neglected by the royalty he served for so long. Incredibly, when he finally died in Hannover in 1716, the Academy that Leibniz had founded took no notice and no one but his secretary attended his funeral.

For More Information

Abbott, David, ed. *The Biographical Dictionary of Scientists: Mathematicians.* New York: Peter Bedrick Books, 1986.

Jolley, Nicholas. *The Cambridge Companion to Leibniz.* Cambridge, England: Cambridge University Press, 1994.

MacTutor History of Mathematics Archive. "Gottfried Wilhelm von Leibniz." http://www-groups.dcs.st-and.ac.uk/~history/Mathematicians/Leibniz.html (accessed on April 23, 1999).

Pappas, Theoni. *Mathematical Scandals.* San Carlos, CA: Wide World Publishing/Tetra, 1997.

Simmons, George F. *Calculus Gems: Brief Lives and Memorable Mathematics.* New York: McGraw-Hill, 1992.

Young, Robyn V., ed. *Notable Mathematicians: From Ancient Times to the Present.* Detroit: Gale Research, 1998.

Gottfried Leibniz

Linear measurement

L inear measurement is the determination of the length of something by comparing it to some standard unit. Length is the number representing the measurement of something from end to end.

Background

When measuring something to find out how long it is from end to end (or for any other type of measurement), it is necessary to compare it to something whose size is already known. The one thing that is most familiar and which has always been available for quick reference is one's own body. Therefore, the earliest standard units for measuring length were parts of the body.

Existing records kept by Babylonians and Egyptians suggest that the hand, span, cubit, and foot were all used as standards for measuring different lengths. The hand was the width of a man's hand (not including the thumb) held up with the fingers together (about 4 inches). This was used to measure the height (vertical length) of a horse, and it is still used today. A span is the width of a man's hand with fingers and thumbs spread fully apart, measured from the tip of the little finger to the tip of the thumb (about 9

Linear measurement

inches). A cubit is the length of the forearm from the elbow to the tip of the middle finger (about 18 inches). A foot was the distance from heel to toe (about 12 inches), and was considered by the Romans to be the equivalent of 12 *uncia,* or thumb-widths. It was the Roman word *uncia* for one-twelfth that resulted in the standard known as the inch.

For the Romans, long distances were measured in paces, one of which was the distance of a normal stride (about 2½ feet). The Roman mile was therefore about 2,000 paces. Around the year 1100, King Henry I of England (1068–1135) decreed that a yard was the distance from the tip of the nose to the tip of the thumb of an outstretched arm. By the fourteenth century, King Edward I of England (1272–1307) made the standard yard from an iron bar about two cubits long (36 inches). Other early English measurements were three barleycorns or grains of barley for one inch. A rod was the total length of the left feet of 16 men (with 320 rods equaling 1 mile).

While the British and the Americans still use a system for measuring length that is based on these standards, most of the rest of the world uses what are called SI units which are based on the meter. (A meter equals approximately 39.37 inches.) Called the "Système Internationale" for its origins in the French-originated metric system, this system is based on powers of 10 and uses prefixes like "deca-," "hecto-," and "kilo-" to designate 10 times, 100 times, and 1,000 times the fundamental unit of one meter.

Description and use

Linear measurement or length is purely a one-dimensional property. It typically involves measuring a straight or curved line (which is a set of points joined together) and a line with no width or thickness. While nothing could seem simpler than measuring the length of a line, in principle it can be extremely complex. This is so if one realizes that when measuring the distance between two points, no matter how close together they are, there is an infinite number of points lying on the path between these two points. Although this idea of infinity is true, it is only considered by theoretical mathematicians. In everyday life, measuring for length is something people do without giving a thought to the notion of an infinity of points between two points.

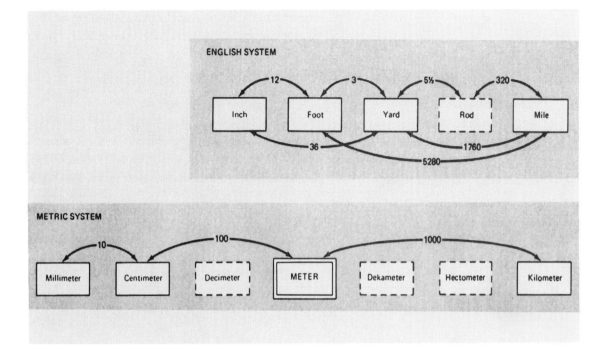

One of the more useful measurements for length is that of **perimeter.** The perimeter is the distance around a two-dimensional or flat figure. For any closed curve figure like a **polygon** (a figure with three or more sides), the perimeter is measured by adding the lengths of all of its sides. For a **circle,** however, the distance around it is called its circumference.

Linear measurement is something humans do all the time. One knows almost intuitively (without having to think about it) most of the lengths of everyday objects and can probably even give an accurate estimate. However, when Americans must work with the metric system of linear measurement, they are usually unfamiliar with it and must consult a conversion table to translate SI units into what Americans call the customary system.

For More Information

Hirschi, L. Edwin. *Building Mathematics Concepts in Grades Kindergarten Through Eight.* Scranton, PA: International Textbook Co., 1970.

Ganeri, Anita. *The Story of Weights and Measures.* New York: Oxford University Press, 1997.

Conversions among English and metric units.

Measuring with thumbs and fingers and feet

Many of today's units of measure come from ancient times when things were measured or compared to a standard that everyone recognized. This process would allow people to compare what they were measuring against something that was familiar and always available. The Babylonians and Egyptians therefore used parts of their body as standards. The Egyptians built their pyramids using parts of their arms as units of length. However, since the size of everyone's fingers, palms, and arm spans differed, they decided to use those of the king or pharaoh (ruler) as the standard.

The smallest Egyptian unit, the digit, was equal to the width of one finger. For the Romans, it was the width of the thumb. The English eventually called the digit an inch. A cubit was the length from the king's fingertips to his elbow. The Greeks and Romans used real feet as a measure; the English later adopted the foot and said it consisted of 12 inches. The yard is said to have come from a decree from King Henry I (1068–1135), who said that one yard was the distance from the tip of his nose to the end of his thumb. Others say that a yard was taken from the length of the arrows used by archers who used the longbow. The word mile comes from the Roman word *mille,* meaning "one thousand." The Romans said one mile was equal to one thousand paces.

Humez, Alexander, et al. *Zero to Lazy Eight: The Romance of Numbers.* New York: Simon & Schuster, 1993.

Walpole, Brenda. *Distance.* Milwaukee: Gareth Stevens Publishers, 1995.

Wheeler, Ruric E. *Modern Mathematics.* Pacific Grove, CA: Brooks/Cole Publishing Co., 1995.

Born December 1, 1792
Nizhniy Novgorod, Russia

Died February 24, 1856
Kazan, Russia

Russian geometer

Nikolay Lobachevsky

As the inventor of non-Euclidean **geometry,** Nikolay Loba-chevsky created a radically different mathematical system. This system eventually proved to be the basis for a true revolution in human thought. His new geometry provided the foundation upon which the great discoveries in physics of the twentieth century would be built. Although he has had as great an influence on mathematics as anyone, Lobachevsky remains one of the least known of all the mathematical greats.

> *"There is no branch of mathematics, however abstract, which may not some day be applied to phenomena of the real world."*

Early life and education

Nikolay Ivanovich Lobachevsky (pronounced luh-buh-CHAFE-skee) was born in Nizhniy Novgorod, a part of northwest Russia known from 1932 to 1990 as Gorky. His father, Ivan Maksimovich Lobachevsky, has been described at times as an architect, a surveyor, or a clerk in a surveying office. He was of Polish heritage and migrated to Russia. The elder Lobachevsky married Praskovia Aleksandrovna, a cultured and educated woman, with whom he had three boys. Nikolay was the middle son. When Nikolay's father died around 1800, his mother moved the family further east to Kazan. Although the family was

Nikolay Lobachevsky

extremely poor, his mother was determined that her children would not grow up uneducated. She taught them herself until they were old enough to attend school. All the boys won scholarships to attend the local school.

Lobachevsky was eight years old when he entered school in Kazan. He immediately impressed his teachers with his quick intelligence. He was especially good in Latin and mathematics. By the age of 13, he had won a scholarship to the recently founded Kazan University. Since the new university had recruited many of its professors from Germany, most of the classes they taught were conducted in Latin—the professors did not speak Russian and the students did not speak German. Lobachevsky accepted his scholarship in 1807 on the condition that he teach in Russia for six years after graduation. This condition was an attempt by the government to develop its own teachers rather than depend on attracting foreigners to Russia. Lobachevsky's two brothers also accepted scholarships on this basis. His younger brother, Alexei, did well at the university, but his older brother, Alexander, committed suicide before he graduated. The motive for the suicide is not known.

Although Lobachevsky had entered the university to study medicine, he began taking mathematics classes under Johann Martin Christian Bartels, a friend of the great German mathematician, **Carl Friedrich Gauss** (1777–1855). Lobachevsky's developing interest in mathematics prompted him to switch his major. Soon thereafter, he was named a "Kammerstudenten," or honor student, in mathematics. However, Lobachevsky began acting up in school, teasing his teachers and classmates, arranging practical jokes, and even setting off firecrackers late at night. When the university threatened to withhold his degree and possibly expel him (kick him out of school), Bartels came to his rescue. Bartels had Lobachevsky apologize and promise he would settle down. So at the age when most boys are beginning college, Lobachevsky received his master's degree in mathematics and physics.

As the university's most brilliant student, Lobachevsky was offered a faculty position in 1814. That year, he became a lecturer in mathematics and mechanics. Having promised to teach for six years after graduation, he actually wound up giving the university 40 years of his life.

Serves the university in many ways

Lobachevsky never forgot that the city of Kazan had educated him and his brothers when they were unable to afford tuition. As a result, he devoted himself to improving the city and its university. His teaching career was one of steadily increasing responsibilities, as he soon was promoted to associate professor and then extraordinary professor. In 1820 he accepted some administrative duties, becoming university treasurer as well as librarian, and soon was serving as dean of two departments. In 1822, Lobachevsky became a member, and then leader, of the committee that supervised new building construction on campus. In addition, he studied architecture to better understand his duties. In 1825, at the age of 33, he was named rector, or president, of the university.

Under Lobachevsky's leadership, the once-unorganized school saw its faculty increase and its standards improve. In 1830, however, the university and all of Kazan were threatened by an outbreak of the plague. This then-incurable and usually fatal disease was highly contagious. The plague had already swept through Europe, killing hundreds of thousands. When Lobachevsky went to see the governor of Kazan, he found the gates to the city locked and realized that the university was on its own. He then ordered faculty members to bring their families on campus and locked the university's gates, allowing no one in except doctors. Because of the strict sanitation rules enforced by Lobachevsky (he insisted on disinfecting objects with steam at a time when no one even knew of the existence of germs), the university survived the threat with few deaths.

With the events of the plague now behind him, the 40-year-old Lobachevsky married in 1832. His bride was a wealthy aristocrat (a member of a privileged class involved in government) named Lady Varvara Aleksivna Moisieva. The couple would have several children.

Creates "imaginary geometry"

Amidst all his other very important duties, Lobachevsky found time to study creative mathematics. As early as 1825, he began work on what would become an entirely new kind of geometry. Starting with postulates, or axioms (facts widely accepted as true) given by Greek geometer **Euclid of Alexandria** (c. 325–c. 270 B.C.), Lobachevsky focused on one postulate that was not "self-evi-

Nikolay
Lobachevsky

**Nikolay
Lobachevsky**

dent," or obviously true to everyone. This famous parallel postulate said that through a point in a given plane, only one line can be drawn parallel to another line on the plane. Although no one doubted the truth of this statement, it was not considered self-evident, which made it stand out from all of Euclid's other axioms.

Once Lobachevsky was able to demonstrate that this axiom could not be proved, he went where no one had tried to go before. He asked, Why not try to disprove it or even find a substitute? Instead of working on a flat plane with straight lines as Euclidean geometry did, Lobachevsky visualized his geometry as made up of lines on a curved or spherical-shaped figure, now called a pseudosphere. He found that on this curved surface, more than one line could be drawn through a point that is parallel to another line. He realized that he had created an entirely different geometry from Euclid's (now called non-Euclidean geometry) that was self-contained and self-consistent. That is, this geometry set its own rules and axioms and contained no contradictions. Because he thought his geometry was universal and could apply to any situation, he called it "pangeometry." (The prefix "pan-" means "all"; so pangeometry meant "all geometries" to Lobachevsky.)

Lobachevsky published his first complete account of this new geometry in a local scientific journal in 1829, but it was mostly ignored in his lifetime. (Carl Friedrich Gauss, Lobachevsky's Kazan professor's friend, also studied the possibility of it, but never carried it out or published anything.) There are other claims to the invention of non-Euclidean geometry as well. In 1832, for instance, Hungarian geometer János Bolyai (1802–60) published an addendum in a mathematical text written by his mathematician father, Farkas Bolyai (1775–1856), that included a description of a new kind of geometry. Bolyai was totally unaware of Lobachevsky's work. When Bolyai saw it years later, he initially assumed that Lobachevsky had copied his own work. Lobachevsky, of course, had not, as he had written on the subject in 1825.

Lobachevsky's career at Kazan ended badly. The Russian government forced its employees to retire after 40 years. Since Lobachevsky had started at the university when he was only 13, the 53-year-old mathematician did not feel ready for retirement. Lobachevsky spent his last ten years in decline. Suffering from various vision problems, he continued to work by dictating to a secretary. He died in his beloved Kazan on February 24, 1856.

Lobachevsky's great discovery would not be used until a half-century had passed. It was finally applied to modern physics by German American physicist and mathematician **Albert Einstein** (1879–1955), via the work of German mathematician **Bernard Riemann** (1826–66). Einstein used non-Euclidean geometry to explain the physics of a new, four-dimensional, space-**time** world.

For More Information

Abbott, David, ed. *The Biographical Dictionary of Scientists: Mathematicians.* New York: Peter Bedrick Books, 1986.

Biographical Dictionary of Mathematicians. New York: Charles Scribner's Sons, 1991.

MacTutor History of Mathematics Archive. "Nikolay Ivanovich Lobachevsky." http://www-groups.dcs.st-and.ac.uk/~history/ Mathematicians/Lobachevsky.html (accessed on April 27, 1999).

Muir, Jane. *Of Men and Numbers: The Story of the Great Mathematicians.* New York: Dover Publications, 1996.

Young, Robyn V., ed. *Notable Mathematicians: From Ancient Times to the Present.* Detroit: Gale Research, 1998.

Nikolay
Lobachevsky

Logarithms

Logarithms are numbers known as exponents that are used to express repeated multiplications of a single number. A logarithm, often shortened to log, is always used in reference to a number or power to which another base number is to be raised. The invention of logarithms reduced the multiplication of large numbers to the simple addition of smaller ones.

Background and history

Until the seventeenth century, mathematicians and astronomers found that problems involving many numbers or very large numbers were extremely difficult and time-consuming. Because of this, Scottish mathematician **John Napier** (1550–1617) sought an easier method of computation and discovered the concept of logarithms. His discovery was no overnight success however. Napier labored for twenty years before he found a system that would greatly shorten the multiple calculations that took a great deal of **time** and often led to regular miscalculations.

At some point in his studies, Napier realized that large numbers could be more easily expressed in terms of "powers." Thus, 100

Logarithms

WORDS TO KNOW

Base number in a logarithm, the numeral or fixed base to be raised to a certain power; for example, in 10^2, 10 is the base

Characteristic in a logarithm that contains a decimal portion, the whole number part of the log is its characteristic; for example, in the log of $427 = 10^{2.6304}$, the 2 is the characteristic

Decibel a unit for measuring the relative loudness of sounds

Exponent in a logarithm, the exponent tells how many times a number is to be multiplied by itself; for example, with 10^2, the exponent 2 tells how many times 10 is used as a factor

Mantissa in a logarithm that contains a decimal portion, the decimal part of the log is its mantissa; for example, in the log $427 = 10^{2.6304}$, the .6304 is the mantissa.

Richter Scale a logarithmic scale ranging from 1 to 10, used to express the total amount of energy released by an earthquake

Trigonometry the branch of mathematics that deals with the relationships between the sides and the angles of triangles and the calculations based on them

equals 10 times 10, which can be written as 10^2. This can be read as "ten squared" and means "ten to the power of two." This smaller numeral 2 above and to the right of the 10 (called the "base" number) is called an **exponent,** and it signifies how many times a number is to be multiplied by itself. One of the truly amazing things about logarithms is that as long as the same base number is used, one can multiply by *adding* exponents and divide by *subtracting* exponents.

The word logarithm is derived from two Greek words—*logos,* meaning "reckoning" or "ratio," and *arithmos,* meaning "number." At first, Napier called his invention "artificial numbers," but soon came up with the more impressive-sounding name logarithms.

Napier made his discovery of logarithms known in 1614 with the publication of his book, *Mirifici logarithmorum canonis descriptio (A Description of the Wonderful Canon of Logarithms).* This work explained the concept and use of his new invention and offered a set of logarithmic tables. The valuable tables contained in his book simplified routine calculations and relieved much of the tedious work that mathematicians faced when doing their calculations. Napier was also able to provide mathematicians with a system that worked with small numbers or even those with different bases. The system he devised, which others later improved, made use of the fact that any number can be stated as ten with an exponent as long as **fractions** and **decimals** are used. In 1615, English mathematician Henry Briggs (1561–1630) suggested to Napier that the base 10 be used with decimal exponents. This system of "common" logarithms was soon adopted.

Description and use

An example of the beauty and simplicity of Napier's discovery is seen in multiplying the fairly small numbers 35 and 27. Consulting a logarithmic table shows that 35 is the same as $10^{1.5441}$, and that 27 is $10^{1.4314}$. The sum of those exponents is 2.9755; a quick check of a log table shows that $10^{2.9755}$ equals 945. Thus, one-step **addition** takes the place of multi-step **multiplication.** In this example, the **whole number** 2 is called the characteristic, and the decimal part (.9755) is called the mantissa.

Napier's invention was embraced by nearly anyone who had to do long or elaborate calculations. The discovery of logarithms proved to be one of the exceptions in the history of science, where many a good idea is not recognized as such in its own time. Napier's log tables were put to immediate use in such fields as astronomy, navigation, trade, engineering, and warfare. They became especially important to the branch of mathematics known as trigonometry, whose convenient formulas depend on logarithmic tables.

Less than ten years after logarithms were invented, they were applied in a mechanical instrument called the slide rule. This device was basically two log tables arranged side by side with a movable piece in the middle that allowed for rapid multiplication and **division.** This new device, which was based on logarithms, proved to be a major technological tool since it was fast and relatively accurate. For well over 300 years, the slide rule served students and professionals who needed to calculate rapidly. But in the 1970s, the slide rule was totally replaced by the electronic calculator. It offered totally accurate logarithmic calculations nearly instantly.

Besides functioning as an aid to computation by reducing multiplication and division to addition and **subtraction** (of exponents), logarithms enable certain quantities to be measured on what is called a logarithmic scale. One such quantity is sound, the intensity of which is measured in decibels. Since a logarithmic scale is designed for the easy computation of both extremely small and large numbers, very delicate readings can be obtained at the low end of the scale. Another phenomenon especially suitable to a logarithmic scale is the measurement of the usually enormous magnitude of an earthquake. This is done on a Richter Scale.

For More Information

Boyer, Carl B., and Uta C. Merzbach. *A History of Mathematics.* New York: John Wiley & Sons, 1989.

Eves, Howard. *An Introduction to the History of Mathematics.* Philadelphia: Saunders College Publishing, 1990.

Rogers, James T. *The Pantheon Story of Mathematics for Young People.* New York: Pantheon Books, 1966.

West, Beverly Henderson, et al. *The Prentice-Hall Encyclopedia of Mathematics.* Englewood Cliffs, NJ: Prentice-Hall, 1982.

Logic

Logic is the science of right or proper reasoning. It is also described as the process of combining statements to arrive at conclusions. While logic is used in many fields, for mathematics it is a tool to establish something that is valid or true.

History and background

Before the Greeks, there was really very little abstract thinking, especially in mathematics. (Abstract thinking refers to thoughts that are not connected to a specific thing.) Neither the Babylonians nor the Egyptians ever reached the point of dealing with numbers as abstract concepts or as ideas. Not until they could think of **whole numbers** like 2, 3, and 4 without having to associate them with any physical objects could they reach an advanced stage of mathematics. The Greeks, however, not only realized the abstract nature of numbers, but insisted on dealing only with these abstractions. Abstractions not only appealed to their inquiring minds, but they allowed them to be able to generalize about things. For them, the study of mathematics was the best way to practice and to learn how to generalize.

Abstraction something that is general and not particular; an idea or concept that is theoretical rather than practical

Analogy a form of reasoning that assumes if two things are alike in some ways, then they are probably alike in other ways as well

Deduction a type of reasoning in which a conclusion follows necessarily from a set of axioms, or givens; it proceeds logically from the general to the specific

Equation a mathematical sentence with an equal sign (=) between two expressions; a statement of equality; for example, $3 + x = 10$ and $a + b = b + a$ are both equations

Induction a type of reasoning conducted first by observing patterns of something and then predicting answers for similar future cases; it proceeds logically from the specific to the general

Proposition a statement that makes an assertion; something that is stated as either true or false

Rational consistent with or based on reason; logical; reasonable

Syllogism a logical argument that involves three propositions, usually two premises and a conclusion, whose conclusion necessarily is true if the premises are true

Symbolic logic a system of mathematical logic that uses symbols instead of words to solve problems, and whose symbols can be manipulated much like an equation

The ancient Greek philosopher Aristotle (384–322 B.C.) was one of the first to use principles of proper reasoning to arrive at sound conclusions. Called the "father of logic," Aristotle developed the technique of starting a single statement and then proceeding in a certain way toward a single, correct conclusion. The word logic is derived from the Greek word *logos,* meaning "speech," "reasoning," and "discourse."

Viewed as a science the way Aristotle saw it, the goal of logic is not to approximate a conclusion or to give an account of what probably is correct. Rather, the goal of logic is to establish truth. As Aristotle viewed it, there were several ways of reasoning or obtaining knowledge. One way was by authority, that is to accept the word of others. Another was by experience or trial and error, which is close to an experiment. A third way was by analogy, in which one learns something about one thing from what occurred in a similar situation. While all three methods may provide useful knowledge, none can dependably and reliably always deliver what is absolutely true.

Two other methods—induction and deduction—came closer to establishing truth. Induction is close to experimentation, in which one observes repeated happenings of the same thing and concludes that it will *probably* always keep doing so. Only deduction, however, can give *necessary* conclusions about something that will always be true. Greek mathematician **Euclid of Alexandria** (c. 325–270 B.C.) adopted Aristotle's methods of logic, or reasoning, to mathematics, in such a way as to provide the mode for classical logic.

The first serious attempt to formalize Aristotle and Euclid's logical methods was made by German mathematician and philosopher **Gottfried Leibniz** (1646–1716). He created a system of logic that used symbols instead of words, but he did not provide a complete and detailed system that could be used. It was not until the nineteenth century however, that English mathematician **George Boole** (1815–64) founded the modern science of mathematical logic. In his book entitled *The Laws of Thought,* Boole created a complete system of symbolic logic that used symbols rather than words to solve problems in logic and which could therefore be actually manipulated much like an equation in **algebra.**

Description and use

Ever since Euclid, logic has been called the glue that holds mathematics together. Because of logic, mathematics can make the claim that it establishes truth or makes statements that follow necessarily from other, given statements. This separates it from many other disciplines. Mathematics is therefore concerned with truth, which is established by proof, which is based on logic.

Ever since Aristotle, the way to establish truth by proof was to use a set of statements called a syllogism. A syllogism is a logical statement that uses three propositions, or assumptions. They are called the major premise, the minor premise, and the conclusion. If the first two are true, then the conclusion is necessarily true. An example of a correct syllogism is: (1) All men are mortal. (2) Aristotle is a man. (3) Aristotle is mortal. There are several detailed rules that a syllogism must follow if it is to be valid. One such rule is that no valid syllogism has two negative premises. A syllogism is an example of deduction, or deductive reasoning; it is the type of reasoning used by mathematics to prove that something is true. (See accompanying sidebar for more information on syllogisms.)

Much of the logic used in everyday life involves inductive reasoning. Inductive reasoning involves arriving at probable, but not necessary, conclusions. This is the type of reasoning doctors use when they diagnose the probable cause of a patient's symptoms. Legal scholars and lawyers use the same kind of reasoning to find out

Syllogisms

Although syllogisms are seldom taught in school today, they were considered an essential part of a good education at least through the nineteenth century. Students used syllogisms to study the structure of an argument. Although syllogisms seem complicated today, they are really not that difficult to grasp since they use sentences rather than symbols. The rules that syllogisms must follow are based on features that are common to all valid syllogisms. If a syllogism breaks any one of the rules, it is considered invalid, or not true.

To begin with, a syllogism has three statements, or propositions. The third statement, which is the conclusion, must necessarily follow from and be the logical consequence of the first two statements, which are called the premises. For example:

> All men are mortal.
> Aristotle is a man.
> Therefore, Aristotle is mortal.

This argument must have exactly three terms (the major term, the minor term, and the middle term) or it is not valid. In the Aristotle example, the major term *(P)* is the word or predicate that describes the subject of the conclusion ("mortal"). The minor term *(S)* is the subject of the conclusion ("Aristotle"). The middle term *(M)* is the remaining word ("men"). To state this symbolically: "All *M* are *P*; *S* is *M*; therefore, *S* is *P*." The symbols *S, P,* and *M* are those most commonly used and stand for the subject *(S)*, the predicate *(P),* and the middle *(M)*.

Other rules apply as well, such as no valid syllogism has two negatives; two positive premises must yield a positive conclusion; and a negative premise and a positive premise must yield a negative conclusion.

Charles Dodgson, a.k.a. Lewis Carroll

"I only took the regular course."

"What was that?" enquired Alice.

"Reeling and writhing, of course, to begin with," the Mock Turtle replied: "and then the different branches of Arithmetic—Ambition, Distraction, Uglification and Derision."

"I never heard of Uglification," Alice ventured to say. "What is it?"

Lewis Carroll, author of the most popular children's books in England, was really the pseudonym or pen name (a made-up name used by an author) for English mathematician and logician Charles Lutwidge Dodgson (1832–98). His famous books, *Alice's Adventures in Wonderland* and *Through the Looking-Glass and What Alice Found There,* are among the most quoted works in English and are enjoyed as much by adults as by children.

In 1854, Dodgson graduated first in his class in mathematics from Christ Church in Oxford. He went on to become a deacon in the Church of England as well as a lecturer in mathematics. Among his more significant mathematical writings are *Euclid and His Modern Rivals* (1879) and *Symbolic Logic* (1896). When Queen Victoria of England (1837–1901) read and enjoyed his two *Alice* books, she immediately requested copies of every book Carroll had ever written. To her confusion, she received a pile of mathematics books!

Dodgson was an extremely shy, quiet man who stuttered, never married, and seemed to get along best with children. Although he was a logician, he was more amused by using logic as a game, not as a method for testing reason. His *Alice* books contain many mathematical references. For example, *Looking Glass* is based on a game of chess, and Alice's changes in size and proportion in *Wonderland* are related to geometry.

which particular law applies to a given case. Knowing how to use logic not only helps organize and present one's thoughts better, but it allows one to analyze the arguments of others as well. Finally, an orderly and civilized society depends a great deal on rational behavior: that is, that people generally think and act in a reasonable manner, and that everyone agrees upon what is considered reasonable.

For More Information

Baum, Robert. *Logic.* Fort Worth, TX: Harcourt Brace, 1996.

Kline, Morris. *Mathematics for the Nonmathematician.* New York: Dover Publications, 1985.

Miles, Thomas J., and Douglas W. Nance. *Mathematics: One of the Liberal Arts.* Pacific Grove, CA: Brooks/Cole Publishing Co., 1997.

Miller, Charles D., et al. *Mathematical Ideas.* Reading, MA: Addison-Wesley, 1997.

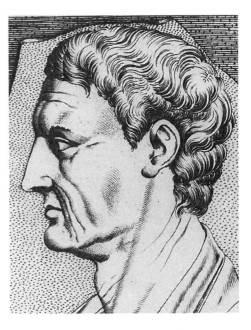

Aristotle, the father of logic.

Born November 20, 1924
Warsaw, Poland

Polish-born Lithuanian geometer

Benoit B. Mandelbrot

As the mathematician who conceived, developed, and named the new field called fractal **geometry,** Benoit B. Mandelbrot created what is now recognized as one of the major developments of twentieth century mathematics. Fractal geometry offers a systematized approach to understanding the basic chaos or irregularities of the natural world and has helped modern science find some order in its apparent randomness. Fractal geometry has proved to be a valuable tool for analyzing and understanding a wide variety of physical, biological, and social phenomena.

> *"Science would be ruined if (like sports) it were to put competition above everything else, and if it were to clarify the rules of competition by withdrawing entirely into narrowly defined specialties."*

Early life and education

Benoit B. Mandelbrot was born in Warsaw, Poland, though his family was originally from Lithuania. Mandelbrot's father, Charles, was well-educated and came from a long line of scholars. As a "starving scholar" however, he became a maker and seller of clothing. Mandelbrot's mother, Belle Lourie, was trained as a doctor and dentist. Fearful of exposing her son to the many epidemics that were then common, she kept him out of school for grades one and two. Mandelbrot later reflected that he

Benoit B. Mandelbrot

thought this might have been the beginning of his intellectual success since from then on, he instinctively avoided "being imprinted by schools." Instead, he was tutored at home by an unemployed uncle who taught him to read and with whom he mastered chess and maps. Mandelbrot remembers that his uncle never made him learn the whole multiplication table or even the entire alphabet, and that learning with his uncle was simply fun.

After finally attending elementary school in Warsaw, Mandelbrot moved with his family to Paris, France, in 1936. Germany's Nazi dictator, Adolf Hitler (1889–1945), was beginning to threaten Europe, and its Jews in particular. Since the Mandelbrot family was Jewish, they left Poland for the apparent safety of France. This was a wise move, since Hitler eventually invaded Poland in 1939, thus beginning World War II (1939–45). He also began to carry out his policy of killing all Jews.

In France, Mandelbrot got to see his uncle, Szolem Mandelbrot, who taught mathematics there as a university professor, and he spent a good deal of time meeting and being around mathematicians. In 1937, Mandelbrot entered the Lycée, which was the secondary school that prepared students for the university. By 1940, the German army was about to take over Paris, so the Mandelbrot family moved to Tulle in south central France. Since family life was so focused on avoiding the Nazis, young Mandelbrot's education was anything but regular. He recalls that having to frequently move around France with his younger brother in order to remain safe made him independent and self-confident instead of timid and fearful.

Mandelbrot continued to move around France until the Germans were driven from the country in 1944. During that time, Mandelbrot had worked as an apprentice toolmaker for a railroad and also cared for horses at an estate near Lyon. During his wanderings, he always tried to keep his books with him. As soon as the universities would allow, he took the entry examinations for the leading science schools in France. These exams were both a physical and intellectual achievement since they consisted of a month-long series of oral and written tests. Although he studied very little for them, his scores were among the highest and he was admitted to the exclusive École Polytechnique. While there, he studied under Professor Paul Lévy (1886–1971) and formulated what he later described as a romantic career goal: "to be the first to find order where everyone else had only seen chaos."

After receiving his engineering degree in 1947, Mandelbrot accepted a scholarship to study at the California Institute of Technology where he obtained his master's degree in aeronautics in 1948. Returning to France, he spent one year in the French Air Force and then entered the University of Paris. The dissertation for which he received his Ph.D. in 1952 was a unique and almost strange blend of mathematics and physics. It dealt with thermodynamics (the part of physics that considers how heat is used as energy), cybernetics (computer theory), and game theory (probability).

Specializes in statistical irregularities

In 1953–54, Mandelbrot joined several other notable European scientists who studied in post-war America at the famous Institute for Advanced Study at Princeton University in New Jersey. For the next three years, he taught in Switzerland and France and continued to explore so many different fields that he never allowed himself to be labeled simply a mathematician. During this period, he married Aliette Kagan, who later became a biologist. They have two children, Laurent and Didier.

In the summer of 1958, Mandelbrot was a faculty visitor at IBM's Thomas J. Watson Research Center in Yorktown Heights, New York, when he decided to take a risk and leave academics. His acceptance of a research position there turned out to be the right decision as he found the Center to be the perfect environment for

Stefan Banach

A generation before the Poland-born Benoit B. Mandelbrot made a name for himself in mathematics, another Polish mathematician lived. Stefan Banach (1892–1945) was abandoned by his parents almost immediately after he was born and was raised by a laundress whose last name he took. Nothing is known of his childhood except that he was self-taught and that by the age of fifteen he was making a living as a tutor of mathematics.

In 1914, an overheard conversation would change Banach's life and give him the chance to pursue his mathematical talents. While sitting on a park bench in Krakow, Poland, talking to a friend about mathematics, a mathematics professor heard Banach say the words "the Lebesque integral." Intrigued that someone would utter a calculus term that few would know, the professor struck up a conversation with Banach. He soon discovered the young man's great natural talent.

From then on, Banach's life changed and he went on to become an accomplished teacher who did major research of his own. His life ended tragically during World War II however, as he was forced by the occupying German army to work in a laboratory where infectious diseases were studied. Given the lowly job of feeding the lice used in experiments, he eventually lost his health and died on August 31, 1945, of lung cancer, in the Ukraine city of Lvov. World War II was particularly tragic for mathematical progress in Poland as many of its finest mathematicians died in Nazi concentration camps.

Benoit B. Mandelbrot

him to pursue the kind of open-ended work he wanted to do. It was in this very free environment that he began the work that would eventually pull together all of his different ideas and interests.

In 1960, Mandelbrot began to notice that certain patterns could be found in what was obviously random data. He then discovered that such patterns could be found in areas or situations that had a significant source of random data (events that seem to have no obvious or predictable cause or which happen erratically). He found these patterns when studying the stock market and he found them while studying the problem of "noise" (interference) on telephone wires used for computer communications.

Creates fractal geometry

In a 1967 paper, Mandelbrot asked, How long is the coast of Britain? In the paper, he showed that there was no single correct answer, for the answer depended upon the scale at which the coast was measured. That is, if one measures it from a map using a ruler, the answer will be quite different than if one took a measuring tape and actually measured all the zigs and zags of the coastline. Further, if the measuring tool was even smaller and therefore more precise, the answer would be different (and greater) yet again. In some ways then, he said, all coastlines have a sort of infinite length, since the more one "zooms in," the more detail a person can see. Mandelbrot then examined other patterns in nature this way—such as the shapes of clouds and mountains, meandering rivers and moon craters, even the structure of human lungs and the holes in Swiss cheese. He went on to show that it is a common property in nature to contain this kind of rough pattern at all scales.

Ever since he was young, Mandelbrot had been inclined toward thinking in terms of shapes. He believed his gift of being able to translate a problem or equation into its geometrical counterpart gave him a special advantage when he took tests in school. He said it was a kind of cheating "without breaking any rules." It was natural for him to want to show these newly discovered mathematical patterns graphically. To do this, he devised a new geometry with "fractional" (meaning fractured or broken up to a very small scale) dimensions. He called it "fractal geometry." He first coined the word "fractal" in 1975 and used it in the title of his classic work in

French, *Les Objets fractals*. Mandelbrot shows in this book and others how his new geometry is a dramatic break from the classic geometry of **Euclid of Alexandria** (c. 325–c. 270 B.C.), and that because it is so different it offers modern science a way to deal with the randomness and uncertainty of nature.

Although fractal geometry was initially only a mathematical curiosity, it has provided valuable insights into such natural phenomena as the distribution of earthquakes, weather forecasting, the distribution of galaxies in the universe, and even the ways to compress pictures so they can be stored more efficiently on a **computer.** In his discovery of fractal geometry, Benoit Mandelbrot realized his youthful ambition of finding the hidden order in what appeared to be chaos. In 1985, Mandelbrot left IBM and became professor of mathematics at Yale University in New Haven, Connecticut.

For More Information

Albers, Donald J., and G. L. Alexanderson, eds. *Mathematical People: Profiles and Interviews.* Boston: Birkhauser, 1985.

Henderson, Harry. *Modern Mathematicians.* New York: Facts on File, 1996.

McGuire, Michael, and Benoit B. Mandelbrot. *An Eye for Fractals: A Graphic and Photographic Essay.* New York: Perseus Press, 1991.

MacTutor History of Mathematics Archive. "Stefan Banach." http://www-groups.dcs.st-and.ac.uk/~history/Mathematicians/Banach.html (accessed on May 5, 1999).

MacTutor History of Mathematics Archive. "Benoit Mandelbrot." http://www-groups.dcs.st-and.ac.uk/~history/Mathematicians/Mandelbrot.html (accessed on May 5, 1999).

Mandelbrot, Benoit B. *Fractal Geometry of Nature.* New York: W. H. Freeman and Co., 1988.

Millar, David, Ian Millar, John Millar, and Margaret Millar. *The Cambridge Dictionary of Scientists.* Cambridge, England: Cambridge University Press, 1996.

Young, Robyn V., ed. *Notable Mathematicians: From Ancient Times to the Present.* Detroit: Gale Research, 1998.

Benoit B. Mandelbrot

Multiplication

Multiplication is the process of finding the total number of elements in a given number of sets where each set has the same number of members (such as 3 sets with 5 things in each set equaling 15 things). As one of the four basic arithmetic operations (**addition, subtraction,** multiplication, and **division**), multiplication can also be described as the process of adding a number to itself a certain number of times. In this way, it is a short way of adding or counting equal numbers.

Description and use

Multiplication was probably not discovered until well after mankind had mastered both addition and subtraction. The most obvious reason for this is that multiplication is a much more complicated idea to understand than the ideas behind addition and subtraction. The other reason is that the time-saving aspects of multiplication (as a quick way of adding) would not have been necessary until mankind had become sophisticated enough in its transactions to need a system that went beyond finger- or pebble-counting. When civilization did reach this stage—probably when people began to specialize in different job trades—the need arose

Associative a property that applies to addition and multiplication (but not subtraction or division) in which addends or factors can be grouped in any order without changing the sum or product; for example, $2 \times (2 \times 3) = (2 \times 2) \times 3$

Binary operation an operation that is performed on exactly two numbers at a time; like addition, subtraction, and division, multiplication is binary since any two numbers can be added, subtracted, divided, or multiplied

Commutative a property that applies to addition and multiplication (but not subtraction or division) in which the order in which the numbers are added or multiplied does not change the sum; for example, $2 \times 3 = 3 \times 2$

Distributive in multiplying one number times a sum of two other numbers, the sum may be taken first and then the multiplication performed, or each of the numbers to be summed can first be multiplied by the common factor and the results added together; for example, with $3 \times (3 + 4)$, 3 and 4 are added and their sum (7) multiplied by 3 equals 21; or 3 and 4 can each be multiplied by 3 and their products (9 and 12) can then be added to get 21

Factors the numbers multiplied to form a product; both the multiplier and the multiplicand

Multiplicand the number that is being multiplied by another number; for example, in $3 \times 4 = 12$, 3 is the multiplicand

Multiplier the number that does the multiplying; for example, in $3 \times 4 = 12$, 4 is the multiplier

for a shorthand way of adding the same number many times. A typical example is that of a baker having three dozen loaves of bread to sell. If someone wanted to buy them all, and one loaf cost 7 cents, if the baker did not know the idea of multiplication, he would have had to add 7 a total of 36 times to find out the price of three dozen loaves.

Eventually, someone did a problem often enough to realize that a certain quantity times a certain number always gave the same answer (such as the number 4 taken 5 times equals 20). When that person noticed that 5 taken 4 times also gave the same answer, that individual was well on his or her way toward putting together what was the first multiplication table.

As with addition, multiplication is a binary operation, meaning that numbers are multiplied two at a time. The numbers being multiplied are called factors, and the result of the multiplication (the answer) is called the product. Of the two factors, the number that is multiplied is called the multiplicand, while the number that does the multiplying is called the multiplier. In $4 \times 6 = 24$, 4 is the multiplicand and 6 is the multiplier.

The properties

Since multiplication is another shorter way of doing addition, it makes sense that it also shares the properties of addition. Therefore, multiplication is both commutative and associative. The commutative property says that the grouping or arrangement of the numbers makes no difference and that the product is always the same (3×4 is the same as 4×3). The associative property says that when three or more factors are being multiplied, the grouping of the factors does not affect the product. Therefore $[(3 \times 4) \times 2]$ is the same as $[3 \times (4 \times 2)]$. Unlike addition, however, multiplication also has a distributive property. This means that if a series of numbers is to be multiplied by the same multiplier, like $[3 \times (3 + 4) = 21]$, the same answer can be reached if their sum is multiplied ($3 \times 7 = 21$). The numbers may also be multiplied individually and their products added $[(3 \times 3 = 9) (3 \times 4 = 12);$ therefore, $(9 + 12 = 21)]$.

Multiplying large numbers (those with three or more digits) is more complicated than adding large numbers because the process results in separate groups of numbers that must be added together to arrive at a final answer. It also assumes a knowledge of the principles of "place value" and "carrying" that come into play.

For example, in the operation 432 × 65, the standard method of multiplying without a calculator is to place the smaller number below the larger number and to add the product of the numbers multiplied by 5 to the product of those multiplied by 6.

$$\begin{array}{r} 432 \\ \times\ 65 \\ \hline 2160 \\ 2592\ \\ \hline 28,080 \end{array}$$

Being able to multiply these numbers assumes a knowledge of place value—that the value a digit represents depends on its place. Thus, in 432, the 4 is in the hundreds place, the 3 is in the tens place, and the 2 is in the ones, or units, place. An understanding of the notion of carrying, or regrouping, is necessary as well. With carrying, a number is renamed from one place value to another. In the example of 32 × 6, the first step multiplies 6 × 2 to get 12; 2 is recorded in the ones place and 1 ten is carried. After multiplying 6 × 30 (to get 18 tens or 6 × 3 tens), the ten that was

Mathematical symbols

Since the earliest times, mathematicians have used symbols instead of words in order to save both time and energy. As a kind of shorthand, mathematical symbols should be simple, brief, clear, and easily understood. Along with the equal sign, the four key mathematical symbols are those that stand for addition, subtraction, multiplication, and division.

With the invention of mechanical printing around 1450, the symbols used in early printed works on arithmetic and algebra were usually only abbreviations or maybe the first letter of a key word (such as a "P" taken from the Italian word *piu* for "plus"). This simply continued the system that copyists had long used when each book was a hand-written manuscript. Eventually, other more simple symbols were suggested, as mathematics started to move from the old, ancient ways to more modern means of expression.

The modern symbol for equality (=) was introduced in 1557 by English mathematician Robert Recorde (c. 1510–58). In his book *The Whetstone of Witte,* he stated that he selected this particular sign "because no two things can be more equal" than two parallel lines.

The plus (+) and minus (–) symbols are of German origin, and first appeared in print in a 1489 book for merchants written by German mathematician Johannes Widman (c. 1462–c. 1498). He used "+" to indicate a surplus (more) and "–" to indicate a deficit (less). The plus sign is believed to be derived from a shorthand form of the Latin word *et* meaning "and." The minus sign was used by some Greeks, and may also come from a bar that medieval traders used to mark the differences in the weights of the same product.

The multiplication sign (×) is said to be based on St. Andrew's Cross, the design on the national flag of Scotland since the twelfth century. The multiplication sign first appeared in print in an appendix to a 1616 book on logarithms. It is thought that the anonymous appendix was the work of English mathematician William Oughtred (1574–1660), who 15 years later published a book that contained about 150 suggested symbols.

Finally, the first printed book to contain today's division sign (÷) was a 1659 introduction to algebra written by Johann Heinrich Rahn (1622–76) of Switzerland.

carried is added, which results in 19 tens (190). Adding the first 2 to the 190 results in 192.

$$\begin{array}{r} 32 \\ \underline{6} \\ 192 \end{array}$$

Multiplication symbol

With the invention of mechanical printing around 1450, the symbols used in early printed works on arithmetic and **algebra** were usually only abbreviations or maybe the first letter of a key word (such as a "P" taken from the Italian word *piu* for "plus"). This simply continued the system that copyists had long used when each book was a hand-written manuscript. (Long before photocopy machines were in existence, copyists duplicated works by copying—word for word—the original documents.) Eventually, other more simple symbols were suggested, as mathematics started to move from the old, ancient ways to more modern means of expression. The multiplication sign ($\times$) is said to be based on St. Andrew's Cross, the design found on Scotland's national flag. (See accompanying sidebar for more information on mathematical symbols.)

For More Information

Heddens, James W. and William R. Speer. *Today's Mathematics: Concepts and Classroom Methods.* Upper Saddle River, NJ: Merrill, 1997.

Julius, Edward H. *Arithmetricks: 50 Easy Ways to Add, Subtract, Multiply, and Divide Without a Calculator.* New York: John Wiley and Sons, 1995.

Math in Action: Multiplication. Belmont, CA: Fearon/Janus/Quercus, 1991.

Rogers, James T. *The Pantheon Story of Mathematics for Young People.* New York: Pantheon Books, 1966.

Stienecker, David L. *Multiplication.* Tarrytown, NY: Benchmark Books, 1996.

West, Beverly Henderson, et al. *The Prentice-Hall Encyclopedia of Mathematics.* Englewood Cliffs, NJ: Prentice-Hall, Inc., 1982.

Wheeler, Ruric E. *Modern Mathematics*. Pacific Grove, CA: Brooks/Cole Publishing Co., 1995.

Multiplication

Born 1550
Edinburgh, Scotland

Died April 4, 1617
Edinburgh, Scotland

Scottish inventor of logarithms

John Napier

Although he never held a professional position of any kind, John Napier used his inquiring mind and creative ability to invent **logarithms,** to introduce the **decimal** point, and to design a mechanical calculating aid. One of the truly great "amateurs" in the history of mathematics, John Napier contributed far more to the field that he loved than did many full-time academics.

Early life and education

John Napier was born in Edinburgh, Scotland, into the Scottish nobility (privileged class). Since his father was Sir Archibald Napier of Merchiston Castle, and his mother, Janet Bothwell, was the daughter of a member of Parliament, John Napier became the eighth laird (property owner) of Merchiston. Napier's father was only 16 when his son, John, was born. As was the practice for members of nobility, Napier did not enter school until he was 13. He did not stay in school very long, however. It is believed that he dropped out and traveled in Europe to continue his studies. Little is known about these years, nor is there any suggestion of what or where he may have studied.

> *"Seeing there is nothing that is so troublesome to mathematical practice . . . than the multiplications, divisions, square and cubical extractions of great numbers, which besides the tedious expense of time are . . . subject to many slippery errors, I began therefore to consider [how] I might remove those hindrances."*

John Napier

In 1571, Napier turned 21 and returned to Scotland. The following year he married Elizabeth Stirling, daughter of Scottish mathematician James Stirling (1692–1770), and built a castle at Gartnes in 1574. The couple had two children before Elizabeth died in 1579. Napier later married Agnes Chisholm, with whom he had ten children. On the death of his father in 1608, Napier and his family moved into Merchiston Castle, where he lived the rest of his life.

Defender of the faith

Napier's father had been deeply interested and involved in religious matters, and Napier himself was no different. Because of his inherited wealth, he needed no professional position. He kept himself very busy by being involved with the political and religious controversies of his time. For the most part, religion and politics in Scotland at this time pitted Catholics against Protestants. Napier was anti-Catholic, as evidenced by his 1593 book against Catholicism and the papacy (office of the pope) entitled *A Plaine Discovery of the Whole Revelation of St. John.* This attack was so popular that it was translated into several languages and saw many editions. Napier always felt that if he attained any fame at all in his life, it would be because of that book.

Inventor

As a person of high energy and curiosity, Napier paid much attention to his landholdings and tried to improve the workings of his estate. Around the Edinburgh area, he became widely known as "Marvellous Merchiston" for the many ingenious mechanisms he built to improve his crops and cattle. He experimented with fertilizers to enrich his land, invented an apparatus to remove water from flooded coal pits, and built devices to better survey and measure land. He also wrote about plans to build elaborate devices that would deflect any Spanish invasion of the British Isles. In addition, he described military devices that were similar to today's submarine, machine gun, and army tank. He never attempted to build any of the military instruments, however.

Invention of logarithms

Napier was led to his greatest invention by his interest in astronomy. He took this hobby seriously: He not only observed the skies but did actual research that required lengthy and time-consuming calculations of very large numbers. Once the idea came to him that there might be a way to do this calculating in a simpler manner, he spent 20 years working on perfecting what came to be known as logarithms.

No one knows for sure exactly how Napier first realized (possibly around 1590) the simple but key truth that makes logarithms work. Once it came to him, though, he worked continuously to perfect it and make it a practical system. Napier realized that all numbers can be expressed in what is now called exponential form, meaning that 4 can be written as 2^2, 8 as 2^3, 16 as 2^4, and so on. (The numbers 2, 3, and 4, in this case, are called **exponents.**) Other numbers like 7 or 9 can be written as 2 to some fractional power between 2 and 3.

The beauty of logarithms is that they simplify what is complicated—logarithms reduce the operations of **multiplication** and **division** to those of **addition** and **subtraction.** When very large numbers are involved, the use of logarithms can save an enormous amount of calculation. These simpler calculations are also easier, more accurate, and less time-consuming. French astronomer Pierre-Simon de Laplace (1749–1827) once said that the invention of logarithms, "by shortening the labors, doubled the life of the astronomer."

A simplified description of a logarithm is that it is the power to which a number must be raised in order to be equal to another number. Therefore, the logarithm 10^2 says that 10 must be raised to the second power (or multiplied by itself—10 × 10), and it will equal 100. The practical aspect behind logarithms is that any number can be expressed in terms of the number 10 to a certain power. So just as 100 is 10^2, so 56 is $10^{1.74819}$. The simplification aspect of logarithms comes into play when it changes multiplication and division of very large numbers into simple addition and subtraction. Thus, in order to find out what 10^2 times 10^5 equals, one only has to add the powers and arrive at 10^{2+5}. ($10^2 \times 10^5 = 10^{2+5} = 10^7 = 10,000,000$.)

Napier first made his logarithm discovery known in 1614 in his book *Mirifici logarithmorum canonis descriptio (A Description of the Wonderful Canon of Logarithms)*. In this work, Napier briefly

John Napier

explained his invention and, more important, offered his first set of logarithmic tables. The availability of these ready-to-use tables and the sheer beauty of Napier's new idea made his book an instant hit. Rarely in the history of science has a new idea or a new invention been so quickly and eagerly accepted. Everyone who ever had to perform long, tedious calculations welcomed Napier's tables. In fact, English mathematician Henry Briggs (1561–1630) was so enamored by the tables, he traveled to Edinburgh to meet Napier. The two of them worked on some improvements, such as the development of base 10.

Napier's second book of logarithms—referred to as the *Constructio* because its title is the same as the title of his first book except for the last word—was published in 1619 after his death. This more detailed work fully explained both how the tables were calculated and what his reasoning process was.

Other achievements

At about the same time, Napier published his first work of logarithmic tables, he was working on an idea for speeding up calculations even more. He reasoned correctly that if one could do elaborate calculations more quickly by using logarithms, more speed could be obtained by using the logarithm tables mechanically. Napier then applied his ingenuity to building a simple but useful mechanical multiplication table. Called "Napier's bones," this system consisted of a series of bones or ivory rods that were mounted in a box that looked like a chessboard with numbers in its squares. Calculations were done by rotating the rods by hand. In many ways, this device was the forerunner of the slide rule.

Napier was also responsible for advancing the notion of the decimal **fraction** by introducing the use of the decimal point. By suggesting that a simple point or dot could be used to separate the **whole number** from the fraction part of a number (for example, 3.1 means three and one-tenth), Napier contributed greatly to the then-new notion of a decimal fraction. The decimal point quickly became accepted and was soon part of standard practice in Great Britain.

Given the range and level of accomplishments that John Napier achieved in his 67 years, it is obvious that he was probably never idle. Although he suffered from gout, it is also not surprising that Napier's death on April 4, 1617, can be partially attributed to overwork.

For More Information

Bergamini, David. *Mathematics*. Alexandria, VA: Time-Life Books, 1980.

Biographical Dictionary of Mathematicians. New York: Charles Scribner's Sons, 1991.

Eves, Howard W. *An Introduction to the History of Mathematics*. Philadelphia: Saunders College Publishing, 1990.

MacTutor History of Mathematics Archive. "John Napier." http://www-groups.dcs.st-and.ac.uk/~history/Mathematicians/Napier.html (accessed on April 27, 1999).

Reimer, Luetta, and Wilbert Reimer. *Mathematicians Are People, Too.: Stories from the Lives of Great Mathematicians*. Palo Alto, CA: Dale Seymour Publications, 1995.

Young, Robyn V., ed. *Notable Mathematicians: From Ancient Times to the Present*. Detroit: Gale Research, 1998.

John Napier

Born December 28, 1903
Budapest, Hungary

Died February 8, 1957
Washington, D.C.

Hungarian American game theorist,
mathematical physicist, and computer scientist

John von Neumann

Considered one of the most creative mathematicians of the twentieth century, John von Neumann made important contributions to many fields. His work in mathematics contributed to the basis of modern **computer** technologies, and he is perhaps best known for his invention of the mathematical theory of games. One of the last individuals to master both pure and applied mathematics, his genius was so profound and impressive that even his peers were in awe of his abilities. His colleagues said of him, "Most mathematicians prove what they can; von Neumann proves what he wants."

> *"[Von Neumann] was the only student I was ever afraid of. If in the course of a lecture I stated an unresolved problem, the chances were he'd come to me as soon as the lecture was over, with the complete solution in a few scribbles on a slip of paper."*
>
> *—Hungarian mathematician*
> *George Pólya*

Early life and education

Born János von Neumann (pronounced NOY-mon) in Budapest, Hungary, von Neumann was the oldest of three sons and was called Jancsi for short. His father, Max Neumann, was a prosperous banker who had married Margaret Kann. Because the family was well off, the children had governesses from whom they learned French and German. Although the family was Jewish, they did not observe that religion and actually had a mix of Jewish and Christian traditions in the home.

John von Neumann

Von Neumann was recognized early as a prodigy (a child with exceptional intelligence). At the age of six, he could divide eight-digit numbers in his head. By then, he was also fluent in classical Greek, a language he and his father would use to tell each other jokes. Sometimes the family would show off von Neumann's photographic memory to guests and friends by having them randomly select a page and column in the telephone book. The young boy would look it over a few times, hand the book to the guests, and then answer correctly any question about a name, address, and number.

Young von Neumann was tutored at home until he was ten, and then entered the Lutheran Gymnasium (a secondary school). Once his teachers realized his mathematical genius, they arranged for him to be tutored by a young university mathematician named Michael Fekete.

Von Neumann's native Hungary began to change following the end of World War I (1914–18). An unpopular Communist government had taken over for a short time, and many of its leaders were Jewish. Once they were removed from power, there was considerable anti-Jewish feeling in Hungary. Consequently, when von Neumann was ready to attend the University of Budapest in 1921, quotas determined how many Jews would be accepted. However, von Neumann's abilities were so great (he had already co-authored a mathematical paper with Fekete) that he was admitted easily. Although he entered the University of Budapest, he did not attend lectures there. He went instead to the University of Berlin in Germany for two years and then on to the Zurich Institute in Switzerland. Altogether, he studied mathematics, chemistry, and physics. In 1926, having returned to Hungary, von Neumann received his Ph.D. in mathematics from the University of Budapest.

Establishes reputation

The following year, von Neumann took a position as a *Privatdozent*, or unpaid lecturer, at the University of Berlin. In 1929, he accepted a teaching position at the University of Hamburg. During those years, he also was awarded a Rockefeller grant for postdoctoral work. This grant allowed him to study at the Göttingen University in Germany under the great German number theorist, David Hilbert (1862–1943). By 1930, von Neumann had published a number of papers and had also become famous in academic circles. Often at a conference he would notice others pointing him out as the famous young genius.

During 1929, von Neumann was invited to lecture on quantum theory at Princeton University in New Jersey. He replied that he would accept as soon as he had taken care of some personal matters. He then headed directly back to Budapest where he married his fiancée, Marietta Kovesi. The newlyweds moved to New Jersey in 1930 and von Neumann became a visiting lecturer at Princeton. A year later, he became professor of mathematics. In 1933, he was invited to join the elite group being formed at the newly created Institute for Advanced Study at Princeton. He became one of the original six mathematics professors there—one of whom was German American physicist and mathematician **Albert Einstein** (1879–1955), and was also its youngest member. He would remain there for his entire career.

During the 1930s, von Neumann solidified his still-growing reputation as an outstanding and productive mathematician. At the beginning of the decade, he held on to his academic positions in Germany, but when the Nazi party came to power there, he resigned the positions and became a naturalized American citizen. During those years, he also published a book on quantum physics, *The Mathematical Foundations of Quantum Mechanics*. It is still a standard textbook on that difficult subject.

Von Neumann and his wife had a daughter, Marina, but in 1937, their marriage ended in divorce. In 1938, von Neumann married Klara Dan, who was from Budapest. At Princeton, the von Neumanns were not typically quiet scholarly types; they both enjoyed socializing. In Germany, von Neumann had always enjoyed going to nightclubs, and now in the United States, he and his wife would host parties at their home that were described by one guest as "frequent, and famous, and long."

World War II research

After von Neumann became a naturalized American citizen, he started consulting for the U.S. Army. When the United States entered World War II (1939–45) in 1941, von Neumann became more involved in defense research. This work opened a new chapter in his life as he began applying his mathematics to projects

John von Neumann

John von Neumann, right, with physicist J. Robert Oppenheimer in 1952.

ranging from wind tunnel research to work on atomic energy. Von Neumann showed he was not just a mathematical genius; he was one who also grasped technical problems quickly and, even better, could come up with creative solutions. His personality also helped. He was a very persuasive person with more than enough administrative ability to get people to work together.

In 1943, von Neumann went to work for American physicist J. Robert Oppenheimer (1904–67) at the Los Alamos Scientific Laboratory in New Mexico to help develop the atomic bomb. His work on a device to make the bomb detonate, or explode, involved so many calculations that they were done by a staff of 20 people using desk calculators. This led von Neumann to investigate the possibility of using electronic machines to help with these enormous computations. After learning which scientists were involved with computers, he met with individuals at Harvard University,

Bell Laboratories, IBM, Columbia University, and the Moore School of Electrical Engineering at the University of Pennsylvania.

Von Neumann eventually joined a team that was building an improved machine called the Electronic Discrete Variable Automatic Computer (EDVAC). In 1945, he wrote a report that presented the first written description of the concept of a stored program, an idea upon which all modern computers are based. This concept meant that a computer could take into its memory whole programs and data which it would then run. Until this time, a computer had to be manually reprogrammed, which required a slow and inefficient process of turning switches on and off. Von Neumann's eventual design of a computer for scientific research at Princeton served as a model for all later computers.

Develops game theory

As early as 1926, von Neumann invented his theory of games. After analyzing strategies used in poker games, he devised a mathematical model that was applicable to all games or situations involving strategy. By creating this quantifiable, or measurable, mathematical model for games of chance in which free (and therefore unpredictable) choices are made, von Neumann essentially introduced an entirely new branch of mathematics. Von Neumann continued work on game theory while at Princeton. When Austrian American economist Oskar Morgenstern (1902–77) joined the Princeton faculty, he and von Neumann collaborated on applying game theory to economic situations. In 1944, they produced the ambitious, 641-page *Theory of Games and Economic Behavior*. Thus, von Neumann's work opened new channels of communication between mathematics and the social sciences.

After the end of World War II, von Neumann continued to consult for and advise the government. In 1954, U.S. president Dwight D. Eisenhower (1890–1969) appointed him to the Atomic Energy Commission. Von Neumann continued to attend Commission meetings even after he became ill with bone cancer. He soon learned he was incurably ill. His genius intellect, which had allowed him to conquer any problem, was becoming less dependable. His friend, Hungarian American physicist Edward Teller (1908–), said, "I think that von Neumann suffered more when his mind would no longer function, than I have ever seen

John von Neumann

any human being suffer." Another friend, mathematical physicist Eugene P. Wigner (1902–95), described how heartbreaking it was when von Neumann finally realized "that he would cease to exist, and hence cease to have thoughts."

Von Neumann lost his battle with cancer on February 8, 1957. Remembering better days, Laura Fermi, the wife of Italian American physicist Enrico Fermi (1901–54), wrote that at Los Alamos, von Neumann was "one of the very few men about whom I have not heard a single critical remark."

For More Information

Aspray, William. *John von Neumann and the Origins of Modern Computing.* Cambridge, MA: MIT Press, 1991.

Biographical Dictionary of Mathematicians. New York: Charles Scribner's Sons, 1991.

Cook, William J. *U.S. News Online.* "A Calculating Man." http://www.usnews.com/usnews/issue/980817/17johy.htm (accessed on June 7, 1999).

Cortada, James W. *Historical Dictionary of Data Processing: Biographies.* New York: Greenwood Press, 1987.

MacTutor History of Mathematics Archive. "John von Neumann." http://www-groups.dcs.st-and.ac.uk/~history/Mathematicians/Von_Neumann.html (accessed on April 27, 1999).

Myhrvold, Nathan. "John von Neumann: Computing's Cold Warrior." *Time,* March 29, 1999, p. 150.

Young, Robyn V., ed. *Notable Mathematicians: From Ancient Times to the Present.* Detroit: Gale Research, 1998.

Born January 4, 1642
Woolsthorpe, England

Died March 31, 1727
London, England

English mathematician and physicist

Isaac Newton

Many consider Isaac Newton to be not only one of the greatest figures in the history of mathematics but also one of the supreme intellects ever produced by the human race. Besides his explanation of the laws of motion and gravitation and his discoveries concerning light and color, his development of calculus is regarded as the greatest creation in all of mathematics. His quarrel with German mathematician and philosopher **Gottfried Leibniz** (1646–1716) over calculus was one of the longest and most bitter scientific disputes.

Early life and education

In the same year that the great Italian mathematician **Galileo** (1564–1642) died, Isaac Newton was born in the village of Woolsthorpe, near Lincolnshire, England. So small and sickly was the premature infant Newton that no one thought he would survive. His mother, Hannah Ayscough, later recalled that he was so tiny, he could have fit in a quart jar. Newton's father, also named Isaac, died before he was born. Both his parents were farmers.

> *"Who, by vigor of mind almost divine, the motions and figures of the planets, the paths of comets, and the tides of the seas first demonstrated."*
>
> —*Epitaph of Isaac Newton*

Isaac Newton

When Newton's mother remarried three years after his father's death, he went to live with his maternal grandmother. Having never known his father and feeling angry and jealous that his mother took another husband, Newton's years with his grandmother were often solitary and resentful. When he was 20 years old, Newton wrote that he remembers as a young boy "threatening my father and mother . . . to burne them and the house over them."

Although he was sent to King's School in Grantham at the age of 12, Newton spent most of his spare time building models and mechanical devices of all sorts. He built water clocks, a mill powered by a mouse, and kites with lanterns in them. He also paid close attention to the natural world and made many sketches of birds, plants, and animals. At school he showed no special ability, but when pushed by the class bully, who was also first in the class, Newton managed to beat him both at academics and in a fight. When his mother took him out of school at 17, intending that he work at home and become a farmer, Newton proved so uninterested, lazy, and distracted that both his uncle and the master of Grantham School agreed that he should make better use of his then-obvious intelligence. They persuaded his mother to change her mind, and she allowed him to prepare for a university education.

In June 1661, Newton was admitted to Trinity College at Cambridge University. He ignored the traditional course work, which was based on Greek philosopher Aristotle (384–322 B.C.), and read many of the great scientific books of the day. Since he also found the work of Greek geometer **Euclid of Alexandria** (c. 325–c. 270 B.C.) to be "trifling" (trivial), he instead read the works of German astronomer and mathematician **Johannes Kepler** (1571–1630), French algebraist and philosopher **René Descartes** (1596–1650), and Italian mathematician Galileo among many others. During his years at Cambridge, Newton's great natural intelligence began to show itself as he read more widely and deeply.

Meets Isaac Barrow

Little or nothing is known about Newton's personal life at college or the subject of his college thesis. At Cambridge, however, he attended the lectures of English mathematician Isaac Barrow (1630–77), who was the first Lucasian professor of mathematics at Cambridge. This new position had been funded by an English-

Isaac Barrow

If Isaac Barrow (1630–77) is remembered at all today, it is usually as the mentor of the greatest of all English mathematicians, Isaac Newton. As the first occupant of the Lucasian chair of mathematics (established at Cambridge University in 1663 by the will of Henry Lucas, a member of Parliament), Barrow is said to have resigned that prestigious position in 1669 and proposed that his talented pupil, Newton, be named his successor. It is not known for certain if this is true.

Barrow was a person of deep contrasts. Although he was an excellent student as a youngster, he was described as extremely rebellious both at home and at school. At the age of 25 he began an adventurous four-year tour of eastern Europe and actually had to fight off a pirate attack during a sea voyage from Italy to Turkey. Returning to England in 1660, he turned to religion and was ordained in the Anglican Church. He began teaching mathematics that year as well. Barrow possessed great physical strength, bravery, a quick sense of humor, and extreme conscientiousness. He died at the age of 47, apparently of a drug overdose following a fever.

man named Henry Lucas (c. 1610–63), and it still exists at Cambridge. Barrow was both an outstanding teacher and an excellent judge of intelligence. He always challenged as well as encouraged his students to do their best, and Newton thrived under his direction. They eventually shared respect and friendship. (See accompanying sidebar for more information on Barrow.)

In 1669, after Newton had received his master's degree, Barrow reportedly resigned the Lucasian professorship, requesting that Newton take his place. This was a remarkable gesture, since Barrow was only 39 years old at the time. Barrow recognized Newton's genius, however. He knew that if Newton took the position, he would remain in mathematics, since it only required that he lecture one hour a week. The job would give him the time, prestige, and resources to do research. Newton accepted the position and would teach at Cambridge for 18 years.

Most people think that by the end of 1664, Newton had mastered all the mathematics there was to know and was ready to

go beyond and make contributions of his own. Immediately after Newton received his bachelor's degree in 1665, Trinity College officially closed down because of the plague. This highly contagious and usually fatal disease seemed to breed and spread rapidly in cities, which in the seventeenth century were dirty and congested. Because there was no cure or even adequate treatment, quarantine or isolation was the only alternative. The university was thus closed down until the disease passed, and its students were sent home. Newton returned to his mother's farm in Woolsthorpe, where he remained for a year and a half until school reopened.

Annus mirabilis

During this time of inactivity, Newton let his great mind wander in the most productive manner. Called a "wonderful year" or *annus mirabilis* in Latin (though it was actually 18 months), this period is recognized by historians as the fertile months during which Newton literally figured out what would become the foundations of his later work in mathematics, optics, astronomy, and physics.

The famous story of Newton's apple occurred during the annus mirabilis. While resting under a tree, he watched an apple fall to the ground. At that moment, he had the brilliantly intuitive thought that perhaps the same force affected both the apple and the moon. From this notion, he eventually came to his great law of universal gravitation. Newton always swore that this story was true.

Throughout his career, Newton would often refer back to the thoughts, calculations, and experiments of the annus mirabilis and would elaborate and eventually publish his findings. For example, in 1684, English astronomer Edmond Halley (1656– 1742) told Newton about a particular problem concerning the movement of planets that no one could solve. After Newton immediately told him the answer, Halley asked how he knew, and Newton said simply that he had calculated it nearly 20 years earlier. (See sidebar on Edmond Halley in the **Statistics** entry.) Eventually, Newton would publish what would become his theories on the nature of light, his laws of motion and gravitation, and his invention of calculus. Any one of these discoveries would have been enough to make him a giant in the history of science.

Opposite page:
A whimsical representation of the moment Isaac Newton conceived of the idea of universal gravitation.

Isaac Newton

Invention of calculus and quarrel with Leibniz

Calculus marks the beginnings of what is called higher mathematics. Its invention provided mathematicians and scientists with a powerful tool to solve problems that had been unsolvable before. A typical problem that can only be solved by calculus involves a relationship that is 1) both dynamic or rapidly changing and 2) also affected by many different factors (like **time,** speed, distance, force) at the same time. Most historians now agree that Newton and Leibniz each invented their own versions of calculus independent of the other, with Newton doing it first by eight to ten years. However, since Newton was typically very late in publishing his work, the publications of Leibniz in 1684 and 1686 were first.

Although the two men did not begin their relationship as rivals, the debate over whether Leibniz had taken Newton's ideas grew into a bitter dispute that eventually reached the patriotic level of England versus Germany. Leibniz's calculus symbolism, or style of notation, was much more convenient to use than Newton's, which made matters even worse. The dispute lived on in both countries long after both men were dead and had a negative effect on English mathematics, which shut itself off for a long time from any other European advances in mathematics.

Lifetime accomplishments

Mathematics was at the core of nearly all Newton's scientific accomplishments. The same year he assumed the Lucasian professorship, he began his work on optics and a theory of colors, and also built the first reflecting telescope, the ancestor of today's massive instruments. He was elected a member of the Royal Society in 1672. In 1687, Newton published his monumental work entitled *Philosphiae naturalis principia mathematica (The Mathematical Principles of Natural Philosophy).* The laws of motion and the universal principle of gravitation contained in this book make it one of the most famous works of Western science.

Always a very private and secretive man who would literally lose himself in his thoughts (many a story about his absent-mindedness exist), Newton suffered a severe mental illness in 1693 during which he experienced deep depression and fears of being persecuted. Eventually he overcame these mental problems and in 1696 left Cambridge to become warden (and eventually master) of the mint. This position placed him in charge of British **currency** and gave him a generous salary. He devoted as much time and energy to this job as he had to his science. In 1703 he was elected president of the Royal Society and was reelected every year after until his death.

German American physicist and mathematician **Albert Einstein** (1879–1955) once said that for Newton, nature "was an open book, whose letters he could read without effort." English poet Alexander Pope (1688–1744) said very much the same thing in a couplet:

> "Nature and Nature's laws lay hid in night;
>
> God said, Let Newton be! and all was light."

Newton absorbed in thought

The legendary absent-mindedness of Isaac Newton makes him the ultimate preoccupied professor. Once, when giving a dinner for some university friends, he left the table to get a bottle of wine. On the way to the wine cellar, he started thinking about his work. Forgetting about his company as well as his errand, he went to his study and did not return that night.

Sometimes Newton would find himself half-dressed on the street. Other times he would be seen strolling in his garden, only to suddenly stop and bolt quickly to his study where he would scribble on the first piece of paper he found. One time, he got off his horse to lead him up a hill and the horse slipped out of the bridle. Newton did not discover that he was holding an empty bridle until he reached the top of the hill.

After getting out of bed in the morning, Newton would often be found by his housekeeper simply sitting on the edge of his bed—still in his nightclothes, totally absorbed in thought. Few know that Newton spent years of his life intensely occupied in trying to find a way to turn base metals into gold. He brought the same intensity to this project as he did to his science. It has been said that there were periods when his furnace fires were not allowed to go out for six weeks!

Such statements from individuals who themselves were great thinkers show just how highly Newton was and is regarded. Although he was an odd person who never married, was suspicious of everyone, held deeply to grudges, and often would not remember to eat, Isaac Newton was a genius who showed the world that mathematics was a highly useful tool for solving the riddles of nature.

For More Information

Anderson, Margaret Jean. *Isaac Newton: The Greatest Scientist of All Time.* Springfield, NJ: Enslow, 1996.

Biographical Dictionary of Mathematicians. New York: Charles Scribner's Sons, 1991.

MacTutor History of Mathematics Archive. "Sir Isaac Newton." http://www-groups.dcs.st-and.ac.uk/~history/Mathematicians/Newton.html (accessed on April 27, 1999).

Isaac Newton

Muir, Jane. *Of Men and Numbers: The Story of the Great Mathematicians.* New York: Dover Publications, 1996.

Rankin, William. *Introducing Newton.* New York: Totem Books, 1994.

Simmons, George F. *Calculus Gems: Brief Lives and Memorable Mathematics.* New York: McGraw-Hill, 1992.

Tiner, John Hudson. *Isaac Newton: Inventor, Scientist, and Teacher.* Milford, MI: Mott Media, 1981.

Westfall, Richard S. *Never at Rest: A Biography of Isaac Newton.* Cambridge, England: Cambridge University Press, 1983.

White, Michael. *Isaac Newton: The Last Sorceror.* Reading, MA: Helix Books, 1999.

Young, Robyn V., ed. *Notable Mathematicians: From Ancient Times to the Present.* Detroit: Gale Research, 1998.

Born March 23, 1882
Erlangen, Bavaria, Germany

Died April 14, 1935
Bryn Mawr, Pennsylvania

German algebraist

Emmy Noether

One of the leading figures in the development of modern abstract **algebra,** Emmy Noether was a mathematical genius whose work became basic to the general theory of relativity. During her career, she worked closely with some of the greatest mathematicians and theoretical physicists of her time. She was described by German American physicist and mathematician **Albert Einstein** (1879–1955) as "the most significant mathematical genius thus far produced since the higher education of women began."

> *"[Emmy Noether] had great stimulating power and many of her suggestions took shape only in the works of her pupils and co-workers."*
> —*German mathematician Hermann Weyl*

Early life and education

Amalie Emmy Noether (pronounced NEUH-ter) was born in Erlangen, Germany, the oldest of the four children of Max Noether and Ida Amalia Kaufmann Noether. She was always known by her middle name, Emmy, rather than by her first name, Amalie. Although her father was a mathematician and university professor, Noether received the traditional education most young German girls were given. She did not make any special mark as an outstanding student. Her home life was warm and secure, and Noether did things that most girls

Emmy Noether

her age did. She learned to cook, do housework, and sew, and she also enjoyed going to dances.

Few, if any, girls in Noether's day received a college education; she, too, did not attend a college preparatory school but instead studied languages at a school that would certify her to teach French and English at a girl's school. After she passed the test that would have qualified her to be a language teacher, Noether suddenly decided that she wanted to continue her own education and study the subject she really loved—mathematics.

Supported by her family in her decision, Noether began to study and prepare for the entrance exam she would have to take to enter the Göttingen University. After sitting in on mathematical classes at the University of Erlangen and completing two full years of study on her own, Noether passed the examination and was admitted to Göttingen in 1900, but only as an auditor. (Auditing meant that although she could attend class, she would not receive official credit for doing so.) She studied in this manner until 1904 when the University of Erlangen allowed women to become regular students with the same rights as male students. She then left Göttingen and enrolled as a regular student at Erlangen, where her father taught.

Nearly all her fellow students were male and were not used to having a woman in class with them. She was one of only two women among nearly one thousand students. Noether did not mind at all since she was finally able to study mathematics all the time. At Erlangen, Noether was able to study with a mathematics professor, Paul Gordan (1837–1912), who was also a good friend of the family. She happily worked very hard, wrote her doctor's thesis, and was awarded her Ph.D. in mathematics in 1907 *summa cum laude*—with the highest honors. During her student years at Erlangen, she also gained experience teaching, since she substituted for her father as a university lecturer whenever he was unable to teach.

Difficult career as a mathematician

Although Noether had encountered and overcome several obstacles to her education, trying to find a teaching job as a mathematician was even more difficult. Times were changing in Germany, but many rules still blocked her way. One rule would not allow women to be part of the university faculty. Since no one would hire her to teach at that high level, she simply continued her research and study and substituted for her father when necessary.

By 1915, Noether's abilities had become known to a wider group of people. In 1915, the great German number theorist, David Hilbert (1862–1943), one of the best known mathematicians in the world, invited her to give lectures at Göttingen University where he taught. Hilbert and his colleagues were working on the mathematical aspects of Einstein's newly announced general theory of relativity, and he thought that Noether's particular type of mathematical knowledge and skill would be helpful. Einstein's theory described the relationship between energy, mass, and the speed of light. Hilbert tried to get her a position at the university but met much resistance, especially from non-mathematical departments like philosophy. He got around this by simply letting her teach his own courses. Finally, in 1919 he was able to obtain a job for her called a *Privatdozent*. This position gave her the right to teach and be paid directly by the students, but she could not be paid by the university.

By this time, Noether had become an outstanding and increasingly well known mathematician who had published nearly 40 papers. Despite her distinguished credentials, it was apparent that she was prevented from being an official member of the university simply because she was female. As one opponent of hers stated near the end of World War I (1914–18), "What will our soldiers think when they return to the university and find that they are expected to learn at the feet of a woman?" During the terrible economic times for Germany that followed because of its loss in the war, Noether remained at the Mathematical Institute at Göttingen in an unpaid position. In 1922, however, she was lucky enough to receive a low but regular salary as an instructor of algebra.

Despite all of this, Noether was happy at Göttingen, where she enjoyed teaching. Having never married, she was able to devote all her time to her mathematics and to her friends and colleagues. As a teacher, she had a very loyal student following, although not everyone was able to keep up with her informal but demanding way of lecturing in which she and her students worked out mathematical problems together.

Emmy Noether

Emmy Noether

Mathematical contributions

During the decade of the 1920s, Noether became a real force in mathematics and actually changed the face of algebra. Her unique ability to work with abstract concepts and to visualize connections that others could not see enabled her to work out ideas in her head that others could only grasp by computations. This very different style of thinking about algebra made it a useful, new connection between mathematics and the modern physics of Einstein.

By the early 1930s, Noether was an internationally recognized mathematician of the first rank whose many speaking invitations came from several countries. Although the Mathematical Institute at Göttingen where she taught was considered the top center of its kind in the world, on April 7, 1933, she suddenly found herself separated from the Institute and "on leave until further notice." The National Socialist Party of Adolf Hitler (1889–1945) had come to power in Germany, and it set out to eliminate anyone it considered a potential enemy. Noether had three strikes against her. She was Jewish, an intellectual woman, and a known liberal and pacifist. Hitler's plans for the Jews proved to be even more terrible, but at first he began by taking away their rights.

Begins new career in the United States

During the difficult times in Germany, Noether was always calm and courageous. She showed more of a concern for the lack of world peace than she did for her own welfare. This was not unusual; Noether was a dedicated pacifist. Fortunately, Noether had many friends in the international community. They arranged for her to leave Germany and take a teaching position at Bryn Mawr, a women's college near Philadelphia, Pennsylvania. So in 1933, she moved to Philadelphia.

Noether immediately began a new, productive life. For the first time she was actually paid for her teaching. She also was part of a department whose head was a woman. Her students took to the warm, friendly teacher at once, and she often took them on long walks during which she would become so absorbed talking about mathematics that her students had to protect her from walking into traffic. Noether also benefitted from the closeness of the Institute for Advanced Study at nearby Princeton University in New

Emmy Noether

Emmy Noether sits at her desk.

Jersey. There, she lectured and discussed mathematics with some of America's leading mathematicians.

Dies suddenly

Noether's new life in America did not last long, however, as she died on April 14, 1935, after what appeared to be routine surgery. Noether underwent surgery to remove a uterine tumor, but died suddenly four days later from an apparent postoperative infection. Thus, one of the most creative mathematicians and a person who broke down many barriers to the success of women had her ashes buried near the library on the Bryn Mawr campus. Today, Noether's pioneering work is recognized as a cornerstone of the modern algebra studied by every graduate student in mathematics.

For More Information

Abbott, David, ed. *The Biographical Dictionary of Scientists: Mathematicians.* New York: Peter Bedrick Books, 1986.

Emmy Noether

MacTutor History of Mathematics Archive. "Emmy Amalie Noether." http://www-groups.dcs.st-and.ac.uk/~history/Mathematicians/Noether_Emmy.html (accessed on April 27, 1999).

Morrow, Charlene, and Teri Perl, eds. *Notable Women in Mathematics: A Biographical Dictionary.* Westport, CT: Greenwood Press, 1998.

Osen, Lynn M. *Women in Mathematics.* Cambridge, MA: The MIT Press, 1974.

Young, Robyn V., ed. *Notable Mathematicians: From Ancient Times to the Present.* Detroit: Gale Research, 1998.

Perimeter

Perimeter is the distance around a two-dimensional or flat figure. Unlike the concept of **area,** which is a measure of how much space the figure takes up (or how much is contained within the sides of a figure), perimeter is concerned only with the total measure of the sides or edges of that figure. It is therefore described as being the sum of the lengths of the sides of a **polygon.**

Background and description

The word perimeter is the result of combining two Greek words. The first, *peri,* means "around"; the second, *metron,* means "measure." Perimeter therefore means to measure around something. As one of the easiest concepts of Euclidean **geometry** to understand, perimeter shows what the lengths of all the sides of a polygon will add up to. A polygon is a figure composed of three or more line segments (called sides). The simple rule for finding the perimeter is that it is the sum of the lengths of the sides of a polygon. Thus, a hexagon whose six sides individually measure in inches 2, 5, 3, 2, 5, and 3 has a perimeter of 20 inches (2 + 5 + 3 + 2 + 5 + 3 = 20).

Perimeter

WORDS TO KNOW

Area the amount of space a flat geometrical shape occupies; the region inside a given boundary

Circumference the distance completely around the outside of a circle; its perimeter

Diameter a line segment that joins two points on a circle and passes through its center; the longest chord possible in a circle

Parallelogram a quadrilateral in which both pairs of opposite sides are parallel

Pentagon a polygon with five sides

Pi (π) a number defined as the ratio of the circumference to the diameter of a circle; it cannot be represented exactly as a decimal, but it is between 3.1415 and 3.1416

Polygon a geometric figure composed of three or more line segments (straight sides) that never cross each other

Ratio the relationship between two quantities, which is obtained by dividing two things; for instance, the ratio of 3 to 2 is written 3:2 or $\frac{3}{2}$

Finding the perimeter for polygons of certain shapes can be shortened by using formulas. For example, knowing that by definition a square is composed of four equal sides enables one to find its perimeter by multiplying the length of one of its sides by four. So a square whose sides are 7 feet each has a perimeter (P) of 28 feet ($P = 7 \times 4$).

A different but still very simple formula is used for rectangles and parallelograms, each of which has opposite sides of equal length. In this case, the perimeter equals twice the length (*l*) plus twice the width (*w*) ($P = 2l + 2w$), which is the same as saying $P = l + w + l + w$. Naturally, the perimeter of a **triangle** is equal to the sum of its three sides. While there are other formulas that could be developed and used to find the perimeter of all different sorts of polygons, it is sometimes easier to simply add up the lengths of all its sides than to try to remember an abstract formula.

For a **circle,** the distance around it is called its circumference, rather than its perimeter, but it nonetheless means the same thing as perimeter. From ancient times it has been known that the ratio of the circumference of a circle to its diameter is an unchanging value that is a little over 3. (See also **Ratio, proportion, and percent.**) This constant value is named for **pi,** the sixteenth letter of the Greek alphabet. To find the circumference of a circle, one multiplies the circle's diameter times pi, or 3.14.

Applications and uses

Initially, there do not seem to be many practical applications for knowing how to obtain the perimeter beyond the straightforward use of finding the total length needed to enclose or draw a boundary around a certain area. However, as perimeter relates to area (the space inside the boundary or sides), it can provide a great deal of valuable and useful information.

For instance, if a farmer has 100 feet of fencing available and wants to know what four-sided shape he should enclose in order to fence in the largest area, a familiarity with basic Euclidean geometry would give him the answer. One of Euclidean geometry's general theorems provides a ready answer: of all rectangles with the same perimeter, a square has the maximum area. When building a house and laying out its rooms, one can conclude that given a certain perimeter, a square-shaped room will give both maximum floor area and offer the most efficient price for building its walls. Related theorems show that for pentagons (five-sided polygons) of the same perimeter, the regular pentagon or one with equal sides, contains the greatest area.

Queen Dido's problem

A famous legend concerns the matter of perimeter and presents this problem: A person has only a certain amount of fencing and wants to enclose as much land as possible along a riverfront so that no fencing would be needed at the shoreline. What shape should the fence be?

Queen Dido was said to have founded the North African city of Carthage after having fled her Mediterranean kingdom. Bargaining for this new land, she was offered as much land as she was able to enclose with the hide of a bull. She then cut the hide into very thin strips and tied them together to form a long rope. After choosing land along a shore, since she would not have to use any hide to close in that side, she then had to decide what shape to use for the boundary. Dido cleverly decided that a circular shape would give her the largest amount of land, and indeed she was correct. It was not until the nineteenth century that mathematicians were able to prove that the greatest area that can be enclosed by a fixed perimeter is that of a circle.

For More Information

Beaumont, Vern, et al. *How to . . . Teach Perimeter, Area, and Volume.* Reston, VA: The National Council of Teachers of Mathematics, 1986.

Green, Gordon W., Jr. *Helping Your Child to Learn Math.* New York: Citadel Press, 1995.

West, Beverly Henderson, et al. *The Prentice-Hall Encyclopedia of Mathematics.* Englewood Cliffs, NJ: Prentice-Hall, 1982.

Wheeler, Ruric E. *Modern Mathematics.* Pacific Grove, CA: Brooks/Cole Publishing Co., 1995.

Pi

Pi is the constant ratio (see **Ratio, proportion, and percent**) of a circle's circumference to its diameter. Although pi is an irrational (see **Rational and irrational numbers**) number and therefore cannot be calculated exactly, it has proven to be a highly useful concept. Many formulas in **geometry** involve pi, most notably the formulas for the **area** of a **circle** and the **volume** of a sphere.

Background

At least 4,000 years ago, the Babylonians recognized that there was a constant formula or shorthand that they could use to find out certain things about a circle, regardless of its size. These ancient people were highly practical and regularly used some forms of geometry in their daily lives. Knowledge of a mathematical rule or formula was essential to how quickly and efficiently they could perform certain tasks. Thus, once they had discovered that there existed a constant ratio or relationship between the circumference of a circle (the **perimeter** of a circle or the complete distance around it) and its diameter (a line drawn from any point on its perimeter through its center to any other point on the perimeter), they were able to put this knowledge to good use. It was often nec-

Area the amount of space a flat geometrical shape occupies; the region inside a boundary

Circumference the distance completely around the outside of a circle; its perimeter

Diameter a line segment that joins two points on a circle and passes through its center; the longest chord possible in a circle

Irrational number a number that is expressed as a nonrepeating decimal fraction and which, when carried out, simply goes on forever; contrasted to a rational number, which has either a terminating decimal (it comes out even with no remainder) or a repeating decimal (as .33333333...)

Perimeter the distance around a polygon, obtained by adding the lengths of its sides; the perimeter or distance completely around a circle is called its circumference

Ratio the relationship between two quantities, which is obtained by dividing two things; for instance, the ratio of 3 to 2 is written 3:2 or 3/2

Volume a number describing the three-dimensional amount of a space; a measure of the capacity or how much something will hold; the number of cubic units in a solid figure

essary to find out exactly how much grain a granary (a building that stores grain) would hold (its volume) or how much land was encompassed by a fence or wall. The Babylonians also were able to divide land and fields or to estimate the number of bricks needed for a construction project.

Description and use

As a ratio, pi is actually a comparison of two numbers by **division** (3.14 to 1) or 22/7. This means generally that a circle's circumference is a little more than three times its diameter. Today it is commonly stated in its **decimal** form with the number 1 being understood and therefore left out. The Babylonians actually were very close to this exact ratio. They calculated pi as 3.1250. At about the same time, the Egyptians were equally knowledgeable and estimated pi to be 3.1605. Around 1100 B.C., the Chinese used the number 3 for pi.

Beginning about 500 B.C., the Greeks began to undertake a serious study of geometry, and it was in their work that the concept of pi was thoroughly analyzed and calculated. Around 240 B.C., Greek mathematician **Archimedes of Syracuse** (287–212 B.C.) found a very close approximation of the value of pi using his "method of exhaustion." He did this by drawing a circle with a square inside it and another with a square outside it. The perimeter of these squares or any other **polygon** (a closed figure composed of three or more line segments that never cross each other) was simple to figure out. This was done by adding the lengths of all of their sides.

Archimedes kept doubling the number of sides of the polygons he would draw inside and outside the circle until he had 96-sided figures. At this point, the polygons on both sides of the circle had extremely short sides and were very close to matching the curved circumference (perimeter) of the circle. He was then able to calculate that the outside polygon had a ratio of 3.1408 and the inside had one of 3.1428. He therefore knew that pi was somewhere between the two (or close to today's 3.1416). However, like the **square root** of two, pi cannot be calculated exactly. It is considered irrational (a number that cannot be expressed as a **fraction**). Pi will go on forever in what is called a nonrepeating decimal expansion.

Pi is taken from the sixteenth letter of the Greek alphabet and is often represented by the Greek symbol π for that letter. It is thought that this letter was chosen because it is the first letter of the Greek word for perimeter, *perimetros*. The perimeter of a circle is the same thing as its circumference. During the seventeenth century, the symbol π was used as part of a fraction to represent the ratio of the circumference of a circle to its diameter. In 1706, William Jones (1675–1749) became the first English mathematician to use the symbol by itself to represent this important ratio. When world-renowned Swiss mathematician **Leonhard Euler** (1707–83) adopted the π symbol in 1737, it soon became accepted by all.

In 1767, Swiss German mathematician Johann Heinrich Lambert (1728–77) proved that pi is irrational and that no fractional or decimal number can *exactly* represent it. Near the end of the nineteenth century, pi was calculated out to just over 700 places. In 1949, the first fully electronic **computer** (called ENIAC) calculated pi to 2,037 decimal places. By 1991, a computer had calculated well beyond the first two billion digits of pi. Since the time of the Babylonians, knowing the approximate value of such a concept as pi has enabled people to compute with confidence the areas and volumes of curved surfaces and circular forms.

Archimedes of Syracuse.

What does pi equal?

The most well-known irrational number is pi. Pi is often represented as the Greek letter pi—π.

Here is the value of pi to one hundred decimal places:

3.1415926535897932384626433832795028841971693993751058209749445923078164062862089986280348253421170679

For More Information

Beckmann, Petr. *A History of Pi.* Boulder, CO: Golem Press, 1977.

Blatner, David. *The Joy of Pi.* New York: Walker and Co., 1997.

Pi

Exploratorium: The Museum of Science, Art and Human Perception. *The Ridiculously Enhanced Pi Page.* [Online] http://www.exploratorium.edu/learning_studio/pi/ (accessed on March 29, 1999).

Hogben, Lancelot T. *Mathematics in the Making.* London: Galahad Books, 1974.

West, Beverly Henderson, et al. *The Prentice-Hall Encyclopedia of Mathematics.* Englewood Cliffs, NJ: Prentice-Hall, 1982.

Polygon

A polygon is a closed geometric figure composed of three or more line segments (straight sides) that never cross each other. In **geometry,** a polygon is a very common shape and serves as an inclusive name for many different types of figures. Polygons are classified by the number of sides they have.

Background

The ancient Greeks studied polygons intensively and it was they who gave polygons their names. The word polygon itself is derived from two Greek words, *polus,* meaning "many," and *gonia,* meaning "angle." Although a polygon is defined as a figure with many sides, the word itself actually means a figure with many angles. No matter what type of polygon a particular shape is, certain parts of a polygon are always called the same thing. For example, each separate line segment is called a side, and the point where two sides connect, or meet, is called the vertex.

Description

Most of the names for the different types of polygons were taken from the Greek prefixes for numbers. Thus, except for **quadrilat-**

Area the amount of space a flat geometrical shape occupies; the region inside a given boundary

Concave polygon a polygon with at least one interior angle that measures more than 180 degrees; at least one straight line can intersect more than two sides

Convex polygon a polygon whose every interior angle measures less than 180 degrees; any straight line intersects no more than two sides

Equiangular polygon a polygon in which every interior angle measures the same number of degrees

Equilateral polygon a polygon in which every side measures the same length

Isosceles triangle a triangle with at least two sides of equal length

Perimeter the distance around a polygon, obtained by adding the lengths of its sides; the perimeter or distance completely around a circle is called its circumference

Regular polygon a polygon in which all sides have equal length and all interior angles have equal measure; a polygon that is both equilateral and equiangular

Side one of the line segments of a polygon; also called "legs" for a triangle

Vertex the point at which any two sides of a polygon meet or intersect; plural is "vertices"

eral (meaning four sides) and nonagon (meaning nine sides), both of which have Latin prefixes, the remaining names are all of Greek origin. (See below.)

Type of polygon	Number of sides
triangle	3
quadrilateral	4
parallelogram	4 (both pairs of opposite sides are parallel)
rhombus	4 (a parallelogram with four sides of equal length)
pentagon	5
hexagon	6
heptagon	7
octagon	8
nonagon	9
decagon	10
hendecahedron	11
dodecagon	12

As a general name for several types of many-sided figures, a polygon can also be classified according to the relationships of its angles or sides. Therefore, a polygon whose every interior (inside) angle has the same number of degrees is called an equiangular polygon. A rectangle is one example of an equiangular polygon since it has four identical interior angles (all right angles equal to 90 degrees). An equilateral polygon has all of its sides of equal length. An example of such a figure is a square (four equal sides). A regular polygon is one whose sides are of equal length and whose angles are of equal measure. While a square and an equilateral **triangle** are examples of a regular polygon, other polygons with even more sides can be regular polygons as well.

Finally, polygons can be concave and convex. A concave polygon has at least one interior angle that measures more than 180 degrees; for a convex, every angle is less than 180 degrees. There is another way to distinguish between the two types of polygons. One straight line drawn through a concave polygon can intersect more than two sides, but for a convex polygon it intersects no more than two. A concave polygon also looks as if it has a dent in it (it "caves in" somewhere). One example of a concave polygon is a star-shaped figure (with five "dents").

Triangle   Parallelogram   Rhombus   Rectangle

Square   Pentagon   Hexagon   Octagon

Eight types of polygons.

For all polygons, the **perimeter** (total distance around its outer edges) is equal to the sum of the lengths of all its sides. Calculating the **area** of an irregularly shaped polygon is more involved, since it requires breaking up the polygon into standard shapes (squares, rectangles, triangles) and then finding the area for each separate part. The area of a regular polygon (equal angles, equal sides) is obtained by dividing it into isosceles triangles (with two sides of equal length) and then using the area formula for triangles.

Certain valuable generalizations can be made concerning area and polygons. For instance, of all polygons with the same perimeter and the same number of sides, the regular polygon has the greatest area. Further, of two regular polygons with the same perimeter, the one with more sides will have the greatest area. However, as one adds more and more sides, the regular polygon approaches a **circle** in shape, leading to the true statement that a circle has more area than any polygon with the same perimeter.

Polygons are all around us—for example, stop signs (octagon), yield signs (triangles), and one-way signs (rectangle). The largest office building in the world, the U.S. Department of Defense

headquarters outside of Washington, D.C., is a five-sided construction named after its shape: the Pentagon. Polygons are found in nature as well. The hexagonal honeycomb that bees build and live in is one of the best examples of a tessellation (a pattern formed by a number of polygons that fit together).

An aerial view of the most famous five-sided building in the world: the Pentagon in Washington, D.C.

For More Information

Burton, David M. *Burton's History of Mathematics: An Introduction.* Dubuque, IA: Wm. C. Brown Publishers, 1995.

Green, Gordon W., Jr. *Helping Your Child to Learn Math.* New York: Citadel Press, 1995.

Heddens, James W. and William R. Speer. *Today's Mathematics: Concepts and Methods in Elementary School Mathematics.* Upper Saddle River, NJ: Merrill, 1997.

Opposite page:
Bees nest in hexagon-shaped honeycombs.

Polygon

Ross, Catherine Sheldrick. *Squares.* Toronto: Kids Can Press, 1997.

West, Beverly Henderson, et al. *The Prentice-Hall Encyclopedia of Mathematics.* Englewood Cliffs, NJ: Prentice-Hall, 1982.

Prime number

A prime number is a natural or counting number greater than 1 that has only two factors—itself and 1. A factor of a number divides the number evenly and has no remainder. A prime number also can be described as a natural number that cannot be made by multiplying smaller numbers together. Prime numbers include 2, 3, 5, 7, 11, 13, 17, and so on.

Background

As far back as the third century, Greek mathematician **Euclid of Alexandria** (c. 325–c. 270 B.C.) wrote about the concept of a prime number and even offered a theorem stating correctly that there was an infinite (never-ending) number of primes. Further, he was able to prove his theorem by an indirect method. First, he made the assumption that primes were not infinite and that such a thing as a largest prime number could exist. Then, by demonstrating that such an assumption led to a contradiction, he was able to show that it was therefore false.

Not long after Euclid, Greek mathematician and geographer Eratosthenes of Cyrene (c. 276–c. 194 B.C.) developed a system

Composite number a whole number that is not a prime number; any number that can be obtained by multiplying two whole numbers other than itself and 1; the first ten composites are 4, 6, 8, 9, 10, 12, 14, 15, 16, 18

Factors the numbers multiplied to form a product; both the multiplier and the multiplicand

Formula a general answer, rule, or principle stated in a mathematical way (with an equal sign between two expressions)

Infinite set a set whose elements cannot be counted because they are unlimited

Least common denominator in the case of two fractions, it is the smallest multiple common to both denominators; for example, with the fractions ⅚, ¼, and ½, the least common denominator is 12 (the lowest number into which 6, 4, and 2 can be divided)

Natural numbers all the cardinal numbers or counting numbers (1, 2, 3, . . .) except 0

Parchment the skin of a goat or sheep that was treated in ancient times so that it could be written on

Prime factorization the process of finding all the prime factors of a given number

Sieve a device with holes or mesh that allows liquid or only particles of a very small size to pass through but which captures larger particles

Theorem a statement or generalization that can be demonstrated to be true

for finding all the primes less than some given number. Called the sieve of Eratosthenes, this system was a way of screening out the primes and eliminating from a certain quantity of numbers all those that were not primes. (See sidebar on Eratosthenes in the **Euclid of Alexandria** entry.) After following his six specific steps or directions—for example, Step 2: cross out all multiples of 2—many numbers would have "fallen through the sieve," and those that remained circled were prime numbers.

When Eratosthenes performed this mathematical exercise with a sieve, he used a piece of parchment (the skin of a goat or sheep) with the numerals arranged in columns. After punching a hole in the parchment after each numeral was eliminated by one of his six steps, he found that when finished, the parchment resembled a sieve. A sieve is a kind of sifter or any type of device that has mesh or holes through which only certain size particles can pass while others remain, thereby separating different types.

Description and use

One of the properties of all prime numbers except 2 is that they are all odd. This is true because every even number has 2 as a factor (and can be divided by it). Every even number greater than 2 has at least three factors (2, itself, and 1) and is therefore not a prime number. If a number is not a prime number it is called a composite number. It is any number that can be obtained by multiplying two **whole numbers** other than itself and 1. For example, 6 is a composite number because it has the factors of 2 and 3 besides itself and 1. The first ten composites are 4, 6, 8, 9, 10, 12, 14, 15, 16, and 18.

Since the time of the ancient Greeks, prime numbers have intrigued mathematicians. Although Euclid was able to prove that there is no largest prime number and that the set of primes is infinite, no one has yet been able to arrive at a formula that will generate only prime numbers. Although the primes seem to be scattered in some sort of pattern, no one has yet been able to precisely describe what it is (which a formula would do). Until computer programming made finding primes somewhat simpler, using a method like the sieve of Eratosthenes was most common. In the nineteenth century, Czech mathematician Yakov Kulik (1783–1863) spent twenty years finding all the prime numbers between 1 and 100,000,000 using the sieve method. Today, such methods as the Great Internet Mersenne Prime Search (GIMPS)—named in honor of French number theorist Marin Mersenne (1588–1648)—in which Internet users can download software in their hunt for large prime numbers, makes finding prime numbers faster. In 1998, in fact, one such user discovered a "new" prime number that is 909,526 digits long!

To mathematicians and teachers, prime numbers are the most basic category of numbers and are therefore regarded as the building blocks from which all numbers are made. The name itself comes from the Latin word *primus,* meaning "first." One very practical application of prime numbers is called prime factorization. Also called complete factorization, this is the process of finding all the prime factors of a given number. When a factor tree is created for a certain number, its bottom line represents the prime factors of the number. Prime factorization becomes very useful when writing **fractions** in their simplest form and when finding least common denominators.

For More Information

Flegg, Graham. *Numbers: Their History and Meaning.* New York: Schocken Books, 1983.

Friedberg, Richard. *An Adventurer's Guide to Number Theory.* New York: Dover Publications, 1994.

Great Internet Mersenne Prime Search (GIMPS). http://www.mersenne.org (accessed on May 7, 1999).

Humez, Alexander, et al. *Zero to Lazy Eight: The Romance of Numbers.* New York: Simon & Schuster, 1993.

Smith, David Eugene. *Number Stories of Long Ago.* Detroit: Gale Research, 1973.

Probability

Probability is a numerical measure of the chance that a certain event will occur, compared to the total number of possible events that could happen. Probability, or the laws of chance, are always expressed as a number, most often as a ratio or a percent (see **Ratio, proportion, and percent**). The laws of probability are much better at predicting what will happen in the long-term with many events than they are predicting what will happen in a short time with only a few cases.

History

Since probability involves chance, a phenomenon that has from the beginning been an inescapable part of human existence, it is perhaps surprising to realize that not until the sixteenth century did anyone have the slightest idea that anything but complete randomness was involved. During that century, Italian mathematician **Girolamo Cardano** (1501–76), who was also a dedicated gambler, decided to try to apply mathematics to games of chance and perhaps improve his chances of success. The work he produced, *De Ludo Aleae (Games of Chance)*, was the first book on the

Probability

mathematics of chance (although it contained as much on cheating and how to detect cheating).

Following Cardano, no attention was paid to the notion of applying mathematics to chance until 1654 when French mathematician and physicist Blaise Pascal (1623–62) began a collaboration with a countryman who was the greatest mathematician of that century, **Pierre de Fermat** (1601–65). Once Pascal took up the notion of probability seriously, he wrote to Fermat describing his goal. Pascal told Fermat that he wanted "to reduce to an exact art, with the rigor of mathematical demonstration, the incertitude [uncertainty] of chance, thus creating a new science which could justly claim the stupefying title: the mathematics of chance." (See accompanying sidebar for more information on Pascal.)

Like Cardano, Pascal and Fermat studied gambling situations, out of which evolved the modern theory of probability, or the laws of chance. By studying the frequency in which certain dice combinations would occur, Pascal and Fermat were able to establish a branch of mathematics dedicated to analyzing how frequently "random" events occur over the long run.

Following the foundation laid by Pascal and Fermat, Swiss mathematician Jakob Bernoulli (1654–1705) wrote *Ars conjectandi (The Art of Conjecturing)*, in which he made his own contributions to the theory of probability. (See sidebar on the Bernoulli family in the **Leonhard Euler** entry.) In 1812, French mathematician and astronomer Pierre-Simon de Laplace (1749–1827) published a major work on probability theory, which is distinguished as the first study to apply probability to subjects and matters other than gambling. Despite the involvement of such major figures, the general mathematical community mostly ignored the notion of probability until the late nineteenth and early twentieth centuries, when three Russian mathematicians, Pafnuty L. Chebyshev (1821–94), Andrey A. Markov (1856–1922), and Andrey N. Kolmogorov (1903–87), fully developed probability as a mathematical theory.

Description and use

Everyday language often includes the word "probably," meaning that something is likely to happen. Very often one knows by experience that one event is more likely to occur than another. For exam-

WORDS TO KNOW

Decimal fraction a fractional number expressed in decimal form; one in which the denominator is some power of ten; for example, .3 is the decimal version of $\frac{3}{10}$

Genetics the branch of biology that deals with heredity, especially the transmission of characteristics

Incertitude uncertainty or doubt about something

Natural selection the process in nature by which only those organisms best suited to their environment survive and transmit their genetic characteristics to succeeding generations

Ratio the relationship between two quantities, which is obtained by dividing two things; for instance, the ratio of 3 to 2 is written 3:2 or $\frac{3}{2}$

Rigor strict precision or exactness

Statistics the branch of mathematics consisting of methods for collecting, organizing, and summarizing data in order to make predictions based on these data

Blaise Pascal

Mathematics has served many different purposes for many different people. But probably no one has ever used it the way French mathematician and physicist Blaise Pascal (1623–62) did. Pascal was a child prodigy (someone with extraordinary talents) whose father tried unsuccessfully to steer him away from mathematics. He deliberately kept all science and math books away from his young son. But when Pascal started figuring out Euclid's theorems on his own—never having seen a book on geometry—his father gave in. Pascal then published a book on geometry at the age of 16, and invented a calculating machine three years later.

Beginning as a child, Pascal was always sick and frail. Besides suffering from terrible headaches, he had indigestion and trouble sleeping. When he was 25 years old, he came under the influence of a strict religious group and soon became obsessed with thoughts of God and eternity. At the age of 27, Pascal promised God that he would abandon mathematics altogether and devote more time to religious study. Three years later he broke his promise, but a narrow escape from death involving a horse and a cliff made him realize that God was reminding him of his promise. Thereafter, the only time he became involved with mathematics was for one week in 1658 when he had a painful toothache. Pascal found that concentrating deeply on a problem in geometry distracted him from the constant pain.

ple, chances are greater that a coin will flip to heads well before a particular playing card is pulled out of a deck. But unless one is familiar with probability theory, it is difficult to tell exactly how much more probable one event is compared to another.

Probability is the branch of mathematics that expresses in numbers (**fractions, decimal**s, or percent) that event A is more or less likely to happen than is event B. Therefore, the probability of an event is the ratio of the number of times an event happens to the total number of outcomes (opportunities to happen). For example, when flipping a coin, the probability of the coin landing heads is ½. (There are two possible outcomes, one of which is heads.) When picking one card from a shuffled deck, the probability of the card being the jack of spades is ½₂. (There are 52 possible outcomes, one of which is the jack of spades.) The probability of the

card being red is $^{26}/_{52}$, or $^{1}/_{2}$. (There are 52 possible outcomes, 26 of which are red cards.) The probability of the card being an ace of any suit is $^{4}/_{52}$, or $^{1}/_{13}$. (There are 52 possible outcomes, 4 of which are aces.)

These numbers or ratios are obtained either experimentally (based on a test made under controlled conditions) or theoretically (relating to an assumption based on speculation or conjecture). Picking cards, flipping a coin, or rolling dice are events that can be tested by actual experiments. Although such experiments have the same possible outcomes all the time (either heads or tail, for instance), the outcome of a single time is impossible to predict. While there are several rules of probability, the main formula used to find the probability of an event occurring is that the probability *(P)* of an event *(A)* is equal to the number of outcomes of an event divided by the number of possible outcomes. Thus, when a single die is rolled once, the chance of rolling a 5 is $P(A) = ^{1}/_{6}$. This can also be stated as a 1-in-6 chance (ratio), or as roughly a 16-percent chance.

Despite its origins in gambling and games of chance, for which it is still very much used, probability theory has entered the fields of serious mathematics and science. Probability has applications in nearly every area of human involvement. Physicists use probability to study the various heat and gas laws as well as in atomic theory. Biologists use probability techniques in genetics and natural selection. Austrian botanist Gregor Johann Mendel (1822–84), for example, used mathematics to establish the laws of inheritance (pertaining to genetic qualities). After compiling 80 years' worth of **statistics** from his breeding experiments on over 30,000 pea plants, Mendel discovered that there were traits that were dominant, or stronger, and others that were recessive, or weaker. This led him to analyze his data and to uncover several basic laws of heredity. For example, he found that mixtures of traits do not "blend" but rather retain their identities. For instance, if a tall plant was crossed with a short one, the result was not a medium plant, but some tall and some short. Mendel observed that these mixed traits combined and sorted themselves out according to fixed rules or ratios.

Swiss mathematician Jakob Bernoulli.

Opposite page:
The probability of rolling snake eyes (two ones) with a pair of dice is 1 in 36.

French mathematician and astronomer Pierre-Simon de Laplace.

Probability theory is also employed in government and industry to assist in the decision-making process. In addition, probability is recognized as forming the theoretical basis for the field of statistics. Overall, the mathematics of probability comes into play in more ways than one realizes, from the intelligence tests children take in school, to the frequency of spot-checks a manufacturer makes on a production line, to the amount of merchandise a store manager must have on hand each day. All of these situations deal with what is basically random phenomena in a way that people are able to obtain a good measure of the *likelihood* of something happening.

For More Information

Cushman, Jean. *Do You Wanna Bet?: Your Chance to Find Out About Probability.* New York: Clarion Books, 1991.

David, Florence N. *Games Gods, and Gambling: A History of Probability and Statistical Ideas.* Mineola, NY: Dover Publications, 1998.

Gigerenzer, Gerd, et al. *The Empire of Chance: How Probability Changed Science and Everyday Life.* Cambridge, England: Cambridge University Press, 1989.

Miller, Charles D., et al. *Mathematical Ideas.* Reading, MA: Addison-Wesley, 1997.

Smith, Karl J. *Mathematics: Its Power and Utility.* Pacific Grove, CA: Brooks/Cole, 1997.

Born c. 580 B.C.
Samos, Ionia, Greece

Died c. 500 B.C.
Metapontum, Lucania (present-day Italy)

Greek geometer and philosopher

Pythagoras of Samos

An ancient Greek philosopher, mathematician, teacher, mystic, and political agitator, Pythagoras was an important early figure in the intellectual development of Western civilization. His influence was especially strong in the field of mathematics which he raised to a very high level. He viewed mathematics as the basis for everything that is known. Beyond his mathematical discoveries and contributions, the school of thought founded by Pythagoras went on to leave its mark on poets, artists, scientists, and philosophers into the twenty-first century.

"Number rules the universe."

Formative years

Pythagoras (pronounced puh-THAG-uh-rus) was born on Samos, a Greek island in the Aegean Sea that is very close to the west coast of Turkey. Although few details are known about his early life, it is believed that his father, Mnesarchus, may have been an engraver of seals or possibly a merchant. Pythagoras was born during what is now called the Golden Age of Greece, when learning was held in high esteem.

Pythagoras of Samos

Pythagoras became a pupil of the great Greek geometer, astronomer, and philosopher **Thales of Miletus** (c. 640–c. 546 B.C.), who is considered the founder of both Greek science and philosophy. As a young man, Pythagoras traveled widely for some thirty years in Egypt and Babylonia, where he is thought to have become acquainted with the mathematics of those regions.

By the age of 50, Pythagoras returned to his native Samos, which he found to be greatly changed under the tyrannical rule of Polycrates. Because of this, Pythagoras left Samos to settle in Crotone, or Crotona, a Greek colony located on the instep of the "boot" of southern Italy. There he founded a religious and philosophical school (some call it a cult; others, a society) whose search for the eternal laws of the universe was marked by secrecy, discipline, self-denial, and mysticism.

The Pythagorean school

Despite its religious, philosophical, and even political aspects, the school that Pythagoras founded was to be most influential in determining both the nature and the content of Greek mathematics. Limited to about 300 wealthy young men, it was not a school for everyone. It is believed that women were allowed to attend some lectures but not to become members. Members were divided into two groups. Beginners, or *akousmatikoi,* never spoke or asked questions but were to memorize the philosophical words of the master. *Mathematikoi* studied mathematics; their advanced training allowed them to ask questions and to express their own opinions. Known as the Order of the Pythagoreans, this group shared not only their worldly goods with each other but all their discoveries as well.

Work in the Pythagorean school was done anonymously. Individuals took no credit for their own work so that the master or the group could be credited. The school also followed some very strict rules of daily living. Members had to become vegetarians and to deny themselves most of life's everyday physical pleasures. Some specific rules seem strange, such as their refusal to wear wool clothing, to eat beans, to stir a fire with iron, or to kill any kind of animal. Since they believed in reincarnation (life after death), they thought they might be harming a dead person whose soul was now in the animal. (A story attributed to Pythagoras states that he begged a man to stop beating a dog, saying that he recognized "by its complaints" the soul of his friend in the dog.)

Pythagoras—"All is number"

At the core of the Pythagoreans' treatment of mathematics was the concept that all things are numbers. By this, they meant that numbers did not just exist as an abstraction or a thought in the human mind; instead, they had a reality all their own that did not depend on one's mind. To Pythagoras and his followers, "all is number" meant that numbers and the relations between numbers formed the basic core out of which everything else came. Numbers were to the Pythagoreans what atoms are to the human race today.

Mathematics of music

Pythagoras may have been led to his conclusion about numbers by any one of his many major mathematical discoveries. Again, since it is not known whether these ideas were discovered by Pythagoras alone or by a member of his school, scholars simply say Pythagoras. One of these discoveries might be described as establishing the mathematical basis of music. Pythagoras discovered, probably to his great delight, that there was a connection between the length of a string (on an instrument like a guitar) and the pitch of its vibrating note. Shorter strings gave a higher pitch than longer ones. Further analysis showed that a string twice as long as another would give a pitch twice as low. Finally, Pythagoras discovered that an instrument's strings would produce harmony when the ratio of the string lengths was a **whole number.** (See also **Ratio, proportion, and percent.**)

Some think that Pythagoras's mathematical theory of music, or harmonics, was solely responsible for his philosophy that numbers ruled the universe and functioned as the basic element that connected all things. Whether or not this is true, the Pythagoreans went on to attempt to explain everything in creation by referring to numbers.

Other mathematical contributions

Besides his theory of harmonics, Pythagoras also invented the terms "odd" and "even." He explained that odd numbers were male, and even numbers were female. Odd (male) numbers were also considered divine and lucky, and even (female) numbers were of the Earth and therefore unlucky. When Pythagoras observed the planets, he naturally interpreted his findings in terms of num-

A 1492 woodcut shows Pythagoras researching the relation between pitch and tone and the size of strings of musical instruments. Pythagoras's mathematical theory of music is called harmonics.

bers. He stated that these heavenly bodies were separated by intervals, or by an understandable number pattern, much like the laws of musical harmony that he had discovered.

Although he did not make any real practical use of his skills in **geometry**, Pythagoras discovered that the sides of a right **triangle** were connected by a law that could be expressed in numbers. Now called the **Pythagorean theorem,** this rule states that the square of the longest side of a triangle (the hypotenuse) is equal to the sum of the squares of its other two sides (its legs).

Finally, Pythagoras is credited with the discovery of irrational numbers. (See also **Rational and irrational numbers** entry.) This discovery came about as a result of his Pythagorean theorem. If a right triangle is pictured with its two legs or short sides of the same length (for example, one inch), then the hypotenuse or longest side is equal to the sum of the two sides squared (or equal to two inches). This means that the length of the hypotenuse is a number that when squared equals 2. Such a number is called the **square root** of 2 (as 10 is the square root of 100). However, the square root of two is not a neat, whole number like 1 or 2. In fact, it consists of a number that can be calculated out forever. Pythagoras called such numbers that had a fractional rather than a whole value "unspeakables," and tried to ignore them and pretend they did not exist. Today, they are called irrational numbers, or numbers whose values cannot be written down in their entirety since they go on to infinity.

Some historians also say that Pythagoras was the first person to use the words "parabola," "ellipse," and "hyperbola" to describe certain shapes. Another first attributed to Pythagoras is his statement that the world is round. After observing the round shadow cast by the Earth on the Moon during a lunar eclipse, Pythagoras concluded that the Earth's shape was spherical. He also argued that the Earth spun on its axis (with one rotation taking 24 hours) and that it orbited some unknown, central point.

Fate of the Pythagorean school

Pythagorean ideas and facts still are influential today. But during his own lifetime, Pythagoras and his followers were driven from Crotone. The rise of a popular or democratic movement in Crotone meant that the secretive and aristocratic Pythagoreans came to be seriously mistrusted, and the school itself was destroyed. Some say that Pythagoras was murdered after he fled to nearby Matapontum. His followers nevertheless spread to other parts of the Greek world and continued his teachings. One of the most famous Pythagoreans was Greek philosopher Plato (c. 428–c. 348 B.C.), who based his own academy on mathematics as the key to understanding the world.

In addition to the major discoveries in mathematics attributed to Pythagoras, his legacy—that nature can be understood by using numbers—can be described as his most significant contribution to modern mathematics and science.

For More Information

Abbott, David, ed. *The Biographical Dictionary of Scientists: Mathematicians.* New York: Peter Bedrick Books, 1986.

Biographical Dictionary of Mathematicians. New York: Charles Scribner's Sons, 1991.

Fey, James. *Looking for Pythagoras: The Pythagorean Theorem.* White Plains, NY: Dale Seymour Publications, 1997.

MacTutor History of Mathematics Archive. "Pythagoras of Samos." http://www-groups.dcs.st-and.ac.uk/~history/Mathematicians/Pythagoras.html (accessed on April 27, 1999).

Rogers, James T. *The Pantheon Story of Mathematics for Young People.* New York: Pantheon Books, 1966.

Young, Robyn V., ed. *Notable Mathematicians: From Ancient Times to the Present.* Detroit: Gale Research, 1998.

Pythagorean theorem

As one of the more important ideas in **geometry**, the Pythagore-an theorem expresses a relationship among the sides of a right triangle (a triangle with a 90 degree angle). It states that the square (a number multiplied by itself) of the hypotenuse (the longest side of a right triangle) is equal to the sum of the squares of its two legs (the shorter sides that meet to form the right angle). It can also be stated that in a right triangle, if the legs have lengths of a and b, and if the hypotenuse has length c, then $a^2 + b^2 = c^2$.

Background

A theorem is basically a generalization that can be demonstrated to be true. As one of the most famous theorems in mathematics, the Pythagorean theorem is named after Greek mathematician **Pythagoras of Samos** (c. 580–c. 500 B.C.), not because he dis-covered it but rather because he offered the first real proof for it. Pythagoras was one of the earliest and wisest of all the ancient Greeks. He founded a school of thought whose followers believed that the entire universe rests on numbers and their relationships. Mathematics to him was therefore the main tool to unlock nature's laws.

Pythagorean theorem

Long before Pythagoras—around 1800 B.C.—the Babylonians knew and used this theorem, but they did not have a proof for it, meaning that they could not explain why it worked. A thousand years before Pythagoras, the Egyptians and the Chinese also knew the theorem, with Egyptian surveyors using ropes that were knotted in segments of equal length which they wrapped around stakes in the ground to create perfect right angles (which enabled them to lay out square corners).

After placing thirteen equally spaced knots in a rope, the surveyors drove a stake into the ground through the first and last knots; another stake went through the fourth knot; and the last stake went through the eighth knot. By stretching the rope as tight as possible before each stake was fully driven in, they ended up with a 3-4-5 triangle, or one whose sides individually measured three units (or spaces between knots), four units, and five units. Each time, the angle opposite the largest or five-space unit was always a right angle. This measuring process had to be done by surveyors every spring in Egypt since the Nile River would overflow and wash out all the past year's property boundaries.

Pythagoras was a frequent traveler and some believe that he learned of the theorem during visits to Egypt. He took this knowledge with him when around 530 B.C. he founded in his hometown of Crotone, Greece, his school of mathematics and philosophy. This school was known as a *homakoeion,* or gathering place for people to learn. Located on the instep of the "boot" of Italy, the port city of Crotone was a Greek colonial outpost.

Theorem description and use

The excitement felt by Pythagoras when he first fully understood the theorem must certainly have been great. The discovery meant that the sides of a right triangle were connected by a law that could be expressed with numbers. Although very ancient peoples could form a perfect right angle knowing the 3, 4, and 5 rule used by Egyptian surveyors, they still did not grasp what the relationship was between those numbers. With a real understanding of the theorem, however, Pythagoras possessed a way to find the length of any side of a right triangle, as long as he knew the lengths of the other two sides. He also was able to use the theorem to find the distance between two

Pythagorean theorem

Greek mathematician Pythagoras of Samos.

points. Over time, it would come to have many similar and very useful applications.

The Egyptians used their practical knowledge of the Pythagorean theorem not only for ground surveying but also for building the Great Pyramid. Modern engineers know that since the largest error of that pyramid's sides and corner angles is only a tiny fraction of one percent, its builders must have known how to make a near-perfect right angle with great accuracy. Today, carpenters still

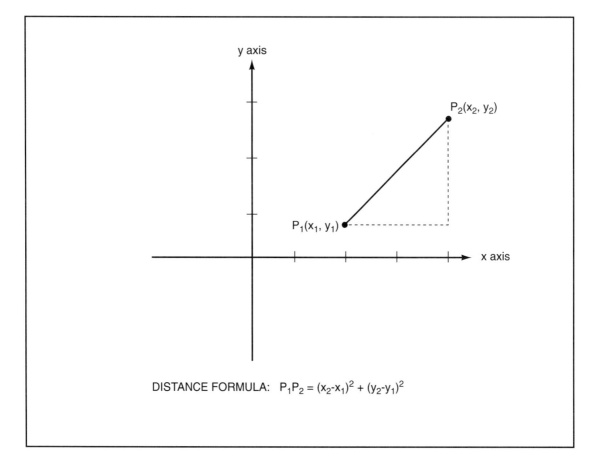

DISTANCE FORMULA: $P_1P_2 = (x_2-x_1)^2 + (y_2-y_1)^2$

Calculation of the shortest distance between two points on a graph, using the Pythagorean theorem.

depend on the principle behind the theorem to be certain that the rooms they build are "square," or perfect rectangles.

The Pythagorean theorem was also important to the development of Greek geometry in general. It extended even further the idea of proof as being a critical or essential part of doing geometry. The Greeks came to realize that there was a great difference between knowing that something was *probably* true and knowing that it was *always* true. The theorem also contributed to the branch of mathematics that deals with the specific functions of angles known as trigonometry. The ability to be able to obtain unknown angles and distances from angles that are known has been useful in such fields as astronomy, map-making, surveying, and artillery range finding. All of these different fields employ the principle that for a right triangle, it is only necessary to know the lengths of two sides to find the length of the third side—

Egyptian mathematics

The Egyptians used mathematics mainly for practical purposes. As early as 3500 B.C., they had a fully developed number system that allowed them to continue counting indefinitely by adding a new symbol from time to time. Mathematics helped with such jobs as counting geese, dividing harvests, measuring the depths of the Nile River at various places along its length, and surveying fields after the Nile floods had receded.

Geometry was what the Egyptians were best at, and they used it in surveying for the great engineering works they built. Surveying is the measurement of land for mapmaking purposes or for determining boundaries. The gigantic sides of the Great Pyramid at Giza are nearly perfectly equal, being less than one inch off from each other. Its corner angles are equal within a fraction of a degree, and its great triangular faces meet perfectly in a point at the top. Egyptian surveyors were also able to lay out roads that ran straight for miles.

whether those two "sides" connect points between three cities, stars, or targets.

For More Information

Bergamini, David. *Mathematics.* Alexandria, VA: Time-Life Books, 1980.

Burton, David M. *Burton's History of Mathematics: An Introduction.* Dubuque, IA: Wm. C. Brown Publishers, 1995.

Hogben, Lancelot T. *Mathematics in the Making.* London: Galahad Books, 1974.

Lappan, Glenda, et al. *Looking for Pythagoras: The Pythagorean Theorem.* White Plains, NY: Dale Seymour Publications, 1997.

Young, Robyn V., ed. *Notable Mathematicians: From Ancient Times to the Present.* Detroit: Gale Research, 1997.

Quadrilateral

A quadrilateral is a geometric figure with four straight sides. It can also be described as a four-sided **polygon.** There are many different types of quadrilaterals, and they are classified according to the relations between their sides and their angles.

Background

The word quadrilateral comes from two Latin words. The first part comes from a variation of the Latin word *quattuor,* meaning "four." The second element of the word is derived from the Latin word *latus,* meaning "side." In ancient Greece, a four-sided polygon was called a tetragon, meaning, literally, that it had four angles. But this name was eventually replaced by the Latin-derived quadrilateral, which stresses the sides more than the angles.

Classification of quadrilaterals

Quadrilaterals are an important class of polygons simply because there are so many different kinds of four-sided figures in this one family of geometric shapes. A property common to all quadrilaterals is that the sum of the interior angles is 360 degrees. This can be proven by know-

Hierarchy a series in which each element is graded or ranked

Parallelogram a quadrilateral in which both pairs of opposite sides are parallel

Polygon a geometric figure composed of three or more line segments (straight sides) that never cross each other

Qualifier a word or phrase that limits or modifies the meaning of another word

Ratio the relationship between two quantities, which is obtained by dividing two things; for instance, the ratio of 3 to 2 is written 3:2 or ⅔

Rectangle a parallelogram whose angles are all right angles

Rhombus a parallelogram whose four sides are of equal length

Square a rectangle whose four sides are the same length

Trapezium a quadrilateral with no pairs of opposite sides parallel

Trapezoid a quadrilateral with only two sides parallel

ing that any quadrilateral can be divided into two **triangles,** and that the sum of the interior angles of any triangle is 180 degrees.

Quadrilaterals are grouped according to their angles and sides. Many people use these distinctions to build a hierarchy of quadrilaterals or a pecking order in which the most inclusive is at the top and the narrowest is at the bottom. The broadest type of quadrilateral is a trapezoid, which is a quadrilateral with only one pair of parallel sides. A trapezium is a quadrilateral with no pairs of opposite sides parallel. The next type is a parallelogram, which is a quadrilateral with two pairs of parallel sides. A parallelogram with a right angle (and therefore four right angles) is a rectangle. A parallelogram with all four sides of equal length is a rhombus. Finally, a square is a rectangle with all sides having equal length.

If the different types of quadrilaterals were diagrammed with trapezoid at the top and square at the bottom, one would see that every square is both a rhombus and a rectangle, every rectangle is a parallelogram, every parallelogram is a trapezoid, and every trapezoid is a quadrilateral. This shows that a certain shape fits more than one type and can be called more than one name. But the general rule is to choose the name that has the greatest numbers of conditions or qualifiers. Therefore, although a typical rectangle is technically called a parallelogram, the name rectangle is more appropriate since it says that the shape has not only parallel opposite sides but four 90-degree angles as well.

One of the more interesting quadrilaterals is a special rectangle called the "Golden Rectangle." Since at least from the time of Greek mathematician **Pythagoras of Samos** (c. 580–c. 500 B.C.), this shape has been considered one of the most pleasing to the eye, and has therefore been used by artists and architects—either deliberately or intuitively (sensing something without any rational thought or reasoning)—ever since. To make a Golden Rectangle, a line must first be divided into two unequal parts so that the ratio of the whole line to the longer part is the same as the ratio of the longer part to the shorter part. (See also **Ratio, proportion, and percent.**) When the new long segment determines the length of the two long sides of the rectangle and the short segments form its two short sides, a Golden Rectangle is created.

The oldest and best known example of this special-ratio rectangle is the Greek Parthenon, built during the fifth century B.C. During

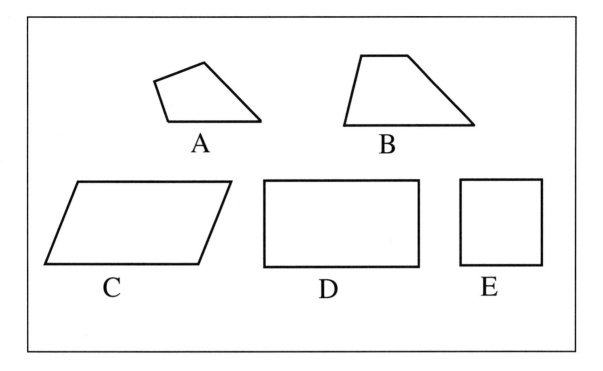

the Renaissance in Europe, such artists as Leonardo da Vinci (1452–1519) used this technique, although it is not known whether he and others actually knew the specific ratio or simply had the ability of a great artist to know what was the most pleasing arrangement of shapes. In terms of an actual numerical value, this "golden ratio" is approximately 1.618 to 1 and is represented by the Greek letter phi (ø).

Five types of quadrilaterals. Figure A: trapezium; Figure B: trapezoid; Figure C: parallelogram; Figure D: rectangle; and Figure E: square.

For More Information

Burton, David M. *Burton's History of Mathematics: An Introduction.* Dubuque, IA: Wm. C. Brown Publishers, 1995.

Green, Gordon W., Jr. *Helping Your Child to Learn Math.* New York: Citadel Press, 1995.

Heddens, James W., and William R. Speer. *Today's Mathematics: Concepts and Methods in Elementary School Mathematics.* Upper Saddle River, NJ: Merrill, 1997.

Ross, Catherine Sheldrick. *Squares.* Toronto: Kids Can Press, 1997.

West, Beverly Henderson, et al. *The Prentice-Hall Encyclopedia of Mathematics.* Englewood Cliffs, NJ: Prentice-Hall, 1982.

**Born December 22, 1887
Erode, Tamil Nadu, India**

**Died April 26, 1920
Kumbakonam, Tamil Nadu, India**

Indian number theorist

Srinivasa A. Ramanujan

As a self-taught prodigy (a child with an exceptionally high level of intelligence), Srinivasa Ramanujan made remarkable discoveries in mathematics and gained a worldwide reputation despite his early death. His remarkable contributions in number theory offered formulas that have today been applied in such different fields as physics, chemistry, and **computer** programming. He was the first East Indian to be elected a fellow of the Royal Society of London and is considered by many to have been India's greatest genius.

> *"[Ramanujan] will return to India with a scientific standing and reputation such as no Indian has enjoyed before, and I am confident that India will regard him as the treasure he is."*
>
> —*English number theorist Godfrey Harold Hardy*

Early life and education

Srinivasa Aaiyangar Ramanujan (pronounced rah-MON-uh-jun) was born in his mother's town of Erode in the Madras province of southern India. His family was poor, and his father served as a bookkeeper and clerk in a fabric shop, while his mother often sang religious songs at a local temple to earn extra money. After Ramanujan was born, the family moved to the city of Kumbakonam in southern India, where he received his early education at an English-language school. At this time, India was a British colony, and its laws and educational system were organized along English lines.

Young Ramanujan was considered a slow child because he did not speak until he was three years old. However, once he attended school, his teachers immediately realized he had unusual mathematical abilities. By the age of ten, he had achieved the highest examination scores in the district. He was therefore eventually allowed to transfer directly to the high school in Kumbakonam. Soon Ramanujan was challenging his teachers with mathematical questions they could not answer. By age 12, he had borrowed a book on trigonometry from a college student, and in a few days he had it read and mastered.

Shortly before Ramanujan graduated from high school, another book would greatly affect his life. After borrowing G. S. Carr's *Synopsis of Results in Pure and Applied Mathematics* from another college student, Ramanujan became obsessed with mathematics to the exclusion of everything else. Carr's book was the perfect stimulant for Ramanujan's inquisitive and original mind: It provided no explanations or proofs for the more than 5,000 mathematical formulas, equations, and results that it compiled. This book so captivated him that he did nothing but pursue his passion for working out each proof as he went along. From then on, mathematics was all he cared about.

Failed university career

Ramanujan's obsession with mathematics to the exclusion of everything else continued when he went to college. In 1904, he won a fellowship to attend Government College in Kumbakonam, but because he spent nearly all his waking hours doing mathematics problems in the notebook he always carried, he neglected his other courses, especially English, and could not graduate. He attended another college in Madras, but eventually lost his scholarship because of his inability to apply himself to anything but mathematics. For the next few years, it is not known exactly what Ramanujan did. Some say he simply wandered the countryside, still always recording his mathematical results in his ever-present notebooks.

In 1909, Ramanujan was forced by his mother to start thinking and living practically since she found a young woman for him to marry. In India, it was the custom for parents to arrange their children's marriage. Ramanujan's mother found a likeable girl named Janaki who was the daughter of a distant relative. His mother had taken the precaution of checking the girl's horoscope to make sure that she would be compatible with her son. On July 14, 1909, the couple was married, although the bride was probably only about 12 years old. In Indian society, Ramanujan was now no longer considered a youth and was expected, as a married man, to be responsible and earn a living.

Meets his benefactors

Still wishing to concentrate on mathematics but knowing he needed to find some type of job, Ramanujan went to the founder of the Indian Mathematical Society, whose assistance led Ramanujan to meet Ramachaudra Rao, a noted mathematician with business connections. Rao later remembered this first meeting, saying that when he asked Ramanujan what he wanted, "He said he wanted a pittance to live on so that he might pursue his researches." Rao was so impressed with the young man's potential that he actually supported Ramanujan himself until he could find him a fellowship. When he could not, Rao found Ramanujan a job as an accounts clerk. By around 1912, Ramanujan had produced his first paper, which was published in the *Journal of the Indian Mathematical Society*.

By the time Ramanujan was in his mid-twenties, he realized that the level of mathematics on which he was focusing was beyond that of anyone he knew in India. Encouraged by friends, he began writing to mathematicians in England for help and guidance. He selected some fairly well known names and sent off his letters. Although he was turned down often, he eventually got a response from English mathematician Godfrey Harold Hardy (1877–1947) of Trinity College at Cambridge.

One of the world's authorities in number theory, Hardy was at first intrigued by Ramanujan's work and then became totally convinced of its merit. He soon began to try to bring the young Indian to England in order to develop further this great but untrained mind, but Ramanujan refused to travel. Although Hardy was able to offer him a full scholarship, Ramanujan's Hindu religion placed restrictions on foreign travel. For example, anyone who crossed the

Srinivasa A. Ramanujan

waters around India would not be allowed to attend Brahmin weddings and funerals. Further, as a strict vegetarian, Ramanujan felt he would have difficulties maintaining a proper diet in a foreign land.

It is said that Ramanujan's mother had a dream in which the Goddess Namagiri appeared and told her to allow her son the freedom to meet his destiny. In 1914, Ramanujan sailed to England.

Collaborates with Hardy

Ramanujan was to spend five years in England with Hardy. Up to this time, Ramanujan had worked in almost total isolation from the rest of European mathematicians. Hardy found that although Ramanujan was a genius in certain areas, he could at times be entirely ignorant of areas that college freshmen had already mastered. To Hardy's credit, he was able to fill the gaps in Ramanujan's education without frustrating the young genius.

Although the styles of Hardy and Ramanujan were so different, they got along with each other very well. Hardy's reputation was based partially on his strict insistence on using rigorous proofs. Ramanujan, on the other hand, not only used unorthodox methods and did his calculations mentally but also depended a great deal on intuition. Despite these differences, they were good friends and colleagues who would collaborate on some twenty papers over the next five years. Ramanujan's flashes of originality and intuition were thus reinforced by Hardy's ability to prove them step by step.

During this period abroad, Ramanujan received several honors. In addition to receiving his bachelor's degree in 1916 from Cambridge, he was elected in 1918 as a fellow of the Royal Society—England's highest scientific body—and of Trinity College as well. For both institutions, he was one of the youngest ever to be so honored. Ramanujan was also the first East Indian to be awarded membership to the Royal Society. As a team, Ramanujan and Hardy produced some of the boldest and most imaginative papers in number theory. Their theory on partitioning, or the many ways a number can be expressed as the sum of other numbers, would eventually prove to be vitally important to modern physicists as well as to the development of computers.

Although Ramanujan initially adapted to living in England, the outbreak of World War I (1914–18) made life more difficult. In India, he was used to having special meals prepared for him by his wife or mother. (Often, he would work for hours lying on a cot; unwilling to stop, he would literally be fed by one of them.) The war had made fresh vegetables scarce, and no restaurants prepared vegetarian meals the way he required.

Lonely and homesick and suffering from the often damp chill of the English climate, Ramanujan eventually became ill. In his weakened state, he caught tuberculosis, a then-incurable lung disease, and returned to India in 1919 as a very sick man. Although he was given an annual allowance by the University of Madras and promised a professorship, his health did not improve and he died at the age of 32, one year after returning home to India. Hardy later commented on his good friend's life and said that if Ramanujan had experienced a more normal youth and better education, "he would have been less of a Ramanujan and more of a European professor."

For More Information

Biographical Dictionary of Mathematicians. New York: Charles Scribner's Sons, 1991.

Golden, Frederic, Leon Jaroff, Jeffrey Kluger, and Michael D. Lemonick. "Cranks . . . Villains . . . and Unsung Heroes: Srinivasa Ramanujan." *Time,* March 29, 1999, p. 197.

Henderson, Harry. *Modern Mathematicians.* New York: Facts on File, 1996.

MacTutor History of Mathematics Archive. " Srinivasa Aiyangar Ramanujan." http://www-groups.dcs.st-and.ac.uk/~history/Mathematicians/Ramanujan.html (accessed on April 27, 1999).

Reimer, Luetta, and Wilbert Reimer. *Mathematicians Are People, Too: Stories from the Lives of Great Mathematicians.* Palo Alto, CA: Dale Seymour Publications, 1995.

Young, Robyn V., ed. *Notable Mathematicians: From Ancient Times to the Present.* Detroit: Gale Research, 1998.

Srinivasa A. Ramanujan

Ratio, proportion, and percent

These three closely related mathematical concepts are among the most useful and common ones in everyday life. Understanding them presumes a knowledge of **fractions** and **decimals.** Ratio is used to compare two related numbers or quantities—it shows a relationship. Proportion indicates that two ratios are equal. Percent is a ratio that compares some number to a hundred.

Ratio

The concept of ratio is the primary idea of the three, since both proportion and percent relate to it. Taken from the Latin verb *ratio,* meaning "to think," a ratio is the relationship of one thing to another. Speaking strictly mathematically, it is the relationship obtained by dividing two things. Put yet another way, it can be called the comparison of two quantities by **division.** An example of a ratio is comparing a boy's height to the length of his shadow. If he stands 4 feet tall and casts a shadow that is 6 feet long, the ratio of his height to his shadow's length is 4 to 6, or 2 to 3 after the numbers have been reduced. A colon is commonly used in place of "to"; so 4 to 6 is shown as 4:6.

Ratio, proportion, and percent

A ratio is basically nothing more than a fraction. Ratio was first studied by Greek mathematician **Pythagoras of Samos** (c. 580–c. 500 B.C.), who was fascinated to find that musical chords are based on ratios. As mathematicians do today when comparing two quantities (such as the boy and his shadow), Pythagoras said the ratio of one to the other was 4:6 or $\frac{4}{6}$. As a fraction, this ratio is reduced or simplified to its lowest terms and then expressed as a ratio of 2:3 or $\frac{2}{3}$. If the comparison were reversed and 6 was compared to 4, the ratio would be 3:2 or $\frac{3}{2}$.

Besides expressing a relationship between two quantities (for example, 2 parts oil and 3 parts gas is 2:3), the notion of ratio can also show the rate at which something *is* happening as well as express the **probability** that something *will* happen. An example of the first is when a car gets 25 miles per gallon of gas (25:1). For probability, if the chances of winning the lottery are 7 million to 1, the appropriate ratio is 7,000,000:1. In a world in which people often must compare things, ratio is the simplest mathematical tool for comparison. It is a highly useful mathematical concept that plays a major role in both science and everyday life.

Proportion

Two ratios that are equal make up what is called a proportion. The statement $\frac{1}{2} = \frac{3}{6}$, which is a statement of equality between two fractions, is a proportion because the 1 is the same portion of 2 that the 3 is of 6. Read sideways from left to right rather than top to bottom, the statement is still in proportion because 1 is the same portion of 3 that 2 is of 6. Over two thousand years ago, **Euclid of Alexandria** (c. 325–c. 270 B.C.) wrote of these very same properties of a ratio in proportion in his great work, *Elements*.

Expressed horizontally (1:2 = 3:6, which is read as "1 is to 2 as 3 is to 6"), the middle two numbers are called the means and the first and last numbers are called the extremes. Means is derived from the Latin *medius,* meaning "in the middle," and extremes is taken from the Latin *extremus,* meaning "the most outside." One of the rules, or properties, of any proportion is that the product of the means equals the product of the extremes ($2 \times 3 = 1 \times 6$). This is also called the cross-**multiplication** rule.

Knowing the cross-multiplication rule makes finding an unknown quantity in a proportion easy when the other three quantities are known. A pharmacist or chemist would use this rule to calculate a particular ratio of chemicals to make a specific quantity of something. The idea of proportion or balance is found as the basis of many principles in biology, physics, and chemistry. It has even crossed over into such technical fields as art and architecture, where symmetry and balance have long proven to be a property pleasing to most people.

Percent

A percent is basically a ratio that compares some number to a hundred. The word itself is derived from the Latin phrase *per centum,* meaning "by the hundred." For centuries, the phrase *per centum* was actually used in place of today's percent, and it can still be found in some very old American arithmetic books. The symbol representing percent (%) is believed to have originated from an early abbreviation of the Italian *per cento,* which included the letters "p" and "c" and a superscript "o" on the letter "c" (pc°). By the seventeenth century, pc° had evolved into what looked like a fraction with zeroes both above and below the bar (%), which is similar to today's % sign.

Since percent expresses a fraction in terms of hundredths and is the same as a fraction with the denominator of 100, percent means computing by the hundredths. Therefore 10 percent (10%) means 10 hundredths ($\frac{10}{100}$) and 90 percent (90%) means 90 hundredths ($\frac{90}{100}$). Just as any fraction can be translated into a decimal fraction, a percent can be converted into a decimal fraction by moving the decimal point two places to the left and removing the percent sign (35% = 0.35). A fraction can be converted to percent by dividing the denominator into the numerator ($\frac{3}{5} = 3 \div 5 = 0.60$ or 60%).

Percent is a concept common to everyday life. Newspapers are filled with stories about prices rising a certain percent and baseball players' batting averages, which are also percentages. The interest that banks pay on savings accounts or that consumers pay on loans is computed on this basis. People who get commissions for selling things receive a fixed percentage of the value of their sales. Probably the oldest application of percent is in figuring how much tax people should pay. Over two thousand years ago, Roman emperor Augustus (63 B.C.–A.D. 14) levied (imposed or collected) a tax of 1% on all goods sold by auction. Each day consumers use percent to figure how much to tip a waiter or cab driver, whether a sale is really a bargain, or whether a garment is made of more or less natural materials.

For More Information

Barnett, Carne, et al. *Fractions, Decimals, Ratios, and Percents.* Portsmouth, NH: Heinemann, 1994.

Curcio, Frances R., and Nadine S. Bezuk. *Understanding Rational Numbers and Proportions.* Reston, VA: National Council of Teachers of Mathematics, 1994.

Eichhorn, Connie. *Ratio and Proportion.* Upper Saddle River, NJ: Globe Fearon, 1996.

Flegg, Graham. *Numbers: Their History and Meaning.* New York: Schocken Books, 1983.

Green, Gordon W., Jr. *Helping Your Child to Learn Math.* New York: Citadel Press, 1995.

Wheeler, Ruric E. *Modern Mathematics.* Pacific Grove, CA: Brooks/Cole Publishing Co., 1995.

Rational and irrational numbers

The notion of rational or irrational numbers has nothing to do with being reasonable, logical, or illogical. Rather, a rational number is a ratio that is symbolically represented as one number over another (as long as the bottom number is not a zero). (See also **Ratio, proportion, and percent.**) A rational number is, therefore, any real number that can be expressed as the ratio of two **integers** (that is, any number that can be expressed as a **fraction**—as 3 can be expressed as the fraction 3 over 1, $\frac{3}{1}$). Since ratio means comparison by **division** or the relationship obtained by dividing two things, a rational number is also described as one that can be expressed as the quotient of two integers. The root of the word rational is "ratio," an example of which is the number $\frac{1}{2}$ being the ratio of 1 to 2. On the other hand, an irrational number is one that cannot be expressed as the ratio of two integers and which, when carried out, simply goes on forever.

Description and use

Rational numbers are an enlarged set of numbers that include both **whole numbers** and integers. Just as the inclusion of negative numbers in the integer set creates a number system in which **subtraction**

Circumference the distance completely around the outside of a circle; its perimeter

Diameter a line segment that joins two points on a circle and passes through its center; the longest chord possible in a circle

Integers a set of numbers that includes the positive numbers, negative numbers, and zero

Irrational number a number that is expressed as a nonrepeating decimal fraction and which, when carried out, simply goes on forever; contrasted to a rational number, which has either a terminating decimal (it comes out even with no remainder) or a repeating decimal (as .33333333...)

Negative numbers a number less than 0; a minus (–) sign is always written before the numeral to indicate it is to the left of 0 on a number line

Pi (π) a number defined as the ratio of the circumference to the diameter of a circle; it cannot be represented exactly as a decimal, but it is between 3.1415 and 3.1416

Quotient the result when one number is divided by another; for example, 2 is the quotient when 10 is divided by 5

Ratio the relationship between two quantities, which is obtained by dividing two things; for instance, the ratio of 3 to 2 is written 3:2 or $\frac{3}{2}$

is always possible, so does the principle behind the idea that rational numbers make division always possible. Rational numbers can be understood as a human invention that allows any portion of a number line to be infinitely divided. For example, the halfway point between 1 and 2 on a number line is 1½; the halfway point between 1 and 1½ is 1¼; and the halfway point between 1 and 1¼ is 1⅛, etc. This process can go on forever (since there is always another fraction between any two fractions), and it is one way of showing that there are many more numbers on the number line than just the integers.

One of the properties of a rational number is that it can be expressed as either a terminating **decimal** or a repeating decimal. A terminating decimal has only a certain number of digits before it comes to an end. An example is the rational number 0.25. When expressed as one-fourth (¼), and 4 is divided into 1.00, the quotient comes out evenly as 0.25. An example of a repeating decimal is the fraction one third (⅓) which, when carried out, repeats the same digit endlessly (0.333333333...).

Numbers that cannot be expressed as a fraction are contrasted to rational numbers and are called irrational numbers. These two very different sets of real numbers are described as being mutually exclusive since they have no elements in common. A well-known example of an irrational number is the **square root** of 2. A square root is the opposite of squaring a number (in which a number is multiplied by itself). A square root answers the question, "What number multiplied by itself equals a certain number?" (The answer to what times itself equals 9 is 3; so 3 is the square root of 9). As for the square root of two, it is obviously somewhere between 1 and 2. It is not 1.5, which multiplied by itself equals 2.25. It is not 1.4, which multiplied by itself equals 1.96. Continuing to figure it out, even with a calculator or a **computer,** only results in the answer getting closer and closer. But one never arrives at a complete solution. No matter how far the number is carried out, it never comes out even or stops. The number starts out 1.41421356237309505... and continues forever. Recalling that a rational number had either a terminating decimal or a repeating decimal, a number with a nonrepeating decimal expansion is therefore an irrational number.

Irrational numbers are actually more common than rational numbers, and one of the most famous and useful is **pi** (pronounced

PIE). Pi is the ratio of the circumference of a **circle** to its diameter. Beginning with the Bible, which says pi equals 3, ancient mathematicians struggled to figure out the ratio exactly. The Babylonians knew it was actually a bit larger than 3, and during the third century B.C., Greek mathematician **Archimedes** (287–212 B.C.) calculated pi to two places. Two thousand years later, Dutch mathematician Ludolph Van Ceulen (1540–1610) calculated pi to 35 places. Finally, Swiss German mathematician Johann Heinrich Lambert (1728–77) proved that, like the square root of two, no matter how many decimal places pi was computed to, it would never come out even. It would go on forever! Lambert proved that the ratio pi is irrational. Like irrational numbers that prove helpful in representing the measure of distances in the practical world, rational numbers allow mathematicians to enter the useful world of fractions.

For More Information

Curcio, Frances R., and Nadine S. Bezuk. *Understanding Rational Numbers and Proportions.* Reston, VA: National Council of Teachers of Mathematics, 1994.

Fey, James T., et al. *Bits & Pieces I; Understanding Rational Numbers.* White Plains, NY: Dale Seymour Publications, 1997.

Fey, James T., et al. *Bits & Pieces II; Using Rational Numbers.* White Plains, NY: Dale Seymour Publications, 1997.

Flegg, Graham. *Numbers: Their History and Meaning.* New York: Schocken Books, 1983.

Friedberg, Richard. *An Adventurer's Guide to Number Theory.* New York: Dover Publications, 1994.

Groza, Vivian Shaw. *A Survey of Mathematics: Elementary Concepts and Their Historical Development.* New York: Holt, Rinehart and Winston, 1968.

West, Beverly Henderson, et al. *The Prentice-Hall Encyclopedia of Mathematics.* Englewood Cliffs, NJ: Prentice-Hall, 1982.

Born September 17, 1826
Breselenz, Hannover (present-day Germany)

Died July 20, 1866
Selasca, Italy

German geometer and mathematical physicist

Bernhard Riemann

No nineteenth century mathematician had as deep an influence on the next century's mathematics as did Bernhard Riemann. An original thinker with a gift for seeing connections where everyone else saw only differences, Riemann laid the foundation for a new kind of **geometry** that later would prove critical to the general theory of relativity. Although Riemann published very little in his short career, all his work was of the highest quality and contained breakthroughs in several areas of mathematics.

> *"[Riemann possessed] a gloriously fertile originality."*
>
> *—German mathematician Carl Friedrich Gauss*

Early life and education

Born in the village of Breselenz in the kingdom of Hannover, now Germany, Georg Friedrich Bernhard Riemann (pronounced REE-mon) was the second of six children. His father, Friedrich Bernhard Riemann, was a Lutheran minister, and his mother, Charlotte Ebell, came from a family that had worked in the courts. The family had very little money, but they were close and supportive. Tuberculosis plagued them however, and Riemann's mother and three sisters would all die from this terrible lung disease, as would Riemann himself.

Bernhard Riemann

As a young boy, Riemann was taught by his father who, with some help from a village schoolmaster, gave him his elementary education. Almost immediately, however, young Riemann showed such considerable mathematical talent that by the age of ten he had gone past both men who were, at times, unable to keep up.

At the age of 14, Riemann went to live with his grandmother in Hannover so he could attend his first school, the Lyceum. Upon her death in 1842, he moved to a school called the Johanneum in Lüneburg. The school was closer to his family's new home (his father having moved to another parish). This move turned into a fortunate occurrence, since it brought him to the attention of a headmaster who recognized his mathematical ability and lent him some classic mathematical books to browse. The 16-year-old Riemann reportedly studied, mastered, and returned the books in six days, one of which was the 880-page *Théorie des Nombres (Theory of Numbers)* by French mathematician Adrien-Marie Legendre (1752–1833).

By the time he was 19, Riemann was ready to enter Göttingen University. Since he was shy, modest, and very respectful of his parents, Riemann agreed to study theology as his father wanted him to do, but he could not deny his love of mathematics. After attending a few mathematics lectures, Riemann knew that he must persuade his father to allow him to become a mathematician. To his father's credit, he soon gave in to his son's sincere request.

Göttingen must have seemed like the center of the mathematical world to Riemann, since it had a living legend, **Carl Friedrich Gauss** (1777–1855), on its faculty. It was in fact not so. Gauss taught only the elementary mathematics courses, and he did so in a way that made students not want to approach him. After an unsatisfactory year at Göttingen, Riemann transferred to the lively and more democratic environment at the University of Berlin. Whereas students at Göttingen were actually discouraged from participating with professors in any creative or original way, those at Berlin were often encouraged by their teachers to openly discuss and share ideas.

Riemann flourished in the open environment of Berlin. He became especially influenced by German mathematician Lejeune Dirichlet (1805–59), who taught there. But in the spring of 1849,

Riemann returned to Göttingen because famous German physicist Wilhelm Weber (1804–91) had returned to teach there. Weber's presence alone changed the formerly unpleasant situation at Göttingen. For three more terms, Riemann studied at Göttingen and then submitted his doctoral dissertation in November 1851.

Challenge and response

In his dissertation, Riemann offered a simple yet sweeping treatment of a mathematical field that had been previously almost impossible to understand. He also contributed an original concept that eventually became known as Riemann surfaces. Even the highly critical Gauss, who usually dismissed most people's work, praised his student's contribution, saying that its author had a "gloriously fertile originality." Despite Riemann's excellent work, the German university system had no room for Riemann or any other scholar who did not have some other means of support. If a poor but bright man like Riemann wanted to work in that system, he could only do so—after qualifying—as a *Privatdozent* (a lecturer paid by his students).

In order to qualify for these Privatdozent positions, candidates were required to give a lecture on a particular subject. The custom was for the candidate to offer the faculty a list of his top three subject choices from which they could select. It was traditional that the department head almost always selected the candidate's first choice. However, when Riemann submitted his three topics, Gauss went against tradition and chose Riemann's third choice—one for which Riemann was fairly unprepared. The topic was a discussion on the hypotheses or assumptions upon which the foundations of geometry are based. Whether Gauss thought he would stump his student or whether he wanted to push his originality is unknown, but Riemann was up to the task. After working intensively for two months, Riemann produced a radically new concept that became one of the great classical masterpieces of mathematics. Some say it was the most important scientific lecture ever given.

Riemann's new geometry

Riemann's lecture was presented in nontechnical language and contained no mathematical formulas or equations. Instead, it was a description of an entirely new kind of geometry that operated in

Bernhard Riemann

Bernhard Riemann

any number of dimensions and situations. Probably no one but Gauss (who was ecstatic) understood it. Most probably thought it was simply an exercise in pure mathematics that had nothing to do with reality. This notion was held until half a century later when German American physicist and mathematician **Albert Einstein** (1879–1955) would finally show that Riemann's ideas of geometry provided a much truer picture of the universe as a whole than any other, especially more so than traditional Euclidean geometry.

Einstein found that Riemannian geometry provided the mathematical tools as well as exactly the right framework for him to develop his general theory of relativity. In his lecture, Riemann suggested a rule that eventually led to the development of what came to be called a Riemann space. For Einstein, this concept led him to treat **time** as a "fourth dimension," and to propose what he called the "curvature of space." Sixty years after he first gave his lecture, Riemann's work was justified by Einstein's general relativity theory.

Tragically short life

Riemann became an unpaid lecturer in 1854 and a year later, Gauss died. When Riemann's good friend, Dirichlet, was called to Göttingen as Gauss's successor, Dirichlet saw to it that Riemann received at least some salary, although still a very small one. When Dirichlet died in 1859, however, Riemann was finally appointed as a full professor to replace him.

In 1862, Riemann married Elise Koch, a friend of his sister, and in 1863 they had a daughter named Ida. Despite his now-secure position, the years of "honored starvation" as a *Privatdozent* and the deaths of his family members, as well as a possible nervous breakdown brought on by overwork, caught up with him. In the same year he was married, the tuberculosis that had plagued him for years had become much more serious. In the mid-nineteenth century, the only treatment for tuberculosis was to visit or move to a warmer climate, so Riemann chose to go to Italy. As a lover of fine art, Riemann traveled throughout Italy and Sicily, often visiting Italian mathematicians as well. He never recovered his health, however. He died at the age of 39 in Selasca, Italy, on Lake Maggiore, while lying under a fig tree, with his loving wife praying nearby.

It is remarkable that a mathematician whose published work consists of literally one volume (his 1854 paper on the foundations of geometry) is so highly thought of and has had such a tremendous impact. Yet many scholars argue that no other single work has had such an impact on modern mathematics.

For More Information

Biographical Dictionary of Mathematicians. New York: Charles Scribner's Sons, 1991.

MacTutor History of Mathematics Archive. "Georg Friedrich Bernhard Riemann." http://www-groups.dcs.st-and.ac.uk/~history/Mathematicians/Riemann.html (accessed on April 28, 1999).

Simmons, George F. *Calculus Gems: Brief Lives and Memorable Mathematics.* New York: McGraw-Hill, 1992.

Stillwell, John. *Mathematics and Its History.* New York: Springer-Verlag, 1989.

Young, Robyn V., ed. *Notable Mathematicians: From Ancient Times to the Present.* Detroit: Gale Research, 1998.

Bernhard Riemann

Born March 1642
Fujioka, Kozuke, Japan

Died October 24, 1708
Edo (present-day Tokyo), Japan

Japanese mathematician

Seki Kōwa

Generally considered to be the founder of Japanese mathematics, Seki Kōwa is credited with inventing his own notation system as well as an early form of calculus. A complete account of his life and accomplishments is difficult because of the secrecy of the times.

Early life and education

Although not a great deal is known about the details of the life of Takakazu Seki Kōwa (pronounced SEH-key KOH-wah), some facts are available. He was born in March 1642 in Fujioka, in the province of Kozuke, not far from present-day Tokyo. He was the second son of Nagaakira Utiyama, a member of the samurai warrior class.

"Mathematics is more than an art form."

Nothing is known of his mother. For reasons that are not clear, Seki Kōwa was adopted as an infant by another noble family, that of accountant Seki Gorozayemon, and was given the name of either Seki Shinsuke Kōwa or Seki Takakazu.

Conflicting stories exist about his education. Some report that he began to study mathematics under Yositane Takahara. Others say he was taught by a servant. Most agree, however, that he was

Seki Kōwa

probably a prodigy (a child with an exceptionally high level of intelligence) and a self-taught genius. It is said that his abilities surfaced when he was only five years old. He was able to point out the calculating mistakes made by his elders. His abilities were so startling that members of the household started calling him "divine child." Another story relates that when he was only nine years old he saw a servant trying to understand a difficult book by the mathematician Yoshida, and he easily showed the servant all the proper solutions.

Whatever early training he may have had, Seki Kōwa is considered by many scholars to have learned most of his mathematics on his own. This talent shows itself in his works, which were highly original and displayed little influence from others. He did not neglect the work of others, however, and he eventually acquired a library composed of both Japanese and Chinese mathematical works.

Attracts students and changes attitudes

As word of his abilities spread, Seki Kōwa became more popularly known, and with the publication in 1674 of his major work, *Hatsubi sampo,* he became famous. In this work, he solved 15 supposedly "unsolvable" problems, which gained him considerable fame. Although he is known to have written hundreds of separate manuscripts, most of them are lost.

During his lifetime, Seki Kōwa was surrounded by pupils who gave him the honored title of "the arithmetical sage." As the descendant of a samurai and therefore part of a noble class, he served the emperor in a public capacity, becoming examiner of accounts to the Lord of Koshu. When his lord eventually became a shogun, or ultimate military and civil ruler of Japan, Seki Kōwa, too, ascended in status.

Besides the actual contributions he would make to mathematics, Seki Kōwa used his popularity and high status to change the role that mathematics played in Japanese society. He changed the study of mathematics in Japan from being merely a hobby practiced by some intellectuals into what would become a real science. By the time of his death, Seki Kōwa had successfully changed attitudes in Japan so that anyone who was capable could take an interest in the subject and teach it to others.

Mathematical contributions

Among Seki Kōwa's major contributions to Japanese mathematics was his creation of a new mathematical system of notation. Because he was familiar with Chinese mathematics, he adapted their system and developed a written system that allowed him to express known and unknown variables in equations, much as letters are used in **algebra** today. His introduction of Chinese ideographs (written or picture symbols that represent a whole word) enabled Japanese mathematics to prepare to enter the modern world of mathematics. Using these new, shorthand techniques, he was able to discover many of the mathematical theories that were being discovered in the West about this same time. His work on **circles** is considered his most significant achievement. The work came to be known as the principles of "Enri" or "Yenri." These principles were actually a form of calculus that he is thought to have invented and passed on to his disciples.

Two geniuses

The greatest Japanese mathematician of the seventeenth century was Seki Kōwa (1642–1708). A child prodigy born of a samurai (military) family, he was correcting the math errors of adults at the age of five and was named the "divine child."

When he became known in the West, he was called the Japanese Newton, and with some justification. Born the same year as English mathematician Isaac Newton (1642–1727), Seki Kōwa learned a great deal on his own and was skilled in mechanics as well as mathematics. Many scholars believe that his invention of the *yenri,* or circle principle, was in fact Japanese calculus, making both men independent inventors of calculus. Seki Kōwa and Newton were each brilliant problem-solvers and were honored by their respective countries.

Stories of his life

Although few hard facts are known about Seki Kōwa's life, many stories and anecdotes survive that give some idea of what he was like as a person and a teacher. One time he was traveling on an official mission from one province to another, transported on a palanquin (somewhat like a covered stretcher that is carried by four men). To amuse himself on the long journey, Seki Kōwa took notes of distances and landmarks and recorded details such as elevations and depressions along the way. Eventually, he prepared such a minutely detailed map of the region that it exceeded what the best geographers had done.

Another story relates how the shogun decided to distribute equal portions of a highly precious piece of incense wood among the

Seki Kōwa

members of his family. No one but Seki Kōwa was able to find the proper way of cutting the wood to make it perfectly equal.

Finally, a story is told of an intricate clock the Emperor had sent to the shogun. The clock suddenly failed after some years. The clock contained a human figure that would strike a bell on the hour, but it no longer would do so. After nearly every expert in the country had tried and failed to fix it, Seki Kōwa repaired the delicate spring on the clock and had it striking the hours correctly again. These stories tell of a resourceful, accomplished, and certainly versatile person who was at home in both the theoretical and the practical world.

When Seki Kōwa died on October 24, 1708, leaving no children behind, he was buried in the Buddhist cemetery at Ushigome in Tokyo. Eighty years later, he was honored as a great teacher and scholar, and his tomb was rebuilt and inscribed with the title given him by his students: the arithmetical sage.

For More Information

Abbott, David, ed. *The Biographical Dictionary of Scientists: Mathematicians.* New York: Peter Bedrick Books, 1986.

Biographical Dictionary of Mathematicians. New York: Charles Scribner's Sons, 1991.

MacTutor History of Mathematics Archive. "Takakazu Seki Kowa." http://www-groups.dcs.st-and.ac.uk/~history/Mathematicians/Seki.html (accessed on April 28, 1999).

Smith, David Eugene, and Yoshio Mikami. *A History of Japanese Mathematics.* Chicago: The Open Court Publishing Company, 1914.

Young, Robyn V., ed. *Notable Mathematicians: From Ancient Times to the Present.* Detroit: Gale Research, 1998.

Born April 30, 1916
Gaylord, Michigan

American mathematician

Claude E. Shannon

Considered by many to be the father of what is now called the information sciences, Claude Shannon established the mathematical foundations of communications theory and laid the groundwork for both **computer** and telecommunications industries.

Early life and education

Claude Elwood Shannon was born April 30, 1916, in the small town of Gaylord, Michigan. He was the son of Claude Elwood Shannon, an attorney and probate judge, and Mabel Wolf, a language teacher and a high school principal. The younger of two children, he had a sister named Catherine who would become a professor of mathematics. His grandfather was an inventor who patented some of his inventions, and one of Shannon's distant cousins was American inventor Thomas Edison (1847–1931).

Young Shannon was a boy who, like his hero Edison, enjoyed the challenge of building things, especially mechanical things, and he tinkered with erector sets and radios. One of the more ambitious

> *"Today Shannon's insights help shape virtually all systems that store, process or transmit information in digital form, from compact disks to computers, from facsimile machines to deep-space probes such as Voyager."*
>
> *—From AT&T biography on Claude Shannon*

Claude E. Shannon

projects he undertook as a youngster was to build a working telegraph system between his and his friend's house. He and his friend built a Morse-code signaling system that connected their houses, which were half a mile apart. After getting some equipment from the local phone company, they even connected a telephone. As he grew older, his interest shifted from mechanics to electronics.

By the time he was ready for college, enrolling at the University of Michigan in the fall of 1932, Shannon had decided he wanted a degree in electrical engineering. At the university, however, he became interested in mathematics as well, and tried to take as many math courses as he could. One of these courses, in symbolic **logic,** would have a major effect on his career. Shannon eventually majored in both electrical engineering and mathematics and received a bachelor's degree from Michigan in both. Shannon later said, "That's the story of my life, the interplay between mathematics and electrical engineering."

After graduating in 1936, Shannon did not know exactly what he wanted to do, but he noticed a note on a University of Michigan bulletin board advertising for a young engineer to run a machine called a differential analyzer. Built by American electrical engineer Vannevar Bush (1890–1974), who was also vice-president of the Massachusetts Institute of Technology (MIT), this machine could solve highly complicated differential equations and was basically the first analog computer. (An analog computer translates continuously changing quantities [such as temperature, pressure, **weight,** or speed] into corresponding voltages or gear movements.) Shannon eventually got the job and spent the next four years at MIT working and pursuing a master's degree in mathematics.

Bush's machine was basically mechanical and used a complicated system of relay circuits (switches operated by an electric current). Shannon tried to find a mathematical way to describe and analyze how relay circuits behaved. He applied the Boolean **algebra** (named after English mathematician and logician **George Boole** [1815–64]) he had learned in the college course on symbolic logic. The resulting master's thesis that he produced in 1937, "A Symbolic Analysis of Relay and Switching Circuits," has been described as one of the most significant works ever done in the history of science. Shannon's ability to somehow perceive some sort of connection between a relay circuit and Boolean algebra was truly inspired. For Shannon however, it was simply a great time. In a 1987 interview, he recalled, "That was a lot of fun, working that out. I had more fun doing that than anything else in my life."

Like everyone else, Bush was highly impressed with Shannon's uniquely important thesis, and he suggested that Shannon pursue a Ph.D. in mathematics from MIT. By 1940, Shannon had received his Ph.D. (as well as another master's degree in electrical engineering). He went to work at Bell Laboratories, where his research would focus on the best ways to transmit information electronically.

Establishes the field of information theory

By the spring of 1941, Shannon was working full-time as part of Bell Labs' secret research on both codes and the aiming of anti-aircraft guns. During this time, he met English algebrist and logician **Alan Turing** (1912–54) and Hungarian American mathematician **John von Neumann** (1903–57), both of whom would become pioneers in the computer field. Although Shannon's work certainly contributed to the war effort, he was also encouraged by Bell Labs to pursue whatever research on communications interested him. After the war, Shannon became increasingly interested in the electronic communication of messages, and in 1949 he published *The Mathematical Theory of Communication*. This book formulated the basic information theory upon which much of today's computer and communications technology is based.

Shannon's book provided for the first time a mathematical way of analyzing the quantification of information. He was able to show how to treat any kind of information mathematically. By reducing pieces of information to an element he called a "bit," he could organize any kind of complicated information by using strict mathematical principles. This concept allowed engineers to be able to deal with the major question of radio and telephone communications: how to measure information and therefore make a truly efficient use of a system. From Shannon's book was born an entirely new field of investigation called information theory. It applies not only to computer design but to almost any subject in which language and communications and the transmission of information is important.

Claude E. Shannon

Claude E. Shannon

Contributes to the field of artificial intelligence

By 1950, Shannon already had become interested in the emerging idea that computers did not have to be only calculating devices, but could also be used to solve other, more complex problems, such as playing chess. Two years earlier, he had published a book entitled *Programming a Computer for Playing Chess,* which was the first such effort on that subject. In 1953, he wrote a paper, "Computers and Automata," that became a pioneering work in the field of artificial intelligence (a field defined by the notion that a machine can solve complex problems, learn from mistakes, and basically think the way humans do).

Career at Bell Labs and MIT

Shannon remained at Bell Laboratories until 1958, when he accepted the position of Donner professor of science at MIT. He remained in that position until 1978 when he retired from MIT. During those years, Shannon received many awards and honors. He received the Morris Liebmann Memorial Award in 1949, the Ballantine Medal in 1955, and the Mervin J. Kelly Award of the American Institute of Electrical Engineers in 1962. In 1956, he was elected to the National Academy of Sciences and later became a member of the Royal Society of London. He was awarded the National Medal of Science in 1966, the Jacquard Award in 1978, the John Fritz Medal in 1983, and the Kyoto Prize in Basic Science in 1985.

Shannon currently lives in Winchester, Massachusetts. In 1949, he married Mary Elizabeth Moore, with whom he had three children. Hailed today as the father of information theory, Shannon still lectures in that field but also spends time working on many diverse subjects, from juggling to the stock market.

For More Information

AT&T Labs Research. "Biography of Claude Elwood Shannon." http://www.research.att.com/~njas/doc/shannonbio.html (accessed on April 26, 1999).

"Interview: Claude Shannon." *Omni,* August 1987, pp. 61–66, 110.

McGraw-Hill Modern Scientists and Engineers. New York: McGraw-Hill, 1980.

Slater, Robert. *Portraits in Silicon.* Cambridge, MA: The MIT Press, 1989.

Square root

The square root of a number is a second number which, when multiplied by itself, equals the first number. Finding or extracting a number's root is the opposite of raising it to a power. There is a particular algorithm or method to extracting the root of a number.

Background

Methods for calculating the square root of a number have been known for many centuries. In Babylonian times, tables were available for mathematicians to consult. As a practical people, the Babylonians's main concern was solving whatever calculating problem they were working on, and even if they only obtained an approximate value, it was usually good enough. Although it is not known exactly how the Babylonians calculated their roots, it is assumed that the later Greeks and Hindus may have obtained their knowledge from the Babylonians. This Greek and Hindu information eventually spread to Western Europe via the Arabs around the thirteenth century.

Description and use

Finding or extracting a root does not always mean that it has to be a number's *square* root. There can be as many roots as there are fac-

Square root

WORDS TO KNOW

Algorithm any systematic method of doing mathematics that involves a step-by-step procedure

Extract to determine or calculate the root of a number

Hypotenuse the longest side in a right triangle

Index the number in the upper left-hand corner of the radical sign that tells which root is to be extracted

Integers a set of numbers that includes the positive numbers, negative numbers, and zero

Irrational number a number that is expressed as a nonrepeating decimal fraction and which, when carried out, simply goes on forever; contrasted to a rational number, which has either a terminating decimal (it comes out even with no remainder) or a repeating decimal (as .33333333...)

Natural numbers all the cardinal numbers or counting numbers (1, 2, ...) except 0

cand the number under a radical

tors of a given number, so that the *sixth* root of 64 is 2 (since 2 × 2 × 2 × 2 × 2 × 2 = 64). It sometimes helps to grasp the concept of a root in order to consider what its opposite is. As with some other mathematical operations that have a reverse operation (**addition/subtraction; multiplication/division**), the opposite or reverse operation to finding a number's root is raising it to a power. Since raising to a power consists of repeated multiplication, its reverse must be some form of repeated division. Raising 3 to its third power (3 × 3 × 3) means multiplying 3 by itself 3 times, resulting in a product of 27. Repeatedly dividing 64 by 2 (resulting in quotients of 32, 16, 8, 4, 2, and, finally, 1) shows that 2 is the sixth root of 64. Another way to look at the idea of root is as a foundation of something. If root means the basis or source of something, than the number 2 is the source or basic number which is raised up until it is 64.

The symbol for a root $\sqrt{}$ is called a radical sign. "Radical" comes from the Latin word *radix*, meaning "root." The number inside and on the right of the radical sign is called the radicand. (In $\sqrt[3]{8}$, 8 is the radicand.) The number in the upper left-hand corner of the radical sign tells which root is to be extracted. It is called the index and is usually written in a smaller type than the radicand. (In $\sqrt[3]{8}$, 3 is the index.) If no number appears in that space, the index is assumed to mean 2, or the square root. Technically, this should be called the second root of a number (for example, 16 divided by 4 divided by 4 = 1 and 4 is the second root of 16). Traditionally, however, the second root $\sqrt[2]{}$, or, more commonly, $\sqrt{}$, is called the square root, and the third root ($\sqrt[3]{}$) is always called the cube root.

Finding the square root of an exact or perfect square is fairly easy, for it is always a **whole number** with no remainder. Thus 9 is a perfect square since its square root is 3. However, if the square root of a number like 3 is sought (what number multiplied by itself gives 3 as an answer?), things look very different. One sees immediately that no **integer** will work since 1 × 1 = 1 (too small) and 2 × 2 = 4 (too large). The answer obviously lies between 1 and 2 and must be a **fraction**. Square roots can therefore be fractional. To continue, 1.7 × 1.7 = 2.89 and 1.8 × 1.8 = 3.24. Although the numbers can be continuously refined (like 1.732 × 1.732 = 2.999824), no matter how many places the numbers are carried out, there will never be a number that is *exactly* the square root of 3. Such roots are called irrational (see also **Rational and irrational numbers**) and are only a close approximation. Since there are so few natural numbers that are perfect squares, it is not surprising that there are many irrational numbers. Thus, the number 64 is rational (see also **Rational and irrational numbers**) because $8 \times 8 = 64$, but 65 is irrational because its square root is somewhere between 8 and 9.

Probably the most famous square root is the square root of 2. When the Greeks used the **Pythagorean theorem** (which was known in principle in much earlier Babylonian and Egyptian times) to estimate distance or to determine the length of something, they eventually realized that there were many numbers which today are called irrational. The Greeks found this out when considering the hypotenuse of a right **triangle** (its longest side).

Specifically, in the case of a right triangle whose two legs or short sides (*a* and *b*) had a length of 1, the square of the hypotenuse *(c)* is equal to the sum of the squares of each leg. If this is the case, and $a^2 + b^2 = c^2$, and since *c* is the number whose square is $a^2 + b^2$, then *c* is equal to the square root of 2. The problem with finding this exact value is that the calculations never stop. No matter how far the calculations are carried out, the result is called a nonrepeating **decimal** expansion. In the time of **Pythagoras of Samos** (c. 580–c. 500 B.C.), consideration of such an "irrational" idea as the square root of two was considered unusual. Eventually, however, being able to prove that the square root of two is irrational is basic to a mathematical education and is thought of as a model of good reasoning.

For More Information

Asimov, Isaac. *Realm of Numbers.* Boston: Houghton Mifflin, 1959.

Flegg, Graham. *Numbers: Their History and Meaning.* New York: Schocken Books, 1983.

Hirschi, L. Edwin. *Building Mathematics Concepts in Grades Kindergarten Through Eight.* Scranton, PA: International Textbook Co., 1970.

West, Beverly Henderson, et al. *The Prentice-Hall Encyclopedia of Mathematics.* Englewood Cliffs, NJ: Prentice-Hall, 1982.

Statistics

Statistics is the branch of mathematics that collects and analyzes numerical facts in order to make predictions. In a more specific way, statistics can also mean just the mass of numerical facts or data that is gathered to identify, study, and solve a problem. Statistics has become an important factor of good decision-making in today's world.

History and background

The Bible tells of data on populations and quantities of grain being collected in ancient times by the rulers of ancient Egypt. Besides taking a population census, Emperor Augustus (27 B.C.–A.D. 17) began counting the property of each Roman family every five years and eventually extended this practice throughout the Roman empire. Even during the Middle Ages, when society was considered backward, there were regular censuses of people made in England, Russia, and Venice. One of the more famous censuses was the *Domesday Book,* which in 1086 compiled a census of the 5,624 watermills in England. Also in London during the sixteenth and seventeenth centuries, "Bills of Mortality" were published that gathered data on deaths from the plague and other epidemics.

Deductive reasoning a type of reasoning in which a conclusion follows necessarily from a set of
axioms or givens; it proceeds logically from the general to the specific

Descriptive statistics the science
of collecting, organizing, and summarizing data that characterize a
particular group

Evolution the theory that groups of
organisms change with the passage of time as a result of natural
selection

Inductive reasoning a type of reasoning conducted first by observing patterns of something and then
by predicting answers for similar
future cases; it proceeds logically
from the specific to the general

Inference the act of reasoning or
making a logical conclusion based
on evidence or something known
to be true

Inferential statistics the science of
making inferences or predictions
about a group based on characteristics of a sample of that group

Mortality tables statistical tables
based on death data compiled over
a number of years

Population all of the individuals,
events, or objects that make up a
group

Probability theory the branch of
mathematics that studies the likelihood of random events occurring
in order to predict the behavior of
defined systems

Random something done unsystematically, without purpose, pattern, or method

It was not until the middle of the seventeenth century that someone realized that data-gathering could be used to make what are
called inferences. An inference is more of a very good educated
guess than it is a prediction of something that will definitely
occur. In 1662, an English merchant named John Graunt
(1620–74) became the first person to use mathematics to analyze
and make sense of large amounts of data about people. Graunt
studied death records in certain cities for causes of death, as well
as data on male and female births and the mortality rates of children in cities and villages. That year he published *Natural and
Political Observations . . . Made Upon the Bills of Mortality*, in
which he became the first to draw inferences based on statistical
information. Reducing 57 years of statistics to a series of tables
from which he drew his conclusions, he stated that more male
babies than female were born and that women lived longer than
men. It is interesting to note his conclusion that 36 out of every
100 people died by the age of six and that hardly anyone lived to
be seventy-five.

Others soon applied what Graunt had discovered. In 1693, English astronomer Edmond Halley (1656–1742) compiled the first
set of detailed mortality tables (statistical tables based on death
data compiled over a number of years) along with a mathematical formula that came to be used by insurance companies. (See
accompanying sidebar for more information on Halley.) In
1749, the word *statistik* was used for the first time by German
mathematician Gottfried Achenwall (1719–72). Both his German and English versions of this word are derived from the
Latin verb *stare*, meaning "to stand." Although the development
of the word is complicated, its basic meaning is to indicate how
things "stand."

In the nineteenth century, many scientists became aware of and
used the power of statistical methods. Two of the most important
were English anthropologist Francis Galton (1822–1911) and
English mathematician Karl Pearson (1857–1936). Galton did
work in the area of inheritance (pertaining to genetic qualities),
and Pearson developed statistical methods to investigate evolution
and heredity. The modern theory of evolution explains both the
appearance of life on Earth and the process by which living things
acquired their present form. By using statistical methods to discov-

Edmond Halley

Most people know that English astronomer and geophysicist Edmond Halley (1656–1742) was the first to predict when a certain comet (which was later given his name) would return. Few, though, know that it was only through his persistence and financial backing that the landmark work of English mathematician Isaac Newton (1642–1727), the *Principia Mathematica*, was ever written and published.

Halley also demonstrated his remarkable perseverance when he translated from Arabic an important mathematical work by Greek geometer Apollonius of Perga (c. 261–c. 190 B.C.). When astronomer Edward Bernard had translated only 13 pages of this recently discovered document, he suddenly died. Despite having no knowledge of Arabic, Halley took up the project, carefully studied the translation, compared it to other Arabic works, and looked for patterns and connections. Through this amazingly difficult process, Halley stumbled his way through the entire document, going over it again and again, until he had translated the entire document with help from no one.

er which traits or characteristics would be inherited, scientists were able to eventually understand and to predict which traits would be passed on. This would prove to be a key factor in explaining how evolution actually works.

Description and use

Statistics, both in its limited meaning of data and larger meaning of conclusions drawn from that data, is something with which everyone is familiar. It is common to be bombarded by statistics in nearly every aspect of everyday lives, most especially from television, radio, and newspapers. Advertisers use them to know to whom they should direct their ads, businesses use them to judge their products as well as their employees, baseball managers use them to decide how to pitch to a batter, and politicians sometimes use them to make policy.

Essential to an understanding of statistics are the concepts of population and sample. Population means *all* the items (or

English anthropologist Francis Galton.

object or events) of interest; sample means only *some* and not all of the items in that group. Thus, for a prediction of an upcoming election, although a candidate may be interested in polling the entire population about people's preferences, he or she can realistically only obtain data from a small sample. To assure that this small portion is representative of the entire population, it should be a random sample that is fully representative.

There are two ways of dividing up the study of statistics. The first is called descriptive statistics, which has to do with the collecting, organizing, and summarizing of data, and is essentially only data-gathering. The second area is called inferential statistics and is described as the science of drawing conclusions and making predictions based on sample information. It is inferential statistics that is most related to the theory of **probability**. A good example of descriptive statistics is the varied data compiled when a new drug is being tested. Researchers gather information on any positive responses to it as well as on its side effects. Inferential statistics comes into play when scientists and administrators must make inferences (predictions) about the drug's effectiveness and safety.

Finally, two types of reasoning processes are possible when making these inferences. One is called inductive reasoning, which is when a prediction is made about a large group using data taken from a sample of it. Turning this around, deductive reasoning is when a prediction about a particular sample is based on complete knowledge of the full group. For both types of reasoning, the principle that the larger the sample the more accurate it will be generally prevails.

For More Information

Kirkby, David. *Handling Data.* Crystal Lake, IL: Rigby Interactive Library, 1996.

Krieger, Melanie Jacobs. *Means and Probabilities: Using Statistics in Science Projects.* New York: Franklin Watts, 1996.

Peters, William Stanley. *Counting for Something: Statistical Principles and Personalities.* New York: Springer-Verlag, 1987.

Riedel, Manfred G. *Winning with Numbers: A Kid's Guide to Statistics.* Englewood Cliffs, NJ: Prentice-Hall, 1978.

English mathematician Karl Pearson.

Born 1548
Bruges, Flanders (present-day Belgium)

Died 1620
The Hague, Holland

Dutch mathematical physicist and engineer

Simon Stevin

A highly versatile individual, the talented Simon Stevin contributed to several areas of science besides mathematics. In addition to introducing the **decimal** system of notating **fractions,** he made discoveries in hydrostatics and mechanics and published original works in other fields like astronomy, navigation, musical theory, and engineering. Until Stevin, mathematicians had always found fractions difficult to handle, but his introduction of decimal fractions greatly simplified any computation that involved fractions. He is sometimes known by "Stevinus," the Latin version of his name.

> *"What appears a wonder is not a wonder."*

Early life and education

Not a great deal of reliable information is available about the early life of Simon Stevin (pronounced STAY-vin), perhaps because he was an illegitimate child. Although both his parents, Antheunis Stevin and Cathelijne van de Poort, were wealthy citizens of Bruges (now in Belgium), they were not married when young Stevin was born in that city.

As a young man, Stevin worked as a clerk in the tax office at Bruges and later moved to Antwerp (now in Belgium), where he

Simon Stevin

was a bookkeeper. Both jobs show that he had at some point been instructed in mathematics. After traveling to Poland, Prussia, and Norway during the years 1571 and 1577, he settled in the Dutch city of Leiden in the new republic of the northern Netherlands in 1581. There, he attended a Latin school and then entered the University of Leiden in 1583. Beginning what was basically his college education at the age of 35 must have been as unusual then as it is now. At the university he was able to add formally to the knowledge of science and engineering that he had acquired on his own.

Joins the army and the Prince of Orange

In the late 1500s, the Netherlands was struggling to free itself from years of being ruled by the Spanish. After attending the University of Leiden, Stevin joined the Dutch army and was given engineering chores. The military leaders quickly came to appreciate Stevin's engineering skills. By 1604, he had become quartermaster-general of the army of the States of the Netherlands. During this time, he designed sluices (gates) that could be used to selectively flood parts of the Netherlands and repel an invading army. He also built windmills, locks, and ports.

While engaged with these engineering projects, Stevin also advised the head of state, Maurice of Nassau, prince of Orange (1567–1625), on constructing fortifications (military defenses) against Spain. Stevin eventually was made the prince's personal science and mathematics tutor. It was for Maurice that Stevin actually wrote several of his textbooks. The prince and his military leaders often consulted with Stevin on defense and navigation matters. With their help, Stevin eventually was able to organize a school of engineering at Leiden. In that school, Dutch rather than Latin was the language of instruction.

Mathematical contributions

After his formal education at Leiden, Stevin began to do his real scientific work, some of which he would then publish. In all of his publications, he pioneered the use of the vernacular, or native language he spoke, which in his case was Dutch. This practice was highly unusual, because Latin was considered the only language for the scholar or scientist. The Dutch owe thanks to Stevin for many of the scientific words and phrases that he coined.

Most of Stevin's early publications were mathematical. His first book, *Tafelen van Interest (Tables of Interest),* published in 1582, was concerned with the principles of bookkeeping. Interestingly, Stevin included in this book tables for rapidly calculating interest; the large banking houses had kept these calculations secret. In his landmark work, *De Thiende (The Art of Tenths),* Stevin introduced decimal fractions and showed that mathematical operations could be performed in a much easier manner using them instead of traditional fractions. Although he did not invent the idea of decimals (long-used by the Arabs and Chinese), Stevin did introduce their use to Western mathematics. By explaining the concept, he was able to overcome the unfamiliarity of most mathematicians and eventually get them to adopt the use of decimals.

Stevin did not view decimal fractions as fractions, and he proceeded to write their numerators without the denominators. For example, he presented the number 2.34 as being 234 items of the unit 0.01. Although he did not use today's decimal point (which would come later), and the **circle**/number system he used was cumbersome, his argument was convincing and his idea made sense and was eventually adopted. Stevin's circle/number system was clumsy since instead of decimals, it used circled numerals to indicate the number of fractional parts like tenths or hundredths. Thus, 5/10 was written as 5①; 7/100 was written as 7②; and 9/1000 was written as 9③. The circled 1, 2, 3 numerals referred to today's places to the right of the decimal point.

At the close of his short book, Stevin suggested that such a decimal system should be adopted by the state for all **weight**s and measures, as well as for its coinage. The European embrace of the metric system made this prediction come true. Before he turned his attention to other fields, Stevin also published a general treatment of arithmetic and **algebra,** a book entirely devoted to **geometry,** and a mathematical treatment of perspective (three-dimensional drawing).

Founds the science of hydrostatics

By 1586, Stevin was already investigating certain aspects of physics or mechanics. In the same year, he published a work that, for the first time since Greek geometer **Archimedes of Syracuse** (287–212 B.C.), contained discussions of the theory of the lever, the inclined plane, and the center of gravity. In his explanation of

Simon Stevin

Simon Stevin

the law of the inclined plane, he included his famous Dutch maxim, "Wonder en is gheen wonder," or "What appears a wonder (or marvel) is not a wonder." He meant that things or results that appear to be marvels or the result of magic are really explainable and understandable if the new tools of science are used.

With his use of these tools, Stevin was able to give the first simple and understandable explanation of the principle of displacement that Archimedes had discovered. Using this explanation, Stevin founded the modern science of hydrostatics (the study of the pressures that fluids exert or transmit). Stevin discovered that the shape of the container holding a liquid does not influence the pressure that the liquid exerts. He then was able to show that what mattered was the height of the liquid above the surface as well as the **area** of the surface. With discoveries like these, Stevin laid the groundwork for the brilliant mechanics of Italian mathematician **Galileo** (1564–1642).

Stevin also published in astronomy. He was one of the first scientists to present the Copernican (Sun-centered) system. He wrote on the science of navigation and on the determination of longitude at sea, as well as on the art of fortification. His ability ranged from writing about mills and drainage to theories of musical tuning. All his work was characterized not only by his amazing versatility but also by his ability to combine theory and practice, without having either suffer. Perhaps his work in the real world long before he obtained his formal education accounted for this unusual ability to excel at both.

Stevin married very late in life. In 1610, at the age of sixty-two, he married Catherine Gray, with whom he would have four children in the remaining ten years of his life. He had two daughters and two sons, one of whom, Hendrick Stevin, was himself a scientist and published some of his father's work. Stevin served his prince until his death.

For More Information

Biographical Dictionary of Mathematicians. New York: Charles Scribner's Sons, 1991.

Katz, Victor J. *A History of Mathematics: An Introduction.* New York: HarperCollins College Publishers, 1993.

MacTutor History of Mathematics Archive. "Simon Stevin." http://www-groups.dcs.st-and.ac.uk/~history/Mathematicians/Stevin.html (accessed on April 28, 1999).

Young, Robyn V., ed. *Notable Mathematicians: From Ancient Times to the Present.* Detroit: Gale Research, 1998.

Simon Stevin

Subtraction

Subtraction can be described as a method of taking away a certain number of things from a larger number of them. It is also the process of finding the difference between the number of elements in one set and the number in another. One of the four arithmetic operations (**addition,** subtraction, **multiplication,** and **division**) and therefore fairly simple, it nonetheless has its share of properties and rules.

Description and use

Subtraction is the inverse, or opposite, of addition. It is so closely tied to addition that it is often taught at the same time, since children sometimes grasp subtraction as the "undoing" of addition. This occurs when they realize that if $4 + 5 = 9$, then if 5 is taken away from 9, they are left with 4. Early man probably started doing simple addition by combining very small sets of things on the fingers of each hand; he probably did the reverse and found that he was able to "take away" a small number from a larger one.

As with addition, probably a great deal of time had to pass before mankind realized that certain numbers or quantities could be

Algorithm any systematic method of doing mathematics that involves a step-by-step procedure

Arithmetic operations the four fundamental actions or processes—addition, subtraction, multiplication, and division—that are performed in a specified sequence and in accordance with specific rules

Associative a property that applies to addition and multiplication (but not subtraction or division) in which addends or factors can be grouped in any order without changing the sum or product

Commutative a property that applies to addition and multiplication (but not subtraction or division) in which the order in which the numbers are added or multiplied does not change the sum; for example, $1 \times 2 = 2 \times 1$

Difference the result of subtraction

Minuend in subtraction, the larger number from which a smaller number is taken away; in $10 - 5$, 10 is the minuend

Place Value (positional notation) the system in which the position or place of a symbol or digit in a numeral determines its value; for example, in the numeral 1,234, the 1 occupies the 1000 place, the 2 is in the 100 place, the 3 is in the 10 place, and the 4 is in the unit (1) place

Set a collection or group of particular things

Subtrahend in subtraction, the smaller number being taken away from a larger number; in $10 - 5$, 5 is the subtrahend

given names (like "one" and "two") and that the *idea* of a certain quantity could be subtracted from a larger one without requiring that the actual things be present or even be represented by fingers or pebbles. This latter type of subtraction is the simplest and is called subtraction by counting. It got its name because to find out how many things are left in a group or set after a smaller number of them is taken away, a person can simply count each one that is left and arrive at the total or answer.

But simple counting is not really subtraction. The faster and best way to find out how many things are left when one set of things is removed from another is by using subtraction by computing. This is sometimes called subtraction by thinking. This process is described as abstract because it can be done in one's head without having to actually count real things. However, it assumes that a person is familiar with certain subtraction facts. Like addition tables (for instance, $2 + 2 = 4$; $2 + 3 = 5$; $2 + 4 = 6$), subtraction tables consist of similar but opposite facts that must be learned or memorized (for example, $4 - 2 = 2$; $5 - 2 = 3$; $6 - 2 = 4$). Having already learned the addition tables makes knowing their reverse much easier. Knowing that $4 + 2 = 6$ makes it easy to figure that 4 taken away from 6 equals 2.

This is a process humans do automatically. But by breaking the process down to its essentials, one can examine some of the properties of subtraction. The number obtained by taking away one set of things from a larger set is their difference, or remainder. (In addition, the answer is called the sum.) The part or larger number from which something is taken away is called the minuend. The part or smaller number being taken away is called the subtrahend. So, in the problem $9 - 5 = 4$, 9 is the minuend, 5 is the subtrahend, and 4 is the difference.

In addition, the commutative property states that it does not matter in what order one finds the numbers being added, or addends. However, subtraction is not commutative. This means that the order of the minuend and the subtrahend is unchangeable. So $5 - 3$ cannot be stated $3 - 5$. For addition, however, the sum or answer is the same whatever the order of the addends. So $4 + 5 = 9$ and $5 + 4 = 9$. Also in addition, the associative property states that when three or more numbers are to be added, the way in which the addends are grouped does not affect the sum. However, subtraction is not associative. Neither minuends nor subtrahends can be grouped the way addends can be in addition. That means "(5 – 3) – 2 = 0" gives an entirely different answer than does "5 – (3 – 2) = 4," since according to the "order of operation" rule in mathematics, the operation contained in the parentheses is always done first. With addition, numbers may be added in any order, but for subtraction, the order of parentheses must be followed.

To subtract large numbers, the subtraction algorithm is used, in which the idea of place value becomes important. A large number (like 512) can be subtracted from a larger one by using column subtraction and by knowing that a number's place determines its value. Thus, starting from the right for 512, the 2 equals 2 single units, the 1 equals 1 tens unit, and the 5 equals 5 hundreds units. So 2 + 10 + 500 = 512. Finally, just as addition can be checked by subtraction (taking away one addend from the sum will equal the other addend), so can subtraction be checked by addition (adding the subtrahend and the difference or remainder will equal the minuend).

Subtraction symbol

The minus (–) symbol is of German origin and first appeared in print in a 1489 book for merchants written by German mathematician Johannes Widmann (c. 1462–c. 1498). He used " + " to indicate a surplus (more) and "–" to indicate a deficit (less). The minus sign was used by some Greeks, and may also come from a bar that medieval traders used to mark the differences in the weights of the same product. (See sidebar on mathematical symbols in the **Multiplication** entry.)

For More Information

Groza, Vivian Shaw. *A Survey of Mathematics: Elementary Concepts and Their Historical Development.* New York: Holt, Rinehart and Winston, 1968.

Heddens, James W., and William R. Speer. *Today's Mathematics: Concepts and Classroom Methods.* Upper Saddle River, NJ: Merrill, 1997.

Julius, Edward H. *Arithmetricks: 50 Easy Ways to Add, Subtract, Multiply, and Divide Without a Calculator.* New York: John Wiley and Sons, 1995.

Rogers, James T. *The Pantheon Story of Mathematics for Young People.* New York: Pantheon Books, 1966.

West, Beverly Henderson, et al. *The Prentice-Hall Encyclopedia of Mathematics.* Englewood Cliffs, NJ: Prentice-Hall, 1982.

Born c. 640 B.C.
Miletus, Asia Minor (present-day Turkey)

Died c. 546 B.C.
Miletus, Asia Minor (present-day Turkey)

Greek geometer, philosopher, and astronomer

Thales of Miletus

Thales of Miletus lived very long ago—over 600 years before Christ and nearly 300 years before Greek philosopher Aristotle (384–322 B.C.). Thales is the first Greek of scientific accomplishment of whom there is significant information. It is not surprising, therefore, that the Greeks considered him to be the first philosopher, the first scientist of any note, and the father of Greek astronomy and mathematics. In mathematics, Thales is credited with introducing the basic concepts of **geometry** to the Greeks.

Early life

Few if any details are known about the life of Thales of Miletus (pronounced THAY-leez of my-LEE-tus), the person considered the first great thinker in Greek history. Most of what is known of him comes from later writers such as Proclus, Eudemus, and Plutarch. The year of his birth could be as early as 640 B.C. or as late as 624 B.C. He may have had a Phoenician mother, and some believe his parents were named Examyes and Cleobuline, but most consider him part of a distinguished but unknown family of the city of Miletus in Ionia. Ionia was the name for a group of Greek

> *"Water is the principle, or the element, of things. All things are water."*

Thales of Miletus

islands in the east Aegean Sea that also included part of the southwest coast of what is now Turkey. Thales was born in Miletus, which was then a trading center as well as the intellectual hub of the Greek world.

Although nothing is known about his education, it is believed that he traveled extensively as a young man, certainly to Egypt and probably to Babylonia. It also is believed that he learned the fundamentals of geometry while in Egypt. He apparently learned a great deal about many other things too, for stories abound about his extensive talents, especially in the practical world. In the field of engineering, one story tells of Thales diverting the river Halys into a channel so that the Greek army led by King Croesus might be able to cross it.

Another story demonstrates that Thales could have been a highly successful merchant if he chose to be one. Once when a colleague criticized him and asked why someone so smart was not rich, Thales used his knowledge of weather and nature to forecast that the coming crop of olives would be extremely large. He then went to the surrounding territory and bought all the olive presses needed for making olive oil. When the bumper crop came in, everyone had to come to Thales to press their olives, and for one season only, he was able to charge extremely high monopoly prices. After becoming rich in one season, he abandoned his business.

Thales has also been described as a wise man of politics. He was able to convince the various Greek city-states of Ionia to form a political union and therefore be able to resist the aggressive push of the neighboring, non-Greek country of Lydia.

Mathematics was the basis of many of Thales' accomplishments in other areas, such as astronomy. Greek philosopher Plato (c. 428–c. 348 B.C.) recounted a humorous story about Thales and his love of astronomy. One night, Thales fell into a well while walking and looking up at the stars. When he was helped out of the well by a servant woman who heard his cries, she mocked him, saying, "Here is a man trying to find out what is going on in the heavens, yet he cannot even see what is at his feet."

The one deed that made Thales most famous and earned him a lasting reputation was his correct prediction of an eclipse of the Sun. A century and a half after the eclipse occurred, it was described by Greek historian Herodotus (c. 484–c. 430 B.C.) as so frightening to the armies of what is now Turkey and Iran, that they stopped a battle and agreed to peace. Modern astronomical techniques indicate that the only eclipse in Asia Minor during Thales' lifetime was on May 28, 585 B.C. This has therefore been described as the first event in human history that can be dated with certainty to a particular day.

The great importance of Thales' mathematics was his introduction of geometry to Greece and his demonstration for the first time that geometry's principles can be proved by a regular series of arguments. Thales did not invent or discover geometry. In fact, his geometry was borrowed from the Egyptians, who knew geometry well and used it in their everyday lives. But prior to Thales, geometry was a real-world, "rule-of-thumb" tool that was used mainly to measure actual surfaces and real solids. For Thales, however, geometry became abstract or theoretical. That is, it became an exact science of lines, **triangles,** and **circles.**

What may have been even more important, however, was Thales' insistence that results be achieved logically. This has been described as his introduction of the notion of proof by the deductive method. Deduction means that a conclusion is reached by following a chain of events, each of which follows from the other, step by step. Today, this is called the reasoning process. But nearly 2,500 years ago, such reasoning was not common or recognized as being important. After Thales, however, Greek geometry or mathematics was distinguished by its requirement of proof. A number of basic theorems in geometry are associated with Thales. One theorem is even named after him. Using these propositions (such as, "If two lines cut across one another, vertical and opposite angles are equal"), he was able to accomplish such astounding feats as telling the height of a pyramid by its shadow or measuring the distance of a ship from shore.

Thales was also a philosopher. He speculated on everything from human nature to the ultimate element in the universe. The maxim "know thyself" is attributed to him. To the basic question, What is the universe made of, Thales answered that the basic element was water, and that the Earth was a flat disk floating on an infinite ocean. Although he was not correct, asking the question itself was more important than the answer he gave, because it would lead

Thales of Miletus

Thales of Miletus

others to ask the same question. As with his insistence on real proof in mathematics, he argued that occurrences on Earth could be explained by seeking their causes in natural events. This emphasis on seeking causes based on nature rather than "Gods" is the reason that Thales is considered one of the first scientists. His attitude and approach is recognized as the first important step in the formation of the modern scientific method.

Thales lived so long ago that in a 1982 book about scientists, he was listed chronologically as the third earliest scientist in history. The book, by American writer Isaac Asimov (1920–92), listed only Egyptian physician Imhotep (twenty-seventh century B.C.) and Egyptian scribe Ahmes (eighteenth-century B.C.) as having preceded Thales. By the time of Plato and Aristotle, Thales was already a legend of the far past, but his modern thinking and exact mathematics set the tone for Greek and later Western progress.

For More Information

Ball, W. W. Rouse. *A Short Account of the History of Mathematics.* New York: Dover Publications, 1960.

Biographical Dictionary of Mathematicians. New York: Charles Scribner's Sons, 1991.

MacTutor History of Mathematics Archive. "Thales of Miletus." http://www-groups.dcs.st-and.ac.uk/~history/Mathematicians/Thales.html (accessed on April 29, 1999).

Moffatt, Michael. *The Ages of Mathematics: The Origins.* Garden City, NY: Doubleday & Company, 1977.

Young, Robyn V., ed. *Notable Mathematicians: From Ancient Times to the Present.* Detroit: Gale Research, 1998.

Time

Described as the human division of the infinite flow of events and occurrences that happen every day, time is one of the most difficult concepts to define. Although everyone has a good sense of what it means, based on life's experiences and intuition, it is nonetheless a real mystery. Time, it seems, can only be thought about or discussed if some change occurs, since it can then be said that something was *before* or *after* that change, thus indicating that time has passed. Despite being unable to define it exactly, one's ability to divide and measure time accurately makes possible human activity that is both predictable and productive.

Background

The expression "time and tide wait for no man" perfectly sums up the continuous, unstoppable nature of the passage of time. Although one cannot stop time from passing, mankind has almost from its beginning regularly attempted to break up its movement into a measurable sequence of events. To human beings, since time and change are closely linked, probably the first things that the earliest humans used to divide time were the natural events that happened with some obvious regularity. The regular, natural divi-

Analog clock an instrument that indicates the time of day by its moving hands on a numbered dial

Circadian rhythm the daily rhythm or cycle of activity that many organisms exhibit during a single 24-hour period

Clepsydra an ancient timekeeping device that marked the passage of time by the regulated flow of water through a small opening; a water clock

Digital clock an instrument that indicates the time of day by giving its reading in actual digits or numbers

Infinite set a set whose elements cannot be counted because they are unlimited

Intuition the act or faculty of knowing or sensing something without having any rational thought or doing any reasoning

Mercantile of or relating to merchants or trade

Prime meridian the zero meridian (0 degrees) used as a reference or baseline from which longitude east or west is measured; by international agreement, it passes through Greenwich, England

Radioactive decay the natural disintegration or breakdown of a radioactive substance that allows it to be dated

Sundial an instrument that indicates solar time by the shadow cast by its central pointer onto a numbered dial

sion of light and darkness marked by the rising and setting of the Sun may have been the first of these. These divisions were called, of course, day and night. Such obvious changes allowed for the concepts of *before* something and *after* it to be easily understood.

Other changes that human beings noticed happened less frequently but with no less regularity. One of these was the cycle the Moon followed as it changed shape every so often. The 29½ days it took the moon to go through one complete cycle came to be called a month. In an even slower and longer cycle, the seasons, and therefore the weather, changed regularly, one into the other. Close observance of the stars at dawn and sunset eventually revealed that the Sun made a complete circle around the sky. The Sun's movement took four full seasons to complete. This cycle of four seasons was found to total about 365½ days (or 12 months), called a year.

For thousands of years, this level of dividing time was probably adequate to the needs of most human beings whose activities primarily revolved around farming. However, as societies became more organized, further and smaller divisions of time were desired. The rise of mercantile societies (involving trade) especially required that people have a more accurate sense of time about them. Consequently, the then-smallest unit of time—the day— was itself divided into smaller units. It was probably the Babylonians, with a numeral system based on 60, who first divided a day into 24 hours, an hour into 60 minutes, and a minute into 60 seconds. This division was not arbitrary, however, as the Babylonians probably used the Egyptian method of "apparent solar time," which considered day and night as 12 hours each.

Once these divisions were decided upon, the next step was to invent a way to keep track of the passage of these cycles. The first device, the sundial, was naturally linked to the Sun's movement and was known by the Egyptians and ancient Chinese. The first mechanical timekeeping device was a water clock called a clepsydra (pronounced KLEP-suh-druh). These devices were used in Greece and operated on the principle that it took a certain amount of time for a steady stream of water to fill a vessel. In the courtrooms of Athens, Greece, for example, the standard water clock allowed a speaker six minutes. The Chinese also used the phenomenon of something burning at a constant rate to keep time, so they used candles and incense sticks as well as sundials, sand in an

hourglass, and water clocks. The first completely mechanical clock was built in Europe around A.D. 1275 and was driven by the slow pull of a falling **weight.** Today's analog and digital clocks and watches powered by electricity are but sophisticated versions of the same principle.

Description and use

At any given moment, it is never the same time everywhere in the world. The time of day changes as the Earth rotates on its axis in relation to the Sun. When it is midnight in London, England, it is 9 A.M. in Tokyo, Japan. Therefore, in order to create a uniform system of measuring time, the concept of standard time zones was developed.

At an international conference in 1884, a system was agreed upon that decreed Greenwich, England, to be the arbitrary starting point for all the world's different time zones. This system divides the entire globe into 12 one-hour time zones to the east and 12 to the west of Greenwich (called the prime meridian).

As technology developed, scientists realized that time based on astronomical measurements was not as accurate as it could be. In

Time

1958, therefore, the measure of or standard for one second was redefined in terms of the billions of electron vibrations per second that occur naturally within an atom of cesium (a rare metal). These vibrations are so consistent that an atomic clock will not lose or gain more than one second in 30,000 years. Today's standard second, therefore, equals 9,192,631,770 vibrations of a cesium beam clock.

Other concepts of time play crucial roles in physics (in which time is a quantity, like mass, that can be measured), biology (in which living things experience natural, circadian rhythms), and geology (in which radioactive decay and carbon absorption are used to date ancient rocks, plants, and animals).

For More Information

Burns, Marilyn. *This Book Is About Time.* Boston: Little, Brown, 1978.

Ganeri, Anita. *The Story of Time and Clocks.* New York: Oxford University Press, 1997.

Goudsmit, Samuel A., and Robert Claiborne. *Time.* Alexandria, VA: Time-Life Books, 1980.

Jespersen, James, and Jane Fitz-Randolph. *Time and Clocks for the Space Age.* New York: Atheneum, 1979.

Macey, Samuel L. *Encyclopedia of Time.* New York: Garland Publishing, 1994.

Triangle

A triangle is a **polygon** with three sides. It is also described as a closed plane (flat) figure that is formed by line segments that join three points but not in a straight line. The various types of triangles are classified by both the length of their sides and the measures of their angles.

Background

The word triangle is derived from a combination of the Latin words *tri,* for "three," and *angulus,* meaning "corner" or "angle." It is known from surviving Babylonian clay tablets and Egyptian papyri (an early form of writing paper made from the papyrus plant) that at least 4,000 years ago, ancient astronomers, surveyors, and navigators used some form of triangle measurement to solve practical problems associated with distances. (See sidebar on papyrus in the **Algebra** entry.) Much later, the ancient Greeks studied the triangle intensively and even made a separate science (trigonometry) of the measurement and use of triangles.

Acute triangle a triangle in which the measure of every angle is less than 90 degrees

Area the amount of space a flat geometrical shape occupies; the region inside a given boundary

Equilateral triangle a triangle in which all three sides are of equal length

Hypotenuse the longest side in a right triangle

Isosceles triangle a triangle with at least two sides of equal length

Obtuse triangle a triangle with one angle that measures greater than 90 degrees

Perimeter the distance around a polygon, obtained by adding the lengths of its sides

Perpendicular when lines intersect and form a right angle

Polygon a geometric figure composed of three or more line segments (straight sides) that never cross each other

Right triangle a triangle in which one of its angles measures 90 degrees (a right angle)

Scalene triangle a triangle in which each side is of a different length

Side the line segment that joins two points on a triangle

Triangulation the location of an unknown point by forming a triangle whose two points are known

Vertex the point at which any two sides of a polygon meet or intersect; plural is "vertices"

Description and use

Triangles are classified in two ways: by the length of their edges (sides) or by the measure of their angles. All triangles are a part of the larger geometric term, polygon; the polygon with the smallest number of sides (3) is a triangle. There are certain properties that are common to all triangles. One is that the sum of the three angles of a triangle always measures 180 degrees. Knowing this rule allows one to find the degrees of a third, unknown angle when the other two angle degrees are given. Another property is that the sum of any two sides of a triangle is always greater than the third side.

Different parts of a triangle have their own names. The vertex is the point where two sides meet. A side is the line segment that joins two points. An angle is what is formed inside the triangle by two sides meeting at the vertex.

There are many different kinds of triangles. Those that are classified according to the relationships of their sides are called scalene, isosceles, and equilateral triangles. In a scalene triangle, no two sides have the same length. An isosceles triangle has at least two sides of equal length. An equilateral triangle has all three sides of equal length. Classified by angles, there are acute, obtuse, and right triangles. An acute triangle is one in which every angle measures less than 90 degrees. An obtuse triangle has one angle greater than 90 degrees. A right angle has one angle that measures exactly 90 degrees.

The **perimeter** (distance around) of a triangle is simply the sum of the lengths of its sides. However, the **area** of a triangle is found by the formula $A = \frac{1}{2}bh$ (area equals half the base times the height, or base times height divided by two). For any triangle except an isosceles triangle, although any side can be the base, it is usually the side on which the triangle is resting (what appears as the bottom of the figure). With any side of a triangle serving as its base, the triangle's height is the side that is perpendicular (usually vertical) to it. This formula for area is important since triangles whose perimeters are equal in length can have different areas.

One of the most famous theorems in mathematics involves a triangle. It is called the **Pythagorean theorem,** although it was known by the Babylonians, Egyptians, and Chinese long before a

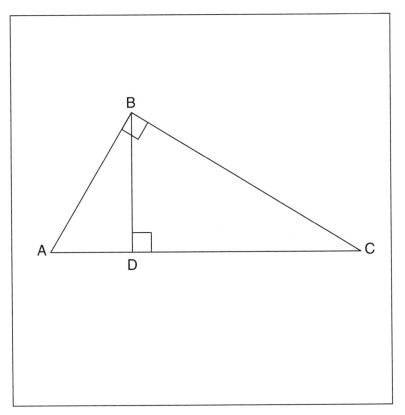

Triangle

ABC, BDC, and ADB are all right triangles.

proof for it was offered by Greek mathematician **Pythagoras of Samos** (c. 580–c. 500 B.C.). The Pythagorean theorem says that the sides of a right triangle have a unique relationship to one another. It states that the sum of the squares of the two shorter sides equals the square of the longest side (called the hypotenuse). Using this theorem, the length of any side of a right triangle can be found as long as the length of the other two sides is known. It has proven very practical in finding the distance between two points. The fields of surveying, astronomy, and navigation have historically employed what they called "triangulation" to measure unknown distances both on Earth and in the skies.

Triangular shapes have very desirable characteristics in the everyday world. Because the triangle is such a rigid figure, it has become basic to the construction of everything from shelves on a wall to bridges and towers. Since a triangular shape holds its form when a force is applied to it, a support that is triangle-shaped will not deform or change shape. What does in fact fail is the material out

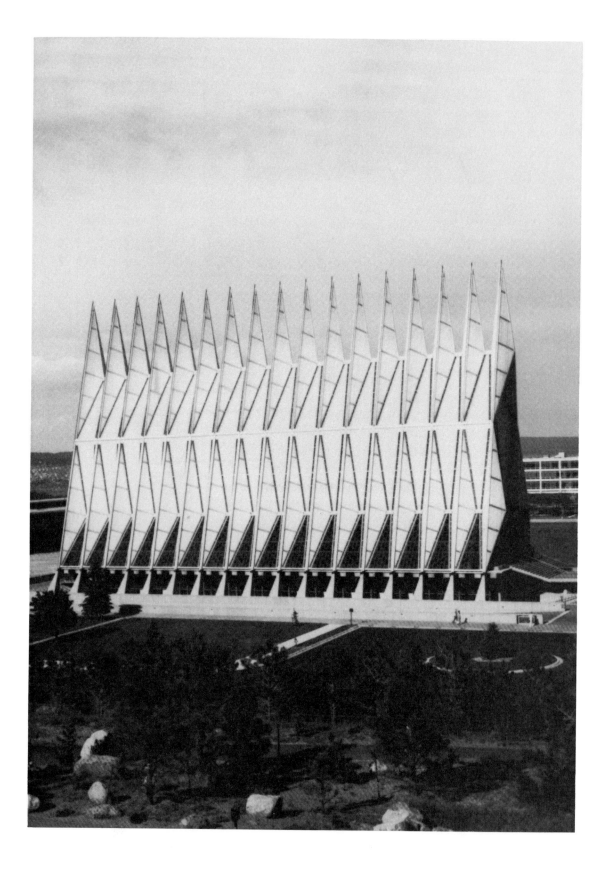

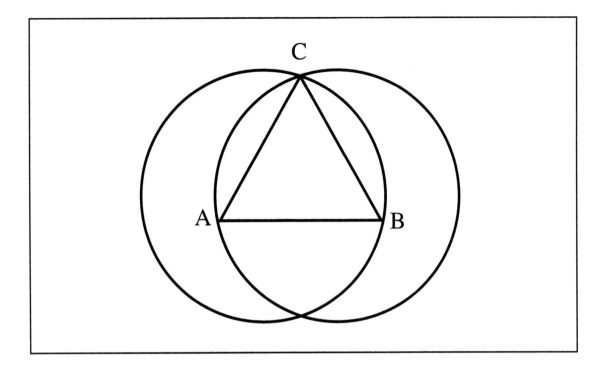

of which the triangle is made. When a triangular support does fail or collapse, what usually happens is that the materials out of which the support is made are not strong enough, and the support fails (or crumbles or bends). Thus, while a triangular support made of common cement might crumble under a heavy load, an identically-shaped support made of reinforced concrete would hold.

Triangular shapes have also been used in classical artworks because they are considered to give a painting or sculpture a desirable look of order, symmetry, or balance. Modern architects use the triangular shape not just for purposes of strength but also as a bold architectural form in its own right. The triangle has proven to be one of the most consistently interesting and fascinating of the basic geometric shapes.

For More Information

Burton, David M. *Burton's History of Mathematics: An Introduction.* Dubuque, IA: Wm. C. Brown Publishers, 1995.

Green, Gordon W., Jr. *Helping Your Child to Learn Math.* New York: Citadel Press, 1995.

An equilateral triangle as shown inside the intersection of two circles.

Opposite page: One of the most dramatic architectural examples of the use of the triangle is the U.S. Air Force Chapel in Colorado Springs, Colorado.

Triangle

Heddens, James W., and William R. Speer. *Today's Mathematics: Concepts and Methods in Elementary School Mathematics.* Upper Saddle River, NJ: Merrill, 1997.

Ross, Catherine Sheldrick. *Triangles: Shapes in Math, Science and Nature.* Toronto: Kids Can Press, 1997.

West, Beverly Henderson, et al. *The Prentice-Hall Encyclopedia of Mathematics.* Englewood Cliffs, NJ: Prentice-Hall, 1982.

Born June 23, 1912
London, England

Died June 7, 1954
Wilmslow, Cheshire, England

English algebraist and logician

Alan Turing

Alan Turing earned his place in the history of mathematics with his pioneering work on the theory of **computers.** As early as 1937, he described a theoretical machine that defined the basics of what essentially became the modern computer. His landmark work also contributed to an understanding of how the thinking process is related to the process of electronic computing. Following his wartime work breaking German codes, he helped design the first British computers.

> *"We can only see a short distance ahead, but we can see plenty there that needs to be done."*

Early life and education

Alan Mathison Turing was born in London, the second son of Ethel Sara Stoney and Julius Mathias Turing, a high official in Britain's colonial government in India. Because his parents were out of the country most of the time, young Turing and his brother were raised in England by relatives and a retired military couple until they were old enough to be sent to boarding school. Turing entered Sherbourne School, a boy's preparatory school in Dorset, when he was 13 years old. There, he was considered to be an inconsistent student who seemed uninterested in any subject except mathematics, especially calculus. However, he often would

Alan Turing

Alan Turing enjoyed running track.

make up for his poor classwork by doing well on year-end exams. At Sherbourne, also, he developed an interest in running track.

Although he failed twice to be admitted to Trinity College in Cambridge, Turing won a scholarship from King's College, also at Cambridge University, and entered there in 1931. By then, Turing had already encountered Einstein's physics and the new science of quantum mechanics on his own. He was ready to take on the newest ideas of modern mathematics. During his years at King's

College, Turing so distinguished himself in mathematics that when he graduated in 1935, he was elected a fellow of the college. This was an honor, since fellows received school salaries and were usually selected from older graduates. His election was based on the brilliance he demonstrated in a 1935 paper on probality theory that also won him the 1936 Smith's Prize in mathematics.

Studies at Princeton University

In 1936, Turing accepted an invitation to work and study with mathematical logician Alonzo Church (1903–95) at Princeton University in New Jersey. There, he began work on a theory of computation and met such influential individuals as Hungarian American mathematician **John von Neumann** (1903–57) and German American physicist and mathematician **Albert Einstein** (1879–1955). While at Princeton, Turing conducted research on such topics as binary numbers (0 and 1) and Boolean **algebra** in the hope of finding a way to apply them to a computing machine that could do problem-solving. He also studied and gained experience working with codes and ciphers (messages in secret codes).

During his two years at Princeton, Turing produced what became his most famous contribution to mathematics. In a paper presented in 1937 to the London Mathematical Society, he described a theoretical computing machine that could solve any mathematical problem, provided it was given the proper problem-solving instructions.

In his description of what came to be called a "Turing machine," Turing detailed an imaginary automatic machine that, using only two commands, could solve a variety of problems, provided they were expressed in binary code (that is, as zeroes and ones). Although Turing described a machine that at the time used paper tape and a typewriter, his 1937 article basically described in detail the digital computer long before it was invented. Further, his concept also contained the basics of the now-familiar notions of program, input, output, and even the processing of information.

Helps crack German war codes

The day after World War II (1939–45) broke out in Europe on September 3, 1939, Turing joined the British government's top

Alan Turing

secret Code and Cypher School at Bletchley Park. Turing had returned to England in 1938 and brought with him an electro-mechanical primitive computer that he had built while at Princeton. His experience at Princeton would be put to good use at Bletchley, and he would play a critical role in the development of a machine that would break the codes of the German's famous machine called Enigma.

The Enigma machine itself was neither new nor secret to the British. The Germans, however, could make it as complex as they wanted and would regularly increase the number of rotors (rotating parts) in the machine and therefore create a more complicated coding system. Each time the Germans did this, they would greatly increase the number of possible combinations, to the point where the British were unable to compute (or search for patterns) fast enough.

What the British needed was a general, programmable machine that could scan for patterns in the Enigma messages. Turing had worked out a theory for just such a machine. According to Turing's mathematical theory, each of the million settings that Enigma used had to have its own internal consistency. Also, certain letters stood for other letters; therefore, certain other letter matchings were not true.

Using a technique called traffic analysis, a machine was built that, by mid-1941, was decoding German messages as fast as they were received. When the Germans improved Enigma, Turing and other British experts responded by building a machine that could check patterns from paper tape and could even store some electronically. In 1943, the team built an early electronic computer called COLOSSUS, and the Allies (the countries who fought against Germany in World War II) could read every German message they intercepted. The cracking of the German code was one of the most important factors in the eventual Allied victory. For his work during the war, Turing was awarded the Order of the British Empire (O.B.E.), a high honor not often given to someone not in military combat.

Postwar work

After the war, Turing turned his attention to general-purpose computers and went to work for the National Physical Laboratory

(NPL) in Teddington, England. In the NPL's mathematics division, he began to work on the design of a machine called the automatic computing engine (ACE). However, working in what was now basically a part of the government bureaucracy was nothing like what Turing had experienced during the war. In wartime, only results were important, and there were few problems with internal politics or budgets. By 1948, Turing had had enough of such an environment in which progress was so slow. He left the laboratory, which eventually produced a scaled-down version of his ACE in 1950.

After leaving the NPL, Turing was appointed reader in the theory of computation at Manchester College and became deputy director of the newly formed Royal Society Computing Laboratory. There, he became concerned with what today is called artificial intelligence. He began considering the question of the ability of a machine to think. In his landmark 1950 paper entitled "Computing Machinery and Intelligence," Turing argued that computers could be designed to mimic the human process of thinking. He said that such a design would be accomplished within 50 years.

Turing also envisioned a computer that would be able to play games like chess, learn languages and translate them, handle code-breaking and building, and perform the functions of mathematics. Near the end of his life, Turing was working on a project that involved yet another computer—the Manchester Automatic Digital Machine (MADAM).

Possible suicide

Throughout his life, Turing was known to be always brilliant and original but also very eccentric. He was a friendly man but very impractical. Turing often resembled the popular image of the absent-minded professor. He sometimes did strange things. For instance, during the war when it looked as if England might lose, he changed all his money into bars of silver and buried them, only to be unable to find them later on. Turing was also a homosexual, and England had harsh laws against gay individuals. In 1952, he was convicted of "gross indecency" and offered the choice of going to jail or being injected with female hormones. He chose the injection.

Although Turing seemed to be coping well with his personal misfortune, he died of cyanide poisoning on June 7, 1954. His death

Alan Turing

Alan Turing

puzzled everyone who knew him. He had been free of the hormone treatments for a year and had seemed to weather the public embarrassment with his career intact. His death was ruled a suicide by the authorities, but Turing's mother suggested it could have been quite accidental, since he often tinkered with chemicals at home. She speculated that he might have accidentally used a spoon coated with poison. Turing left no note suggesting his state of mind or motives, but few who knew him well seriously questioned the official ruling.

For More Information

Biographical Dictionary of Mathematicians. New York: Charles Scribner's Sons, 1991.

Cortada, James W. *Historical Dictionary of Data Processing: Biographies.* New York: Greenwood Press, 1987.

Gottfried, Ted. *Alan Turing: The Architect of the Computer Age.* New York: Franklin Watts, 1996.

Gray, Paul. "Alan Turing." *Time,* March 29, 1999, pp. 147–50.

Henderson, Harry. *Modern Mathematicians.* New York: Facts on File, 1996.

MacTutor History of Mathematics Archive. "Alan Mathison Turing." http://www-groups.dcs.st-and.ac.uk/~history/Mathematicians/Turing.html (accessed on April 29, 1999).

Young, Robyn V., ed. *Notable Mathematicians: From Ancient Times to the Present.* Detroit: Gale Research, 1998.

Volume and surface area

Volume is a measure of the capacity of a figure. Since volume always refers to an amount of three-dimensional space, it is measured in cubic units. Volume is similar to the concept of **area** in that it is a measurement of what is inside of something. Surface area is the total area of all of the exterior sides of a figure. It can also be described as the total area that would be covered if a three-dimensional figure, like a box, were peeled apart and laid out flat. Surface area is measured in square units.

Volume

The word volume comes from the Latin word *volumen,* meaning "something that is rolled up," like a scroll. When printed books replaced the rolled-up scroll during the sixteenth century, the term volume came to apply to books. The word's meaning soon changed, however, to indicate more specifically the size or the bulk of a book. By the seventeenth century, the emphasis was more on the size of the book than on the book itself, and volume came to mean the size or mass of any object. By the nineteenth century, volume took on the additional meaning of amount.

Volume and surface area

Long before the Greeks, volume was calculated by the ancient Babylonians and Egyptians, whose taxes were often stated as a certain volume of grain. Since the tax authorities knew how to calculate the **perimeter** (the distance around a two-dimensional figure) and area of land being farmed, they eventually learned how to estimate the volume of grain that was likely to be produced from a given plot of land. The ancients were able to work out formulas that gave them the volume of simple shapes, like a rectangle, cylinder, and cone.

Calculating the volume of a three-dimensional figure is similar to finding the area of a rectangle, which involves finding how many same-size squares fit in it. Finding the volume of a rectangular solid, like a real box that has not only length and height but width as well, involves determining how many cubes fit inside the box. The resulting answer is the volume. As with area, it is unnecessary to count the number of cubes; a formula is used instead. For a rectangular solid, the formula is: volume $=$ length $\times$ width $\times$ height ($V = lwh$). For a cube, which is a solid whose sides are all the same length, one side is multiplied by itself three times (corresponding to length, width, and height). Thus, a cube whose edges all measure 2 feet will have a volume of 8 cubic feet ($2^3 = 2 \times 2 \times 2 = 8$). Formulas also exist for other shapes such as cylinders, pyramids, and cones.

Surface area

When the concept of area is applied to a three-dimensional or solid object, it is called surface area. The surface area of a solid figure is simply the total area of all of its exterior sides if the figure were broken apart at its edges or seams and laid out flat. For example, a box that is cube-shaped has six sides of equal dimensions. Since its surface area is the total area of the surfaces that form the cube, the area (length $\times$ width) of each face or side is found and then added up. With a (six-sided) cube unfolded and laid out flat in which each side is 3 feet, the area of each square totals 9 feet. Adding the six equal sides ($9 + 9 + 9 + 9 + 9 + 9 = 54$) to find its surface area is the same as multiplying 6 times 9 ($6 \times 9 = 54$). For other shapes like a cylinder, surface area is calculated by breaking it into its component shapes (two **circles** and a rectangle) and computing accordingly.

The concepts of volume and surface area have many useful applications in everyday life. One of the more interesting but lesser-

Volume and surface area

A large animal such as the polar bear has a smaller ratio of surface area to volume than does a smaller animal. This means the polar bear loses less heat than its smaller fellow mammals.

known facts concerning the interaction of the two is found in how certain aspects of an animal's size affects its behavior. The **weight** of an animal depends upon its volume, as does the energy an animal uses up during activity. However, the loss of heat that an animal experiences depends upon its surface area (how much of its skin is in contact with the air).

From a mathematical standpoint, a very large animal has a smaller ratio of surface area to volume than does a much smaller animal. In the natural world, this means that a large animal like a polar bear suffers less heat loss (in proportion to its weight or volume) than does a small dog, because the polar bear has less surface area per volume. (See also **Ratio, proportion, and percent.**) Also, in proportion to the sizes of their bodies, a polar bear has to eat much less food to keep its heat than does a dog which has a higher ratio of surface area to volume. In this way, mathematics can explain why a polar bear is better suited to a winter climate than a small dog.

For More Information

Beaumont, Vern, et al. *How to . . . Teach Perimeter, Area, and Volume.* Reston, VA: The National Council of Teachers of Mathematics, 1986.

Green, Gordon W., Jr. *Helping Your Child to Learn Math.* New York: Citadel Press, 1995.

Miller, Charles D., et al. *Mathematical Ideas.* Reading, MA: Addison-Wesley, 1997.

Smoothey, Marion. *Let's Investigate Area and Volume.* New York: Marshall Cavendish, 1993.

Weight

In physics, weight is the gravitational pull on a body or object. Commonly thought of as how heavy something is (which is really its mass), weight is in fact a force exerted on a smaller object by a massive one (the Earth). In everyday life, however, weight and mass are considered nearly identical since large masses have large weights, and for mathematical purposes, weight will therefore be considered synonymous (having the same or similar meaning) with mass.

Background

In everyday mathematics, the word "weight" is informally used to mean mass. Since weight is therefore thought of by most people as meaning how much matter or "stuff" there is in an object, technically the two are different phenomena, although intimately related. For example, in order to push a stalled automobile, a good amount of force must be exerted. Most people attribute this to the great "weight" of the car. However, weight has nothing to do with it since the force of gravity acts downward and has no effect on motion along the ground. A large force is needed to push the car because its mass naturally resists being moved. Thus, it is the *mass*

Weight

WORDS TO KNOW

Avoirdupois weight a system of weights and measures based on a pound containing 16 ounces

Equivalent equal as in value, force, or meaning

Force strength, energy, or power that causes motion or change

Gravitation the natural phenomenon of attraction between massive celestial bodies

Inertia the tendency of a body to resist being moved and to remain at rest

Mass the measure of the quantity of matter that a body contains

Troy weight a system of weight in which a pound contains 12 ounces

of the automobile rather than its weight that requires the large push. Over 300 years ago, English mathematician **Isaac Newton** (1642–1727) described this as "inertia," a property of matter that makes it wants to remain at rest (unmoving) unless something outside gives it a push.

Another major difference between weight and mass (from the standpoint of physics) is that weight can vary, but mass stays the same. This is proven whenever an astronaut enters outer space and becomes weightless. Having gone beyond the gravitational influence of the Earth, the astronaut has not changed his or her mass in any way. What has changed is the *force* exerted on that mass.

Description and use

For everyday life on Earth, for all practical purposes, weight and mass mean the same thing. What something weighs indicates simply how heavy it is. In order to measure the weight of something, therefore, a standard unit of measure must be used. Today there are two major systems for measuring weight. One is the customary system of the United States. The other is the metric system, which is used by the rest of the world.

The American system was actually developed in England around the beginning of the thirteenth century. This system of measure was based on the "pound," although two separate pounds were used. The commercial world used the *avoirdupois*, taken from the old French term meaning "goods having weight." The "troy" system was used to weigh metals and gems and was named after the city of Troyes, France, where the system was first used.

The customary system began its standard units with the grain, its smallest unit of weight. This harks back to medieval England when a single grain of wheat was chosen as the basic unit. This system proceeds from the grain to the dram, which is a little over 27 grains, and then on to the ounce, which is 16 drams. The pound (avoirdupois) comes next, composed of 16 ounces, followed by the short ton, which is made up of 2,000 pounds. This system was adopted by the United States after its independence was achieved mainly because it had used the old English system for so long.

The new United States did have a choice, however. In 1795, revolutionary France formally adopted an entirely new system of weights and measures. Called the metric system because its basic unit is the meter, which is a unit of length, it is a **decimal** system created on a base of ten. For measuring weight, its basic unit is the gram. Beginning with its smallest unit, the milligram (one one-thousandth of a gram), it proceeds to a centigram (one hundredth), decigram (one tenth), gram, and up to kilogram (1,000 grams), and finally to metric ton (1,000 kilograms).

The **logic** of the metric system's base ten and its demonstrated usefulness to science appealed to more and more countries. Eventually, it was adopted internationally in 1960 as the International System of Units (known by its French name "Système Internationale d'Unites, which is abbreviated to SI). Today, nearly every country in the world except the United States has officially adopted SI. Despite legislation that made the metric system the preferred system of weights of measures for America, actually changing over will require people learning and accepting an entirely new system of weights and measures. Until then, there will always be a need for conversion tables that allow a person to convert from one system of units to another. It is also helpful if children are taught in school the metric equivalents of the more common weights and measures.

For More Information

Ganeri, Anita. *The Story of Weights and Measures*. New York: Oxford University Press, 1997.

Kline, Morris. *Mathematics for the Nonmathematician*. New York: Dover Publications, 1985.

Smith, Karl J. *Mathematics: Its Power and Utility*. Pacific Grove, CA: Brooks/Cole Publishing Co., 1997.

West, Beverly Henderson, et al. *The Prentice-Hall Encyclopedia of Mathematics*. Englewood Cliffs, NJ: Prentice-Hall, 1982.

Weight

Whole numbers

The numbers used in everyday counting (1, 2, 3, 4,...) are called natural numbers. Since there is no such thing as the largest number, the entire group of these numbers is called an infinite set. When the number zero is added to this set, it is called a set of whole numbers. Whole numbers are therefore the set of natural numbers plus the number zero (0, 1, 2, 3, 4,...).

Description and use

A number is easily recognized as the idea or concept that refers to a certain number of things or that answers the question, "How many?" The development of the idea of numbers predates written history. Whether using number words ("five") or number symbols ("5") or holding up five fingers, people have an abstract notion in their minds of what is meant by the general idea of "fiveness." A number is not the same thing as a numeral, however. While a number is basically an idea, a numeral is the written expression of that idea. Roman numerals (like "III") and Arabic numerals (like "3") refer to the actual symbols that represent the idea. (See sidebar on Arabic numerals in the **al-Khwārizmī** entry.) It can be said that a numeral can be erased, but a number cannot (because it is an idea).

Whole numbers

WORDS TO KNOW

Factor in a given number, that which divides that number evenly; for example, the factors of the number 12 are 1, 2, 3, 4, 6, and 12

Infinite set a set whose elements cannot be counted because they are unlimited

Natural numbers all the cardinal numbers or counting numbers (1, 2, 3, . . .) except 0

Number theory a branch of mathematics concerned generally with the properties and relationships of integers

Numeral a symbol or name that stands for a number

Subset a set contained within a set

Whole numbers have four basic axioms (statements) that are obvious to everyone and do not need proof.

1. The first counting number is zero.

2. Every counting number has a successor. (1 is followed by 2, which is followed by 3, and so on.)

3. Every counting number except zero has a predecessor. (100 is preceded by 99, which is preceded by 98, and so on.)

4. Of any two different counting numbers, one number is always greater than the other. (Of 5 and 10, 10 is greater than 5; of 10 and 20, 20 is greater than 10.)

The elementary operations of whole numbers are simply the basic arithmetic operations of **addition, subtraction, multiplication,** and **division.** Besides the ground rules that prevail when doing any one of those operations, there are also rules that govern in what order or sequence these operations must be carried out when solving a problem that requires doing more than one operation. An example of such a two-step operation is the following: How much money would a man collect if he sold a single $5 ticket today and three $10 tickets tomorrow? The problem would look like this:

$$\$5 + 3 \times \$10 = ?$$

If done simply from left to right, 5 is added to 3 and then multiplied by 10 equalling $80. This is obviously wrong. The rule that applies for order of operations is to do the multiplication (or division) first, as if they were in parentheses, and then proceed from left to right. The correct answer is therefore obtained by first multiplying the 3 by 10 (30) and then adding from left to right.

$$\$5 + (3 \times \$10) = ?$$

$$\$5 + \$30 = \$35$$

Subsets

Whole numbers are used by more people in everyday life than any other type of number. People regularly perform operations with them and do not give them a second thought. Whole numbers also have what are called subsets that are taken for granted. Subsets are part of an aspect of mathematics called number theory, which deals with the properties of numbers.

The simplest property or subset of whole numbers are those that are called odd and even. Even numbers are defined as whole numbers that have 2 as a factor. A factor is the same as a divisor, the number by which another number is divided. That means that if 2 will go into a number evenly (with no remainder), then that number is called an even number. For instance, $10 \div 2 = 5$; there is no remainder, so 10 is an even number.

Early Greek mathematicians gave even numbers a sort of mystical significance, saying that even numbers were unlucky and female, while all the odd numbers were male and therefore lucky. (Obviously, Greek mathematicians were nearly all men.) Odd numbers were then defined as whole numbers that did not have 2 as a factor (and therefore give a remainder of 1). So $9 \div 2 = 4$, with a remainder of 1; so 9 is an odd number.

Another subset of whole numbers is that of a factor. Any factor of a given number divides that number evenly (or has a zero remainder). Thus the factors of 18 are 1, 2, 3, 6, 9, and 18. So 18 divided by only those six numbers results in a number that has a zero remainder. One of the principles of factoring is that every number except 1 has at least two factors (since it can always be divided by 1 and by itself).

As people and society became more civilized and sophisticated, and business and science grew more complex, many other types of numbers were developed to meet these new needs (such as **decimals, fractions,** and **rational and irrational numbers**).

For More Information

Eichhorn, Connie, and Mary Garland. *Whole Numbers: Multiplication and Division.* Upper Saddle River, NJ: Globe Fearon, 1996.

Friedberg, Richard. *An Adventurer's Guide to Number Theory.* New York: Dover Publications, 1994.

Ganeri, Anita. *The Story of Numbers and Counting.* New York: Oxford University Press, 1996.

Smith, David Eugene. *Number Stories of Long Ago.* Detroit: Gale Research, 1973.

West, Beverly Henderson, et al. *The Prentice-Hall Encyclopedia of Mathematics.* Englewood Cliffs, NJ: Prentice-Hall, 1982.

Whole numbers

Born November 26, 1894
Columbia, Missouri

Died March 18, 1964
Stockholm, Sweden

American logician

Norbert Wiener

A creative and highly original mathematician, Norbert Wiener established an entirely new branch of science that he named cybernetics. Considered one of the most outstanding mathematicians born in the United States, his work led to research on how the brain works and on artificial intelligence. This work has been applied in such areas as communication theory and **computer** design. The common use of such everyday terms as "input," "output," and "feedback" is largely due to Wiener's writings.

> *"One of the chief duties of a mathematician in acting as an advisor to scientists is to discourage them from expecting too much of mathematicians."*

Early life and education

Norbert Wiener (pronounced WEE-ner) was born in Columbia, Missouri. His father, Leo Wiener, was born in Byelostok, Poland (then Russia), and immigrated to the United States in 1880. As an accomplished linguist, Leo Wiener taught languages at Harvard University in Cambridge, Massachusetts, and met his wife, Bertha Kahn, at a poetry club meeting. When his son, Norbert, was born, Leo Wiener had ambitious education plans for him.

Norbert Wiener

To Leo Wiener's delight, he soon realized that he was blessed with an abnormally bright child. As a prodigy (a child with an exceptionally high level of intelligence), young Wiener responded to his father's educational efforts and was able to read at the age of three. Despite his father's sometimes harsh disciplinary methods, young Wiener progressed rapidly and entered high school at the age of nine, graduating two years later. When the family moved to the Boston area, Wiener entered Tufts University as an 11-year-old. He graduated four years later.

Upon graduating, Wiener enrolled at Harvard to study zoology. Dissatisfied with his choice of subject, he transferred to Cornell University in Ithaca, New York, in 1910 and switched to philosophy. Unhappy with that choice as well, he returned to Harvard in 1911 and decided to specialize in the philosophy of mathematics. He earned his master's degree from Harvard in 1912 and received his Ph.D. a year later. At Harvard, Wiener earned a Sheldon Fellowship, which allowed him to study in Europe after he received his doctoral degree. Since his father still played an active role in his life, he arranged for his son to study **logic** under English mathematician and philosopher Bertrand Russell (1872–1970) in England. Wiener also benefited from working with German mathematician David Hilbert (1862–1943) and others at Göttingen University in Germany.

Joins MIT

After returning to the United States in 1915 but still not sure of the mathematical direction he wanted to take, Wiener accepted a variety of teaching jobs. The outbreak of World War I (1914–18) led him to join a group of scientists and engineers at the Aberdeen Proving Ground in Maryland where they worked on designing range tables for artillery. After the war, he obtained a teaching position at the Massachusetts Institute of Technology (MIT) in Cambridge, Massachusetts. He would remain with that institution all his life, becoming assistant professor in 1924, associate professor in 1929, and full professor in 1932. In 1926, Wiener married Margaret Engemann, an assistant professor of modern languages, and the couple had two daughters.

In the decades between World War I and World War II (1939–45), Wiener taught and established his reputation as a standout mathematician with his work on two very complex subjects, Brownian motion and the Dirichlet problem. Brownian motion is the name given to the apparently random movement of particles suspended in a liquid. This phenomenon is now known to occur because of the existence of molecules and atoms that constantly move. The Dirichlet problem involves the complicated mathematical equations related to the flow of heat, electricity, and fluids.

World War II research

With the outbreak of World War II in Europe in 1939, Wiener worked on getting jobs for German scholars who had fled Adolf Hitler's Nazi Germany. Since Wiener did not learn until he was almost grown that his heritage was Jewish, he must have had special sympathy for his colleagues who were put in danger simply because they were Jewish.

By 1940, Wiener put his wide mathematical interests and abilities to work for the military and joined his many MIT colleagues who were working on war-related projects. Among one of the practical military problems he tried to solve mathematically was that of aiming a gun at a moving target—specifically, using an anti-aircraft gun. This research and the necessary calculations of its many variables—speed, wind, **weight** of shells, distance, evasive action, and the gunner himself, among others—would later prove valuable to his mathematical analysis of even more complicated systems involving aspects of communication and control. Some historians feel that this work led him to the notion of feedback. Feedback is the process by which an organism or a machine is able to monitor itself and then control, adjust, or regulate itself. One example is a typical home thermostat that maintains a desired common temperature by sensing the room temperature and then switching itself (and therefore the furnace) on or off. Feedback has also come to mean the information used in this process.

Creation of cybernetics

From Wiener's work during the war, it was but a small step to his creation of an entire new field whose object was the study of communications and control in living systems as well as in machines. During 1947, he pulled together all his experience with mathematics, physics, medicine, and even ballistics (the study of a projectile shot from artillery) and produced in 1948 his most impor-

Norbert Wiener

$$q^{ik}_{+-}il=0;\ \Gamma_i^l=0;\ R_{ik}=0;$$
$$q^{is}=0$$

A cigar-toting Norbert Wiener discusses a mathematical formula at a chalkboard in 1949.

tant work, entitled *Cybernetics, or Control and Communication in the Animal and Machine.* In searching for a term to describe his new theory of messages, he first considered the Greek word for "messenger," *angelos,* but it was too close to the word angel. He then selected *kubernes,* the Greek word for "helmsman" (a person who steers a ship) and came up with the word *cybernetics.*

Thus Wiener developed and named a new area of scientific investigation whose theory involves a mathematical description of the flow of information. Although cybernetics has found applications outside of mathematics—from how the brain works, to artificial intelligence, to the body's biochemical regulation—it is not surprising that its main use has been in the field of computers and what is called information theory.

In many ways, Wiener's book was very much like Wiener the man. It was eloquent and rich in ideas, which easily crossed the boundaries of different fields. However, it was also badly organized, difficult to read, and often full of misstatements. Wiener himself was a mixture of these two extremes. Although obviously brilliant, in his appearance and behavior he was short and quite round, with vision so poor that he wore very thick glasses. He wrote the way he spoke and often rambled from one unrelated topic to another. He quickly became famous for being self-centered and unaware of how he appeared to other people. However, he was also a basically good-natured person who would not deliberately offend anyone. He always looked very much like the stereotypical "absent-minded professor" who was permanently absorbed in his work. His two-part autobiography is considered to be frank and honest.

In the final years of his life, Wiener studied the impact of machines on humankind. In his book *The Human Use of Human Beings: Cybernetics and Society*, he calls attention to what the impact of computers might be on people. He also warns of the dangers that might be associated with the abuse of such a potentially powerful technology. By the early 1960s, Wiener had given up research entirely and devoted himself to the consideration of the social and philosophical implications of what might be called automation. He is best remembered today, however, for popularizing the terms and meanings used in the field of communication theory. Today's everyday use of such terms as "feedback," "information," "control," "input," and "output" are, for the most part, due to his research and writing.

In 1964, Wiener received the National Medal of Science. Awarded by the president of the United States, this honor recognizes individuals who have made outstanding contributions to science and engineering. It is highly prestigious and can be compared with the Nobel prizes in science. On March 18 of that year, Wiener collapsed and died while traveling through Stockholm, Sweden. An interfaith ceremony held at MIT in his memory proved to be especially fitting for a man who spent his life refusing to be placed into any one category.

For More Information

Abbott, David, ed. *The Biographical Dictionary of Scientists: Mathematicians.* New York: Peter Bedrick Books, 1986.

Norbert Wiener

Norbert Wiener

Biographical Dictionary of Mathematicians. New York: Charles Scribner's Sons, 1991.

Cortada, James W. *Historical Dictionary of Data Processing: Biographies.* New York: Greenwood Press, 1987.

MacTutor History of Mathematics Archive. "Norbert Wiener." http://www-groups.dcs.st-and.ac.uk/~history/Mathematicians/Wiener_Norbert.html (accessed on April 29, 1999).

Wiener, Norbert. *I Am a Mathematician.* Cambridge, MA: MIT Press, 1964.

Wiener, Norbert. *Invention: The Care and Feeding of Ideas.* Cambridge, MA: MIT Press, 1993.

Young, Robyn V., ed. *Notable Mathematicians: From Ancient Times to the Present.* Detroit: Gale Research, 1998.

Born April 11, 1953
Cambridge, England

English number theorist

Andrew J. Wiles

After seven years of concentrated study and work, Andrew Wiles conquered the world's most famous mathematical problem: Fermat's last theorem. Called by *The New York Times* "the most notorious mathematical puzzle of all time," this seventeenth-century challenge by French number theorist **Pierre de Fermat** (1601–65) frustrated professional and amateur mathematicians for well over 300 years. An instant celebrity and the recipient of many awards, Wiles has been especially praised for the innovative techniques he applied toward his eventual solution.

> *"I hope that seeing the excitement of solving [Fermat's last theorem] will make young mathematicians realize that there are lots and lots of other problems in mathematics which are going to be just as challenging in the future."*

Early life and education

Andrew John Wiles was born in Cambridge, England. As was the case with several other major figures in the history of mathematics, his father was a theologian and taught religion at Oxford University. There are no stories of Wiles possessing astounding mathematical gifts as a child, but his interest in Fermat's last theorem when he was only ten years old suggests that he was much more than an above-average youngster.

Andrew J. Wiles

Recalling his first encounter with Fermat's last theorem at a local library, Wiles remembers: "It looked so simple, and yet all the great mathematicians in history couldn't solve it. Here was a problem that a ten year old could understand, and I knew from that moment that I would never let it go." Wiles also recalls that he spent many of his teenage years trying to prove the theorem.

After earning a bachelor's degree from Oxford University in 1974, he entered Clare College at Cambridge University the same year in pursuit of his master's degree. At Clare, he studied elliptical curves. He received his master's degree in 1977 and his Ph.D. in 1980. In 1982, Wiles traveled to the United States to become a professor of mathematics at Princeton University in New Jersey.

Fermat's last theorem

As a schoolboy of ten, Wiles was visiting his local library in Cambridge when he first read about Fermat's last theorem. He immediately became intrigued by this seventeenth-century mathematician who wrote about a puzzling equation that was very similar to the **Pythagorean theorem.** Fermat's last theorem states that $a^n + b^n = c^n$ when n equals 2. But according to Fermat, there is no solution to this equation when n is greater than 2. Fermat also went beyond that statement however, and said that he could *prove* that this was so. Interestingly, Fermat made this claim when he jotted a note in the margin of a book, saying, "I have found a rather marvelous proof of this, but the margin is too small to hold it." This almost throwaway note would tantalize mathematicians for the next three centuries.

As a youngster, Wiles was fascinated by the challenge. He told his teachers about it, and they advised him to concentrate on his homework instead. As a teenager, Wiles decided to try to solve the problem in the manner in which he thought Fermat might have done. This proved useless. When he reached college, Wiles decided to study the methods that others had used during the eighteenth and nineteenth centuries to try to solve it. Although he learned a lot, he still was no closer to a solution.

After college, Wiles began serious research, so he put the problem aside. Although he never forgot about it completely—it was always in the back of his mind—he knew realistically that as long as he continued with the same techniques that everyone else had used, he would end up wasting years and getting nowhere. Unless he could find an entirely different approach, Wiles decided not to take on the theorem again.

Andrew J. Wiles

Chance for a solution

In the early 1980s, a possibility for such a new approach began to show itself to Wiles. A German mathematician, Gerhard Frey, suggested that an elliptical curve (one that results in an egg-shaped **circle**) might be used to represent solutions to Fermat's equations. This notion was, in turn, based on a 1954 idea proposed by two Japanese mathematicians, whose "Taniyama-Shimura conjecture" linked elliptical curves to certain equations. (In mathematics, a conjecture is a fascinating but unproven theory.) In 1986, American mathematician Kenneth A. Ribet showed that Frey was correct. Wiles paid close attention to Ribet's argument, which stated that if the Taniyama-Shimura conjecture could be proved, then logically, Fermat's last theorem could also be proved.

Seven-year journey to prove theorem

Wiles clearly remembers the moment he heard of Ribet's proof and knew that there was indeed a link between Taniyama-Shimura and Fermat. He states that he was electrified: "I knew that moment that the course of my life was changing because this meant that to prove Fermat's last theorem all I had to do was to prove the Taniyama-Shimura conjecture." Up until then, Wiles had resisted any impulses he had to work on Fermat's theorem because his theorem was not considered to be a respectable focus for one's entire career. Academically, it was thought of as a fascinating dead-end.

By the end of 1986, Wiles had decided to dedicate himself to Fermat's last theorem, but he also resolved to work totally alone and to tell no one but his wife, Nada, and his closest colleague. To the outside world, Wiles was now working on a modern problem—the Taniyama-Shimura conjecture—rather than an old one and was doing mainstream mathematics. From Wiles's point of view, however, he had the best of both worlds. He had what he called "the romance of Fermat, which held me all my life," combined with a specific mathematical problem that was professionally acceptable.

*Andrew Wiles at a
mathematics lecture.*

Wiles had another reason for working in isolation—competition.
If he announced what he was doing, he had no doubt that other
experts would become interested and, at the very least, would
want to collaborate with him. He also wanted to be able to devote
his undivided concentration to the problem. Wiles realized that if
his work on the problem were publicized, he would probably be
distracted by what he called "spectators."

Success at last

During the seven years Wiles spent working on Fermat's last theorem, he was totally consumed by it. Except for his responsibilities
at Princeton and the time he spent with his family, Wiles did
nothing else but work on it. "It was on my mind all the time," he
later recalled. "Once you're really desperate to find the answer to
something, you can't let it go."

Wiles began his work by trying to find patterns and attacking
small pieces of the problem that he hoped would eventually fit
together and provide a broader understanding. As the years of
work passed, he made slow progress, but one thing never changed.
"I carried this problem around in my head basically the whole

time," he said. "I would wake up with it first thing in the morning, I would be thinking about it all day, and I would be thinking about it when I went to sleep. The only way I could relax was when I was with my children [two daughters]. Young children aren't interested in Fermat. They just want to hear a story and they're not going to let you do anything else."

Finally, in May 1993, Wiles made a crucial breakthrough. With only one last remaining problem to solve, he happened to stumble upon a reference in a colleague's research paper that mentioned a particular nineteenth-century construction. Suddenly, Wiles realized that this was what he needed to solve his last problem. Having done so at last, telling no one but his wife that he had solved Fermat, Wiles arranged to deliver a series of three lectures at Cambridge University's Newton Institute. Because Wiles had been out of circulation for so long, his sudden appearance drew quite a bit of interest. Never mentioning Fermat until his final lecture on June 23, 1993, Wiles finally revealed that Fermat's last theorem had been proved. What really impressed the mathematical world, however, was Wiles's 200-page solution of the "incredibly deep, very difficult" Taniyama-Shimura conjecture.

Although an error was soon discovered in a crucial part of Wiles's argument, he collaborated with Cambridge mathematician Richard Taylor, and resolved the difficulty with 18 more months of work. Wiles's proof was then considered complete and final.

Since the idea of Fermat's last theorem had attained the status of a legend, its resolution by one man made Wiles an instant celebrity. He was named one of the most intriguing people of the year by *People* magazine, and *The New York Times* announced his achievement on its front page. Described by a reporter as a "quiet, diffident [bashful] man with a shy smile," Wiles later reflected on Fermat the mathematician and decided that he did not believe that he actually had the same proof that Wiles discovered: "It's a twentieth-century proof. It couldn't have been done in the nineteenth century, let alone the seventeenth century. The techniques used in this proof weren't around in Fermat's time." Further, Wiles doesn't believe that Fermat ever had a proof. "I think he fooled himself into thinking he had a proof."

Andrew J. Wiles

Andrew J. Wiles

Wiles remains a professor of mathematics at Princeton. Since his achievement in 1993, he has received special tributes from the International Center for Mathematical Sciences and the International Mathematical Union. In 1998, he also was given the King Faisal International Prize, which awarded him $200,000 for his accomplishment.

For More Information

Aczel, Amir D. *Fermat's Last Theorem: Unlocking the Secret of an Ancient Mathematical Problem.* New York: Four Walls Eight Windows, 1996.

"But How Did Fermat Do It?" (editorial). *The New York Times,* June 27, 1993, p. E14.

Current Biography Yearbook. New York: H. W. Wilson, 1996.

Ribenboim, Paulo. *Fermat's Last Theorem for Amateurs.* New York: Springer-Verlag, 1999.

Singh, Simon. "Andrew Wiles—Fermat's Last Theorem." http://www.vertigo.co.uk/fermat/wiles10.htm (accessed on April 29, 1999).

Singh, Simon. *Fermat's Enigma: The Epic Quest to Solve the World's Greatest Mathematical Problem.* New York: Walker & Co., 1997.

NOVA Online. "Solving Fermat: Andrew Wiles." http://www.pbs.org/wgbh/nova/proof/wiles.html (accessed on April 29, 1999).

Young, Robyn V., ed. *Notable Mathematicians: From Ancient Times to the Present.* Detroit: Gale Research, 1998.

Selected Bibliography

General sources

Asimov, Isaac. *Realm of Numbers*. Boston: Houghton Mifflin, 1959.

Ball, W. W. Rouse. *A Short Account of the History of Mathematics*. New York: Dover Publications, 1960.

Bergamini, David. *Mathematics*. Alexandria, VA: Time-Life Books, 1980.

Borman, Jami Lynne. *Computer Dictionary for Kids—and Their Parents*. Hauppauge, NY: Barron's Educational Series, 1995.

Boyer, Carl B., and Uta C. Merzbach. *A History of Mathematics*. New York: John Wiley & Sons, 1989.

Bunt, Lucas N. H., et al. *The Historical Roots of Elementary Mathematics*. Englewood Cliffs, NJ: Prentice Hall, 1976.

Burton, David M. *Burton's History of Mathematics*. Dubuque, IA: Wm. C. Brown Publishers, 1995.

Cajori, F. *A History of Mathematics*. New York: Chelsea, 1985.

**Selected
Bibliography**

Dictionary of Mathematics Terms. New York: Barron's Educational Series, Inc., 1987.

Duren, Peter, ed. *A Century of Mathematics in America.* 3 vols. Providence, RI: American Mathematical Society, 1989.

Eves, Howard. *An Introduction to the History of Mathematics.* Philadelphia: Saunders College Publishing, 1990.

Flegg, Graham. *Numbers: Their History and Meaning.* New York: Schocken Books, 1983.

Friedberg, Richard. *An Adventurer's Guide to Number Theory.* New York: Dover Publications, 1994.

Green, Gordon W., Jr. *Helping Your Child to Learn Math.* New York: Citadel Press, 1995.

Green, Judy, and Jeanne Laduke. *A Century of Mathematics in America.* Providence, RI: American Mathematical Society, 1989.

Groza, Vivian Shaw. *A Survey of Mathematics: Elementary Concepts and Their Historical Development.* New York: Holt, Rinehart and Winston, 1968.

Heath, T. L. *A History of Greek Mathematics.* New York: Dover Publications, 1981.

Heddens, James W. and William R. Speer. *Today's Mathematics: Concepts and Methods in Elementary School Mathematics.* Upper Saddle River, NJ: Merrill, 1997.

Hirschi, L. Edwin. *Building Mathematics Concepts in Grades Kindergarten Through Eight.* Scranton, PA: International Textbook Co., 1970.

Hoffman, Paul. *Archimedes' Revenge: The Joys and Perils of Mathematics.* New York: Ballantine, 1989.

Hogben, Lancelot T. *Mathematics in the Making.* London: Galahad Books, 1974.

Humez, Alexander, et al. *Zero to Lazy Eight: The Romance of Numbers.* New York: Simon & Schuster, 1993.

Immergut, Brita. *Arithmetic and Algebra—Again.* New York: McGraw-Hill, 1994.

Julius, Edward H. *Arithmetricks: 50 Easy Ways to Add, Subtract, Multiply, and Divide Without a Calculator.* New York: John Wiley and Sons, 1995.

Katz, Victor J. *A History of Mathematics: An Introduction.* New York: HarperCollins College Publishers, 1993.

Kline, Morris. *Mathematics for the Nonmathematician.* New York: Dover Publications, 1985.

Kline, Morris. *Mathematics in Western Culture.* New York: Oxford University Press, 1953.

Miles, Thomas J., and Douglas W. Nance. *Mathematics: One of the Liberal Arts.* Pacific Grove, CA: Brooks/Cole Publishing Co., 1997.

Miller, Charles D., et al. *Mathematical Ideas.* Reading, MA: Addison-Wesley, 1997.

Moffatt, Michael. *The Ages of Mathematics: The Origins.* Garden City, NY: Doubleday & Company, 1977.

Rogers, James T. *The Pantheon Story of Mathematics for Young People.* New York: Pantheon Books, 1966.

Slavin, Steve. *All the Math You'll Ever Need.* New York: John Wiley and Sons, 1989.

Smith, David Eugene. *Number Stories of Long Ago.* Detroit: Gale Research, 1973.

Smith, David Eugene, and Yoshio Mikami. *A History of Japanese Mathematics.* Chicago: The Open Court Publishing Company, 1914.

Smith, Karl J. *Mathematics: Its Power and Utility.* Pacific Grove, CA: Brooks/Cole, 1997.

Stillwell, John. *Mathematics and Its History.* New York: Springer-Verlag, 1989.

Temple, George. *100 Years of Mathematics.* New York: Springer-Verlag, 1981.

Selected Bibliography

West, Beverly Henderson, et al. *The Prentice-Hall Encyclopedia of Mathematics.* Englewood Cliffs, NJ: Prentice-Hall, 1982.

Wheeler, Ruric E. *Modern Mathematics.* Pacific Grove, CA: Brooks/Cole Publishing, 1995.

Wheeler, Ruric E., and Ed R. Wheeler. *Modern Mathematics for Elementary School Teachers.* Pacific Grove, CA: Brooks/Cole Publishing, 1995.

Wulforst, Harry. *Breakthrough to the Computer Age.* New York: Charles Scribner's Sons, 1982.

General biographical sources

Abbott, David, ed. *The Biographical Dictionary of Scientists: Mathematicians.* New York: Peter Bedrick Books, 1986.

Albers, Donald J., and G. L. Alexanderson, eds. *Mathematical People: Profiles and Interviews.* Boston: Birkhauser, 1985.

Albers, Donald J., Gerald L. Alexanderson, and Constance Reid. *More Mathematical People.* New York: Harcourt, 1991.

Alec, Margaret. *Hypatia's Heritage: A History of Women in Science from Antiquity through the Nineteenth Century.* Boston: Beacon Press, 1986.

Asimov, Isaac. *Asimov's Biographical Encyclopedia of Science and Technology.* Garden City, NY: Doubleday & Company, 1982.

Bell, Eric T. *Men of Mathematics.* New York: Simon and Schuster, 1986.

Biographical Dictionary of Mathematicians. New York: Charles Scribner's Sons, 1991.

Cortada, James W. *Historical Dictionary of Data Processing: Biographies.* New York: Greenwood Press, 1987.

Daintith, John, et al. *Biographical Encyclopedia of Scientists.* London: Institute of Physics Publishing, 1994.

Dunham, W. *The Mathematical Universe: An Alphabetical Journey through the Great Proofs, Problems, and Personalities.* New York: John Wiley & Sons, 1994.

Elliott, Clark A. *Biographical Dictionary of American Science: The Seventeenth Through the Nineteenth Centuries.* Westport, CT: Greenwood Press, 1979.

Gillispie, Charles C., ed. *Dictionary of Scientific Biography.* New York: Charles Scribner's Sons, 1990.

Grinstein, Louise S., and Paul J. Campbell, eds. *Women of Mathematics: A Biobibliographic Sourcebook.* New York: Greenwood Press, 1987.

Haber, Louis. *Black Pioneers of Science and Invention.* New York: Harcourt, Brace & World, 1970.

Henderson, Harry. *Modern Mathematicians.* New York: Facts on File, 1996.

Hollingdale, Stuart. *Makers of Mathematics.* London: Penguin Books, 1989.

Hudson, Wade, and Valerie Wilson Wesley. *Afro-Bets Book of Black Heroes From A to Z: An Introduction to Important Black Achievers for Young Readers.* East Orange, NJ: Just Us Books, 1997.

Itô, Kiyosi, ed. *Encyclopedia Dictionary of Mathematics.* Cambridge, MA: MIT Press, 1987.

McGraw-Hill Modern Scientists and Engineers. New York: McGraw-Hill, 1980.

McMurray, Emily J., ed. *Notable Twentieth-Century Scientists.* Detroit: Gale Research, 1995.

Metcalf, Doris Hunter. *Portraits of Exceptional African American Scientists.* Carthage, IL: Good Apple, 1994.

Millar, David, Ian Millar, John Millar, and Margaret Millar. *The Cambridge Dictionary of Scientists.* Cambridge, England: Cambridge University Press, 1996.

Selected Bibliography

Morgan, Bryan. *Men and Discoveries in Mathematics.* London: John Murray Publishers, 1972.

Morrow, Charlene, and Teri Perl, eds. *Notable Women in Mathematics: A Biographical Dictionary.* Westport, CT: Greenwood Press, 1998.

Muir, Jane. *Of Men and Numbers: The Story of the Great Mathematicians.* New York: Dover Publications, 1996.

Ogilvie, Marilyn Bailey. *Women in Science: Antiquity through the Nineteenth Century.* Cambridge, MA: MIT Press, 1986.

Osen, Lynn M. *Women in Mathematics.* Cambridge, MA: The MIT Press, 1974.

Pappas, Theoni. *Mathematical Scandals.* San Carlos, CA: Wide World Publishing/Tetra, 1997.

Perl, Teri. *Math Equals: Biographies of Women Mathematicians.* Menlo Park, CA: Addison-Wesley Publishing Company, 1978.

Porter, Roy, ed. *The Biographical Dictionary of Scientists.* New York: Oxford University Press, 1994.

Potter, Joan, and Constance Claytor. *African Americans Who Were First: Illustrated with Photographs.* New York: Cobblehill Books, 1997.

Reimer, Luetta, and Wilbert Reimer. *Mathematicians Are People, Too: Stories from the Lives of Great Mathematicians.* Palo Alto, CA: Dale Seymour Publications, 1995.

Ritchie, David. *The Computer Pioneers.* New York: Simon and Schuster, 1986.

Shasha, Dennis E. *Out of Their Minds: The Lives and Discoveries of 15 Great Computer Scientists.* New York: Copernicus, 1998.

Simmons, George F. *Calculus Gems: Brief Lives and Memorable Mathematics.* New York: McGraw-Hill, 1992.

Slater, Robert. *Portraits in Silicon.* Cambridge, MA: The MIT Press, 1989.

Spencer, Donald D. *Great Men and Women of Computing.* Ormond Beach, FL: Camelot, 1999.

Young, Robyn V., ed. *Notable Mathematicians: From Ancient Times to the Present.* Detroit: Gale Research, 1998.

Internet sites

Readers should be reminded that some Internet sources change frequently. All of the following web sites were accessible as of May 27, 1999, but some may have changed addresses or been removed since then.

The Abacus
http://www.ee.ryerson.ca:8080/~elf/abacus/

American Mathematical Society (AMS)
http://e-math.ams.org/

Ask Dr. Math
http://forum.swarthmore.edu/dr.math/

Biographies of Women Mathematicians
http://www.scottland.edu/lriddle.women/chronolo.htm

Brain Teasers
http://www.eduplace.com/math/brain/

Canadian Mathematical Society
http://camel.cecm.sfu.ca/CMS

Eisenhower National Clearinghouse for Mathematics
and Science
http://www.enc.org/

Elementary School Student Center
http://forum.swarthmore.edu/students/students.elementary.html

Explorer
http://explorer.scrtec.org/explorer/

Flashcards for Kids
www.edu4kids.com/math/

Fraction Shapes
http://math.rice.edu/~lanius/Patterns/

Galaxy
http://galaxy.einet.net/galaxy/Science/Mathematics.html

Selected Bibliography

The Geometry Center
http://www.geom.umn.edu/

MacTutor History of Mathematics Archive
http://www-groups.dcs.st-and.ac.uk/~history/index.html

Mandelbrot Explorer
http://www.softlab.ntua.gr/mandel/mandel.html

Math-Forum: Women and Mathematics
http://forum.swarthmore.edu/social/math.women.html

Math League Help Topics
http://www.mathleague.com/help/help.htm

Math Magic!
http://forum.swarthmore.edu/mathmagic/

A Math Website for Middle School Students
http://www-personal.umd.umich.edu/~jobrown/math.html

Mathematical Association of America
http://www.maa.org/

Mathematical Programming Glossary
http://www-math.cudenver.edu/~hgreenbe/glossary/glossary.html

The Mathematics Archives
http://archives.math.utk.edu/

Mathematics Web Sites Around the World
http://www.math.psu.edu/MathLists/Contents.html

Mathematics WWW Virtual Library
http://euclid.math.fsu.edu/Science/math.html

Measure for Measure
http://www.wolinskyweb.com/measure.htm

Mega Mathematics!
http://www.c3.lanl.gov/mega-math/

Past Notable Women of Computing and Mathematics
http://www.cs.yale.edu/~tap/past-women.html

PlaneMath
http://www.planemath.com

Project Athena
http://inspire.ospi.wednet.edu:8001/

Women in Math Project
http://darkwing.uoregon.edu/~wmnmath/

The Young Mathematicians Network WWW Site
http://www.youngmath.org/

Organizations

American Mathematical Society
P.O. Box 6248
Providence, RI 02940
Internet site: http://www.ams.org

American Statistical Association
1429 Duke Street
Alexandria, VA 22314-3402
Internet site: http://www.amstat.org

Association for Women in Mathematics
4114 Computer and Space Science Building
University of Maryland
College Park, MD 20742-2461
Internet site: http://www.awm-math.org

Association of Teachers of Mathematics
7 Shaftesbury Street
Derby DE23 8YB England
Internet site: http://acorn.educ.nottingham.ac.uk/SchEd/pages/atm

Institute of Mathematical Statistics
3401 Investment Boulevard, Suite 7
Hayward, CA 94545-3819
Internet site: http://www.imstat.org

The Madison Project
c/o Robert B. Davis
Rutgers University
Graduate School of Education

Selected Bibliography

10 Seminary Place
New Brunswick, NJ 08903

Math/Science Interchange
c/o Department of Mathematics
Loyola Marymount University
Los Angeles, CA 90045

Math/Science Network
Mills College
5000 MacArthur Boulevard
Oakland, CA 94613
Internet site: http://www.elstad.com/msngoal.html

Mathematical Association of America
1529 18th Street N.W.
Washington, DC 20036
Internet site: http://www.maa.org

National Council of Supervisors of Mathematics
P.O. Box 10667
Golden, CO 80401
Internet site: http://forum.swarthmore.edu/ncsm

National Council of Teachers of Mathematics
1906 Association Drive
Reston, VA 20191-1593
Internet site: http://www.nctm.org

School Science and Mathematics Association
400 East 2nd Street
Bloomsburg, PA 17815
Internet site: http://www.ssma.org

Society for Industrial and Applied Mathematics
3600 University City Science Center
Philadelphia, PA 19104-2688
Internet site: http://www.siam.org/nnindex.htm

Study Group for Mathematical Learning
c/o Robert B. Davis
501 South 1st Avenue
Highland Park, NJ 08904

Women and Mathematics Education
c/o Charlene Morrow
Mount Holyoke College
302 Shattuck Hall
South Hadley, MA 01075

Selected
Bibliography

Picture Credits

The photographs appearing in *Math and Mathematicians: The History of Math Discoveries Around the World* were reproduced by permission of the following sources:

The Library of Congress: pp. 1, 21, 31, 34, 49, 53, 59, 62, 65, 99, 110, 125, 127, 153, 164, 177, 207, 213, 219, 235, 253, 271, 285, 299, 313, 345, 348, 399, 400; **Daytona International Speedway/Dennis Winn:** p. 19; **Fisk University Library:** p. 37; **David Blackwell/Jean Libby:** p. 45; **The Wolf Foundation:** pp. 71, 119, 451; **AP/Wide World Photos, Inc.:** pp. 73, 116, 180, 195, 198, 216, 284; **The Stock Market:** p. 79; **Hans & Cassidy, reproduced by permission of The Gale Group:** pp. 80, 89, 335, 358, 363, 423, 425; **CorbisBettmann:** pp. 83, 84, 132, 133, 171, 185, 225, 305, 331, 379, 403, 419; **PhotoEdit/Anna Zuckerman:** p. 94; **The Granger Collection, New York:** pp. 102, 114, 141, 147, 189, 263, 308, 365; **The Bettmann Archive/CorbisBettmann:** p. 111; **Photo Researchers, Inc.:** pp. 131, 247, 413, 427; **U.S. Fish & Wildlife Service:** p. 139; **Archive Photos, Inc.:** pp. 163, 261, 323; **Jim Sugar Photography/Corbis:** p. 166; **Convention & Visitors Bureau of Greater Cleveland:** p. 186; **The University of Texas at Tyler:** p. 201; **U.S. National Aeronautics and Space Administra-**

Index

Italic type indicates volume number; **boldface** indicates main entries and their page numbers; (ill.) indicates photos and illustrations.

Index

Cantor, Georg, *1:* 53–57
Granville, Evelyn Boyd, *1:* 201–205
Analytic geometry, *1:* 88, 99, 141, 143
Analytical engine, *1:* 33, 82
Analytical Society, *1:* 32
Angle, *2:* 422
Apollonius, *1:* 142, 226; *2:* 237
Applied mathematics
    Acoustics, *1:* 192
    Elasticity, *1:* 192
    Geodesy, *1:* 181
    Germain, Sophie, *1:* 189–93
    Granville, Evelyn Boyd, *1:* 201–205
Arabic numerals. *See* Hindu-Arabic numerals
Arago, François, *1:* 135
Archimedean screw, *1:* 22
Archimedes of Syracuse, *1:* 21–26, 21 (ill.), 23 (ill.), 137; *2:* 330, 331 (ill.)
Area, *1:* 27–29, 78; *2:* 326, 330, 334, 422, 434. *See also* Perimeter
Aristotle, *2:* 282, 285 (ill.)
Arithmetic operations, *1:* 108; *2:* 410
Artificial intelligence, *2:* 392
    Turing, Alan, *2:* 431
    Wiener, Norbert, *2:* 445–50
Artin, Emil, *1:* 73
Associative property, *1:* 8, 108; *2:* 294, 410
Astronomy
    Banneker, Benjamin, *1:* 37–43
    Galileo, *1:* 163–69
    Gauss, Carl Friedrich, *1:* 177–82
    Huygens, Christiaan, *1:* 219–23
    Hypatia of Alexandria, *1:* 225–29
    Kepler, Johannes, *2:* 235–40
    Khwārizmī, al-, *2:* 241–45
    Thales of Miletus, *2:* 413–16
Atomic bomb, *1:* 117; *2:* 308

Avoirdupois weight, *2:* 438
Axes, *1:* 88

B

Babbage, Charles, *1:* 31–36, 31 (ill.), 34 (ill.), 82
Ballantine Medal, *2:* 392
Banach, Stefan, *2:* 289
Bank note, *1:* 92
Banneker, Benjamin, *1:* 37–43, 37 (ill.), 40 (ill.)
Barrow, Isaac, *2:* 262, 312, 313, 313 (ill.)
Bartels, Johann Martin Christian, *2:* 272
Barter system, *1:* 91
Base (exponent), *1:* 138
Base number, *2:* 278
Beeckman, Isaac, *1:* 100
Berlin Academy of Sciences, *2:* 264
Bernoulli, Daniel, *1:* 132, 133, 133 (ill.)
Bernoulli family, *1:* 132 (ill.)
Bernoulli, Jakob, *1:* 132; *2:* 344, 347 (ill.)
Bernoulli, Johann, *1:* 132, 132 (ill.), 133
Bernoulli, Nicholas, *1:* 133
Bezout, Etienne, *1:* 153
Binary, *1:* 82
Binary mathematics, *1:* 51
Binary notation, *2:* 262
Binary operation, *1:* 108; *2:* 294
Bit (computer term), *2:* 391
Blackwell, David, *1:* 45–48, 45 (ill.)
Blaschke, Wilhelm, *1:* 72
Bolyai, János, *2:* 274
Bonaparte, Napoléon, *1:* 66, 154–55, 180; *2:* 256
Boole, George, *1:* 49–52, 49 (ill.); *2:* 282, 390
Boolean algebra, *1:* 49; *2:* 390
Bordin Prize, *2:* 250
Bossut, Charles, *1:* 154
Boundary, *1:* 28
Boyle, Robert, *2:* 260
Brahe, Tycho, *2:* 237

Index

Index

Index

Lincoln, Abraham, *1:* 128

Linear equation, *1:* 18, 20

Linear measurement, *2:* 267–70, 269 (ill.)

Liouville, Joseph, *1:* 174

Literary mathematics, *1:* 118

Lobachevsky, Nikolay, *2:* 271–75, 271 (ill.)

Logarithmic tables, *2:* 278, 302

Logarithms, *2:* 277–79, 299, 301

Logic, *1:* 184; *2:* **281–85**

    Agnesi, Maria, *1:* 11–15

    Boole, George, *1:* 49–52

    Euclid of Alexandria, *1:* 125

    Gödel, Kurt, *1:* 195–99

    Leibniz, Gottfried, *2:* 259–65

    Symbolic logic, *1:* 51; *2:* 259, 261

    Turing, Alan, *2:* 427–32

    Wiener, Norbert, *2:* 445–50

Logos, *2:* 282

Longitude, *1:* 88, 89

Lucasian professor of mathematics, *1:* 35; *2:* 312, 316

M

Maestlin, Michael, *2:* 236

Magnetism, units of, *1:* 181

Mandelbrot, Benoit B., *2:* **287–91,** 287 (ill.)

Manhattan Project, *1:* 118

Mantissa, *2:* 278

Maps, Mercator, *1:* 185

Maric, Mileva, *1:* 114 (ill.), 115

Mark I (computer), *1:* 82, 215

Mark II (computer), *1:* 215

Markov, Andrei A., *2:* 344

Mass, *2:* 437, 439

Mathematical logic. *See* Logic

Mathematical physics. *See* Physics, mathematical

Mathematics, applied. *See* Applied mathematics

Means, *2:* 372

Mechanical computation, *1:* 31–36

Mechanics, *1:* 134, 166, 174; *2:* 253–58

Memory, *1:* 82

Mendel, Gregor Johann, *2:* 347, 373

Mercantile, *2:* 418

Mercator, Gerard, *1:* 185

Mersenne, Marin, *1:* 143, 220; *2:* 340

Meter (measurement), *2:* 268

Metric system, *1:* 96; *2:* 253, 257, 269, 269 (ill.), 438–39

Millay, Edna St. Vincent, *1:* 118

Minuend, *2:* 410–11

Minus symbol, *1:* 9; *2:* 295, 411

Minute, *1:* 160; *2:* 418

Mixed number, *1:* 160

Molecules, *1:* 113

Money. *See* Currency

Monge, Gaspard, *1:* 154

Month, *2:* 418

Moon, *1:* 136

Morgenstern, Oskar, *2:* 309

Mortality tables, *2:* 398

Muhammad Ibn Musa al-Khwārizmī, Abu Ja'Far. *See* Khwārizmī, Al-

Multiplicand, *2:* 294

Multiplication, *2:* **293–97,** 302

Multiplication symbol, *2:* 295, 296

Multiplication tables, *2:* 302

Multiplier, *2:* 294

Music, *2:* 351

N

Napier, John, *1:* 82, 96; *2:* 277, **299–303,** 299 (ill.)

"Napier's bones," *1:* 82; *2:* 302

National Academy of Sciences, U.S., *1:* 45, 75, 210; *2:* 392

National Medal of Science, *1:* 75; *2:* 392, 449

National Medal of Technology, *1:* 217

National Physical Laboratory (NPL), *2:* 430

Natural numbers, *2:* 340, 394, 441, 442

Natural selection, *2:* 344

Negative numbers, *1:* 209; *2:* 231, 232, 376

Index